Everyman, I will go with thee,
and be thy guide

EVERYMAN'S BOOK OF EVERGREEN VERSE

Edited by
DAVID HERBERT

EVERYMAN
J. M. DENT · LONDON

First published in Everyman 1981
This edition first published 1993
Reprinted 1994, 1995, 1996, 1997, 1998, 1999

J. M. Dent
Orion Publishing Group, Orion House
5 Upper St Martin's Lane
London WC2H 9EA

Typeset by Deltatype Ltd, Ellesmere Port, Cheshire
Printed in Great Britain by
The Guernsey Press Co. Ltd, Guernsey, C.I.

British Library Cataloguing-in-Publication Data for this
title is available upon request.

ISBN 0 460 87273 7

CONTENTS

Note on the Editor   xx

Introduction   xxiii

Note on the Text   xxvii

ANONYMOUS
'Sumer is icumen in'   1

GEOFFREY CHAUCER
From The Book of the Tales of Caunterbury   1

ANONYMOUS
A Lykewake Dirge   3

ANONYMOUS
The Twa Corbies   4

ANONYMOUS
Edward, Edward   5

ANONYMOUS
Barbara Allan   6

ANONYMOUS
Lord Randal   8

ANONYMOUS
Sir Patrick Spens   9

ANONYMOUS
Greensleeves   10

ANONYMOUS
'There is a lady sweet and kind'   12

THOMAS WYATT
'And wilt thou leave me thus?'   13

CONTENTS

NICHOLAS BRETON
'In the merry month of May' 13

WALTER RALEIGH
From The Passionate Man's Pilgrimage 14

EDMUND SPENSER
From Prothalamion 15
From The Faerie Queene 16

ANTHONY MUNDAY
'Beauty sat bathing by a spring' 17

PHILIP SIDNEY
'My true love hath my heart, and I have his' 18

EDWARD DYER
'My mind to me a kingdom is' 18

MICHAEL DRAYTON
'Since there's no help, come, let us kiss and part' 19
'Fair stood the wind for France' 20

CHRISTOPHER MARLOWE
From Hero and Leander 23
From Dr Faustus 23
The Passionate Shepherd to His Love 24

WALTER RALEIGH
The Nymph's Reply to the Shepherd 25

WILLIAM SHAKESPEARE
From The Passionate Pilgrim 25
From The Sonnets 26
From Richard III 28
From The Two Gentlemen of Verona 29
From Romeo and Juliet 29
From A Midsummer Night's Dream 31
From Richard II 32
From The Merchant of Venice 33
From Henry V 34
From As You Like It 35
From Julius Caesar 38
From Hamlet 40
From Twelfth Night 43
From Othello 44

From Macbeth 45
From Antony and Cleopatra 47
From Cymbeline 48
From The Tempest 49

THOMAS CAMPION
'There is a garden in her face' 50

HENRY WOTTON
The Character of a Happy Life 51

BEN JONSON
From Cynthia's Revels 51
To Celia 52
From The Silent Woman 53

JOHN DONNE
Song 53
The Sun Rising 54
'Batter my heart, three-personed God; for you' 55
'Death, be not proud, though some have called thee' 55

ROBERT HERRICK
Delight in Disorder 56
To the Virgins, to Make Much of Time 56
To Daffodils 57
Night-Piece, to Julia 57
Upon Julia's Clothes 58
Cherry-Ripe 58

GEORGE HERBERT
Virtue 58
The Collar 59
The Pulley 60

ANONYMOUS
'If all the world were paper' 61

JAMES SHIRLEY
'The glories of our blood and state' 62

EDMUND WALLER
'Go, lovely rose!' 62

JOHN MILTON
Lycidas 63
Sonnet [on His Blindness] 68

viii CONTENTS

From Paradise Lost: Book I 68
From Paradise Lost: Book XII 69

JOHN SUCKLING
'Why so pale and wan, fond lover?' 70
'Out upon it, I have loved' 70

JAMES GRAHAM, MARQUIS OF MONTROSE
To His Mistress 71

RICHARD LOVELACE
To Lucasta, Going to the Wars 72
To Althea, from Prison 72

ANDREW MARVELL
To His Coy Mistress 72

HENRY VAUGHAN
Peace 75

JOHN BUNYAN
From The Pilgrim's Progress 75

JOHN DRYDEN
From Absalom and Achitophel 77

ISAAC WATTS
Against Idleness and Mischief 78
The Sluggard 78

JOHN GAY
From The Beggar's Opera 79
From Acis and Galatea 79

ALEXANDER POPE
Ode on Solitude 80
From An Essay on Criticism 80
From The Rape of the Lock 81
From An Essay on Man 81

HENRY CAREY
'Of all the girls that are so smart' 82

ANONYMOUS
The Vicar of Bray 84

JAMES THOMSON
Rule Britannia 85

ANONYMOUS
God Save the King   86

THOMAS GRAY
Elegy Written in a Country Churchyard   87
On a Favourite Cat, Drowned, in a Tub of Gold Fishes   90

OLIVER GOLDSMITH
From The Deserted Village   91
From The Vicar of Wakefield   92

WILLIAM COWPER
'God moves in a mysterious way'   93
From The Task   93
'I am monarch of all I survey'   95

ISAAC BICKERSTAFFE
From Love in a Village   96

RICHARD BRINSLEY SHERIDAN
From School for Scandal   96

WILLIAM BLAKE
From Songs of Innocence: The Lamb   97
From Songs of Experience: The Tiger   98
The Sick Rose   98
Infant Sorrow   99
The Chimney Sweeper   99
From Auguries of Innocence   99
From Milton   101

ROBERT BURNS
Auld Lang Syne   101
Song   102
To a Mouse   103
'Scots, wha hae wi' Wallace bled'   104
'Ae fond kiss, and then we sever'   105

WILLIAM WORDSWORTH
'My heart leaps up when I behold'   106
To the Cuckoo   106
'She dwelt among the untrodden ways'   107
'A slumber did my spirit seal'   107
'I wandered lonely as a cloud'   108
Lines Composed a Few Miles above Tintern Abbey, on revisiting

the banks of the Wye during a tour, July 13, 1798   108
'The world is too much with us; late and soon'   112
The Solitary Reaper   113
Composed upon Westminster Bridge   114
London: 1802   114

WALTER SCOTT
From The Lay of the Last Minstrel   115
Lochinvar   115

SAMUEL TAYLOR COLERIDGE
Kubla Khan   116

ROBERT SOUTHEY
The Inchcape Rock   118
The Old Man's Comforts   120

THOMAS CAMPBELL
'Ye mariners of England'   121

WALTER SAVAGE LANDOR
'I strove with none, for none was worth my strife'   122

THOMAS MOORE
'Oft in the stilly night'   122

FRANCIS SCOTT KEY
The Star-Spangled Banner   123

LEIGH HUNT
Abou Ben Adhem   124

THOMAS LOVE PEACOCK
The War Song of Dinas Vawr   125

GEORGE GORDON, LORD BYRON
'When we two parted'   126
From Childe Harold's Pilgrimage   127
She Walks in Beauty   129
The Destruction of Sennacherib   129
'So, we'll go no more a roving'   130

CHARLES WOLFE
The Burial of Sir John Moore after Corunna   130

JOHN HOWARD PAYNE
Home, Sweet Home   131

CONTENTS xi

PERCY BYSSHE SHELLEY
Ozymandias 132
From To a Skylark 132
'Music, when soft voices die' 133
'One word is too often profaned' 133

FELICIA D. HEMANS
Casabianca 134

JOHN KEATS
On First Looking into Chapman's Homer 135
From Endymion 136
La Belle Dame Sans Merci 136
To Sleep 138
Ode to a Nightingale 138
Ode on a Grecian Urn 140
To Autumn 141

THOMAS HOOD
The Song of the Shirt 142
'I remember, I remember' 145

THOMAS BABINGTON, LORD MACAULAY
From Horatius 146
From The Armada 149

RALPH WALDO EMERSON
Hymn 150

ROBERT STEPHEN HAWKER
The Song of the Western Men 151

ELIZABETH BARRETT BROWNING
Grief 151
A Musical Instrument 152
'How do I love thee? Let me count the ways' 153

HENRY WADSWORTH LONGFELLOW
The Village Blacksmith 154
Paul Revere's Ride 155
The Wreck of the 'Hesperus' 158
From The Song of Hiawatha 161
Excelsior 163
A Psalm of Life 164

SAMUEL FRANCIS SMITH
America 165

EDGAR ALLAN POE
The Raven 166
Annabel Lee 169

EDWARD FITZGERALD
From The Rubaíyát of Omar Khayyám of Naishapur 170

ALFRED, LORD TENNYSON
The Lady of Shalott 172
From The May Queen 176
The Lotos-Eaters 177
'Break, break, break' 178
From The Princess 178
From In Memoriam 180
The Charge of the Light Brigade 181
From Maud 183
From The Brook 185
The Revenge 186

OLIVER WENDELL HOLMES
Old Ironsides 190

ROBERT BROWNING
From Pippa Passes 191
How They Brought the Good News from Ghent to Aix 191
The Lost Leader 193
Home-thoughts, from Abroad 193
Home-thoughts, from the Sea 194
Meeting at Night 194
Parting at Morning 195

EDWARD LEAR
The Owl and the Pussy-Cat 195
The Jumblies 196

EMILY BRONTË
'No coward soul is mine' 197

CHARLES KINGSLEY
The Sands of Dee 198
The Last Buccaneer 199

ARTHUR HUGH CLOUGH
'Say not the struggle nought availeth' 200

WALT WHITMAN
O Captain! My Captain! 201
From Song of Myself 201

JULIA WARD HOWE
Battle-Hymn of the Republic 203

MATTHEW ARNOLD
From Sohrab and Rustum 204
Dover Beach 205
Requiescat 206

WILLIAM JOHNSON CORY
Heraclitus 206

WILLIAM ALLINGHAM
Four Ducks on a Pond 207

ADELAIDE ANNE PROCTER
A Lost Chord 207

DANTE GABRIEL ROSSETTI
From The Blessed Damozel 208
Sudden Light 209

EMILY DICKINSON
'Because I could not stop for death' 210
'Success is counted sweetest' 211
'My life closed twice before its close' 211

CHRISTINA ROSSETTI
From Goblin Market 211
Remember 212
A Birthday 213
Echo 213
Song 214
Up-Hill 214

THOMAS EDWARD BROWN
My Garden 215

GEORGE A. STRONG
From The Song of Milkanwatha 215

LEWIS CARROLL
Jabberwocky 215

The Walrus and the Carpenter   216
From The Hunting of the Snark   219

WILLIAM MORRIS
A Garden by the Sea   222

ANONYMOUS
Frankie and Johnny   223

WILLIAM SCHWENCK GILBERT
The Yarn of the Nancy Bell   225

ALGERNON CHARLES SWINBURNE
From A Forsaken Garden   227

THOMAS HARDY
Weathers   228
In Time of 'The Breaking of Nations'   228
Snow in the Suburbs   229

JOACHIN MILLER
Columbus   229

GERARD MANLEY HOPKINS
Heaven-haven   230
The Windhover   231
Pied Beauty   231

ROBERT BRIDGES
A Passer-by   232
London Snow   232

JAMES WHITCOMB RILEY
When the Frost is on the Punkin   233

WILLIAM ERNEST HENLEY
Invictus   234

ROBERT LOUIS STEVENSON
Requiem   235

ELLA WHEELER WILCOX
Solitude   235
Worthwhile   236

OSCAR WILDE
From The Ballad of Reading Gaol   237

JOHN DAVIDSON
A Runnable Stag 238

DOROTHY FRANCES GURNEY
'The Lord God planted a garden' 240

KATHARINE LEE BATES
America the Beautiful 241

FRANCIS THOMPSON
From The Hound of Heaven 242

ALFRED EDWARD HOUSMAN
'Loveliest of trees, the cherry now' 242
'Is my team ploughing' 243
'When I was one-and-twenty' 244
Epitaph on an Army of Mercenaries 244

HENRY NEWBOLT
Drake's Drum 245
Vitaï Lampada 245

RUDYARD KIPLING
Danny Deever 246
Gunga Din 247
Recessional 249
The Way through the Woods 250
If – 251
Mandalay 252

J. MILTON HAYES
The Green Eye of the Yellow God 253

WILLIAM BUTLER YEATS
Down by the Salley Gardens 255
The Lake Isle of Innisfree 255
When You Are Old 255
An Irish Airman Foresees His Death 256
The Second Coming 256
Sailing to Byzantium 257

EDWIN ARLINGTON ROBINSON
Richard Cory 258
Miniver Cheevy 258

LAURENCE BINYON
For the Fallen 259
From The Burning of the Leaves 261

HILAIRE BELLOC
Tarantella 261
Ballade of Genuine Concern 262
Matilda 263

WILLIAM HENRY DAVIES
Leisure 264

WALTER DE LA MARE
The Listeners 265
Fare Well 266
The Scribe 267

GILBERT KEITH CHESTERTON
The Donkey 267
From Lepanto 268

ROBERT FROST
Fire and Ice 269
The Road Not Taken 269
Mending Wall 270

ROBERT SERVICE
The Shooting of Dan McGrew 271

EDWARD THOMAS
Adlestrop 274

JOHN MASEFIELD
Cargoes 274
Sea-Fever 275

ALFRED NOYES
The Highwayman 275

JOHN DRINKWATER
Moonlit Apples 279

WILLIAM CARLOS WILLIAMS
This is Just to Say 279

JAMES ELROY FLECKER
From Hassan 280

DAVID HERBERT LAWRENCE
Snake 281

JOYCE KILMER
Trees 283

FRANCES CORNFORD
To a Fat Lady Seen from the Train 283

SEIGFRIED SASSOON
Everyone Sang 284

RUPERT BROOKE
The Old Vicarage, Grantchester 284
The Soldier 288

THOMAS STEARNS ELIOT
The Love Song of J. Alfred Prufrock 288
Journey of the Magi 292
The Song of the Jellicles 293

WALTER JAMES TURNER
Romance 294

EDNA ST VINCENT MILLAY
First Fig 295

WILFRED OWEN
Strange Meeting 295

e. e. cummings
'anyone lived in a pretty how town' 296
'next to of course god america i' 297

ROBERT GRAVES
Welsh Incident 298

OGDEN NASH
Peekaboo, I Almost See You 299
Song of the Open Road 300

STEVIE SMITH
Not Waving but Drowning 300

CECIL DAY LEWIS
Birthday Poem for Thomas Hardy 300

CONTENTS

JOHN BETJEMAN
A Subaltern's Love-song   301
Hunter Trials   303

LOUIS MACNEICE
Bagpipe Music   304
Prayer before Birth   305

WYSTAN HUGH AUDEN
Lullaby   306

STEPHEN SPENDER
'I think continually of those who were truly great'   307

DYLAN THOMAS
Do Not Go Gentle into That Good Night   308
Poem in October   308
And Death Shall Have No Dominion   310

HENRY REED
From Lessons of the War   311

CHARLES CAUSLEY
Nursery Rhyme of Innocence and Experience   312

PHILIP LARKIN
The Whitsun Weddings   314
This Be the Verse   316

ELIZABETH JENNINGS
One Flesh   316

GEORGE MACBETH
Owl   317

SYLVIA PLATH
Daddy   318

TONY HARRISON
Long Distance II   320

ROGER MCGOUGH
Let Me Die a Youngman's Death   320

PETE SEEGER
Where Have All the Flowers Gone?   321

SEAMUS HEANEY
Personal Helicon   323

WENDY COPE
Summer Villanelle   323

Acknowledgements   325

Index of Authors   329

Index of First Lines and Titles   333

NOTE ON THE EDITOR

DAVID HERBERT was educated at Rugby and Trinity College, Cambridge. For short periods he was a bookseller, a stage manager (at the Maddermarket Theatre, Norwich), a teacher of English in Spain and of Spanish and French at Eton. From 1955 to 1961 he taught English at Christ's Hospital, where he produced and acted in a great many plays. But for most of his working life he has been in publishing, first with Penguin and later as Publisher at Studio Vista and then at Rainbird. In 1976 he and his wife formed their own company, The Herbert Press. Books he has written or edited for other publishers include *The Operas of Benjamin Britten*, *Romeo and Juliet* (in the Kennet Shakespeare series), *The Everyman Book of Narrative Verse*, *The Gallery of World Photography: The Human Figure* and selections of *John Keats*, *George Herbert* and *Comic Verse*.

To my mother

INTRODUCTION

'The boy stood on the burning deck', 'To be or not to be', 'Come into the garden, Maud', 'I wandered lonely as a cloud', 'There's a breathless hush in the Close tonight', *The Song of Hiawatha*, 'Lars Porsena of Clusium', Masefield's *Cargoes*, Kipling's *If*: these are some of the most prized old favourites included here. For one reason or another, few of them find a place in modern anthologies. Yet to Everyman (who may or may not be a serious poetry reader) they are among the poems he (or she) knows best and loves most in the English language: poems studied, learned by heart, recited at school (or later), poems read aloud by parents and passed on again to children, poems endlessly quoted, misquoted, half-remembered, or remembered with glee from beginning to end. They are evergreen – or green at least for several generations past and several more to come.

This is a collection of all manner of evergreen verse – English and American – from before Chaucer's time to modern times. I have not avoided overlaps with other anthologies (few would exclude *Kubla Khan*, *Ozymandias*, or Blake's *Tiger*). Nor have I preferred one poem to another on aesthetic grounds: the criterion for inclusion being that a piece is sufficiently well known. Beyond this, I have tried to represent fairly as wide a range of periods, poets and kinds of verse as possible, within the number of pages allowed me by the publishers. But exceptionally rich periods (above all the Victorian) and exceptionally popular poets (Keats, Tennyson, Longfellow, Kipling and, above all, Shakespeare) need extra space – and even then cannot have quite what they deserve; whereas some major poets (Dryden, Rossetti, Swinburne) wrote very few poems that could be described as evergreen.

Limits, of course, had to be set. This is an adult selection, so nursery rhymes and children's verse (including, somewhat sadly, *The Pied Piper of Hamelin*, *The Jackdaw of Rheims* and *The King's Breakfast*) do not appear, although 'adult' children's evergreens, such as Belloc's *Matilda*, do. Extracts from the Bible

are excluded, as are all carols: both would fill similar books of
their own. So, too, are songs and hymns, except for national or
near-national anthems and those which, in my view, belong as
much to literature as to the hymnal or song-book. Comic verse,
where the field is also enormous, is represented by the better-
known classics of Lear, Carroll, Belloc, W.S. Gilbert, Ogden Nash
and a few others. On the whole I have resisted parodies, even
preferring the original versions of 'How doth the little busy bee'
and ''Tis the voice of the sluggard; I hear him complain' to
Carroll's versions; but I could not leave out George Strong's *The
Song of Milkanwatha* or Ogden Nash's *Song of the Open Road*.
Finally, lack of space – and only lack of space – dictated the
omission of *John Gilpin* and *The Ancient Mariner*, two poems
which could only be included in their entirety and which, between
them, would have taken up almost a twelfth of the book.

   I hope to have catered not only for my own generation but for
older and younger generations too. But with poems written after
the turn of the century (and particularly after World War I), it
becomes increasingly difficult to maintain a fair balance between
the tastes and memories of young and old. New favourites have
emerged with each generation, not only from the work of new
poets but from the later work of poets already well known for
earlier anthology pieces. It is hard to say whether Eliot's *Old
Possum's Book of Practical Cats*, for example, is more widely
known today than *The Love Song of J. Alfred Prufrock*, or Yeats's
The Second Coming than *The Lake Isle of Innisfree*. Recent
poetry, of course, simply has not had time to become evergreen. In
its first edition I found the book came naturally to an end with the
early 1950s; and essentially, the position has not changed – or has
only changed marginally – in the twelve years since then. But
recently various factors have contributed to a greatly increased
interest in poetry, one of which is the accessibility, in terms of
approach, style and subject matter, of much that has been written
since World War II. Many new poems have become popular with
a very wide audience, and it is reasonable to speculate that some of
these have already become evergreen. For this revised edition,
therefore, I have selected those postwar poems that I think are best
known and most likely to last, preferring older ones which have
already been tested by time, but ending with a very young one by

Wendy Cope. Because the field is so vast on both sides of the Atlantic (and space limited), I have not attempted to represent America in this period, though one or two American poems are here.

I am most grateful to all those of varying ages who have given me advice, and especially to my wife and to Ayeshah Haleem who have helped me put the book together and criticized the selection at every stage.

DAVID HERBERT

NOTE ON THE TEXT

The poets are in chronological order of birth-date. Ballads have been printed in a group after Chaucer, even though some are obviously later in the form in which we have them and others may well be earlier. For the texts of the ballads I have gone to F.J. Child's *English and Scottish Popular Ballads*, Walter Scott's *Minstrelsy of the Scottish Border* and Bishop Percy's *Reliques*. Where Child printed several versions of the same ballad, I have made, out of a combination of them, what I think is the best single version; where the version in this book is supplied by Scott or Percy, I have retained their modernized spelling. In neither case have I altered or added to the text. Other anonymous poems appear in approximate chronological order. For extracts from Chaucer and Spenser I have retained the original spelling (and Spenser's deliberately archaic capital letters). Otherwise I have modernized spelling and capital letters throughout, except where some definite purpose of the author's demanded the old form.

Anonymous

'Sumer is icumen in'

Sing cuccu nu! Sing cuccu!
Sing cuccu! Sing cuccu nu!

Sumer is icumen in,
    Lhude sing cuccu: *Loud*
Groweth sed and bloweth med   *seed; mead*
    And springth the wode nu.
      Sing cuccu!
Awe bleteth after lomb,   *Ewe*
    Lhouth after calve cu;   *Loweth*
Bulluc sterteth, bucke verteth;   *breaks wind*
    Murie sing cuccu.
      Cuccu, cuccu,
Wel singes thu, cuccu,
Ne swik thu naver nu.   *cease*

Geoffrey Chaucer

From The Book of the Tales of Caunterbury

Whan that Aprill with his shoures soote   *sweet*
The droghte of March hath perced to the roote,
And bathed every veyne in swich licour
Of which vertu engendred is the flour;
When Zephirus eek with his sweete breeth   *also*
Inspired hath in every holt and heeth   *Quickened; wood*
The tendre croppes, and the yonge sonne   *shoots*
Hath in the Ram his halve cours yronne,
And smale foweles make melodye,   *birds*
That slepen al the nyght with open ye
(So priketh hem nature in hir corages);   *incites; hearts*
Thanne longen folk to goon on pilgrimages,
And palmeres for to seken straunge strondes,
To ferne halwes, kowthe in sondry londes;
And specially from every shires ende
Of Engelond to Caunterbury they wende,   *go*
The hooly blisful martir for to seke,   *blessed; visit*

That hem hath holpen whan that they were seeke.   *helped*
  Bifil that in that seson on a day,
In Southwerk at the Tabard as I lay   *stayed*
Redy to wenden on my pilgrymage
To Caunterbury with ful devout corage,
At nyght was come into that hostelrye
Wel nyne and twenty in a compaignye,   *At least*
Of sondry folk, by aventure yfalle
In felaweshipe, and pilgrimes were they alle,
That toward Caunterbury wolden ryde.   *intended to*
The chambres and the stables weren wyde,
And well we weren esed atte beste.
And shortly, whan the sonne was to reste,   *(gone) to rest*
So hadde I spoken with hem everichon   *each one*
That I was of hir felaweshipe anon,
And made forward erly for to ryse,   *agreement*
To take oure wey ther as I yow devyse.
  But nathelees, whil I have tyme and space,   *opportunity*
Er that I ferther in this tale pace,   *Before; proceed*
Me thynketh it acordaunt to resoun
To telle yow al the condicioun
Of ech of hem, so as it semed me,
And whiche they weren, and of what degree,
And eek in what array that they were inne;   *attire*
And at a knyght than wol I first bigynne.
  A Knyght ther was, and that a worthy man,
That fro the tyme that he first bigan
To riden out, he loved chivalrie,   *To go campaigning*
Trouthe and honour, fredom and curteisic.
Ful worthy was he in his lordes werre,   *war*
And therto hadde he riden, no man ferre,   *also; farther*
As wel in cristendom as in hethenesse,   *heathendom*
And evere honoured for his worthynesse.
At Alisaundre he was whan it was wonne.
Ful ofte tyme he hadde the bord bigonne
Aboven alle nacions in Pruce;   *Prussia*
In Lettow hadde he reysed and in Ruce,
No Cristen man so ofte of his degree.
In Gernade at the seege eek hadde he be
Of Algezir, and riden in Belmarye.
At Lyeys was he and at Satalye,
Whan they were wonne; and in the Grete See   *Mediterranean*
At many a noble armee hadde he be.   *armed expedition*

At mortal batailles hadde he been fiftene,
And foughten for oure feith at Tramyssene
In lystes thries, and ay slayn his foo.   *lists; thrice*
This ilke worthy knyght hadde been also   *same*
Somtyme with the lord of Palatye   *Once; Palatia*
Agayn another hethen in Turkye.
And everemoore he hadde a sovereyn prys;
And though that he were worthy, he was wys,   *eminent*
And of his port as meeke as is a mayde.   *bearing*
He nevere yet no vileynye ne sayde
In all his lyf unto no maner wight.
He was a verray, parfit gentil knyght.
But, for to tellen yow of his array,   *outfit*
His hors were goode, but he was nat gay.   *horses*
Of fustian he wered a gypon
Al bismotered with his habergeon,
For he was late ycome from his viage,   *military expedition*
And wente for to doon his pilgrymage.

Anonymous

A Lykewake Dirge

This ae night, this ae night,
  Every night and all,
Fire and fleet and candle light,
  And Christ receive thy soul.

When thou from hence away art past,
  Every night and all,
To Whinny-Muir thou com'st at last,
  And Christ receive thy soul.

If ever thou gavest hosen and shoon,
  Every night and all,
Sit thee down and put them on,
  And Christ receive thy soul.

If hosen and shoon thou ne'er gav'st none,
  Every night and all,
The whins shall prick thee to the bare bone,
  And Christ receive thy soul.

From Whinny-Muir when thou mayest pass,
   Every night and all,
To Brig o' Dread thou com'st at last,
   And Christ receive thy soul.

From Brig o' Dread when thou mayest pass,
   Every night and all,
To Purgatory fire thou com'st at last,
   And Christ receive thy soul.

If ever thou gavest meat or drink,
   Every night and all,
The fire shall never make thee shrink,
   And Christ receive thy soul.

If meat or drink thou ne'er gav'st none,
   Every night and all,
The fire will burn thee to the bare bone,
   And Christ receive thy soul.

This ae night, this ae night,
   Every night and all,
Fire and fleet and candle light,
   And Christ receive thy soul.

The Twa Corbies

As I was walking all alane,
I heard twa corbies making a mane;   *moan*
The tane unto the t'other say,
'Where sall we gang and dine to-day?'

'In behint yon auld fail dyke   *turf*
I wot there lies a new-slain knight;
And naebody kens that he lies there
But his hawk, his hound, and his lady fair.

'His hound is to the hunting gane,
His hawk to fetch the wild-fowl hame,
His lady's ta'en another mate,
So we may mak' our dinner sweet.

'Ye'll sit on his white hause-bane,   *neck-bone*
And I'll pike out his bonny blue een:
Wi' ae lock o' his gowden hair
We'll theek our nest when it grows bare.   *line*

'Mony a one for him makes mane,
But nane sall ken where he is gane;
O'er his white banes, when they are bare,
The wind sall blaw for evermair.'

Edward, Edward

'Why dois your brand saw drap wi' bluid,
    Edward, Edward?
Why dois your brand sae drap wi' bluid,
    And why sae sad gang ye, O?'
'O I hae killed my hawke sae guid,
    Mither, mither;
O I hae killed my hawke sae guid,
    And I had nae mair bot he, O!'

'Your hawkis bluid was never sae reid,
    Edward, Edward;
Your hawkis bluid was never sae reid,
    My deir son, I tell thee, O.'
'O I hae killed my reid-roan steid,
    Mither, mither;
O I hae killed my reid-roan steid,
    That erst was sae fair and frie, O.'

'Your steid was auld, and ye hae gat mair,
    Edward, Edward;
Your steid was auld, and ye hae gat mair;
    Sum other dule ye drie, O.'   *sorrow you suffer*
'O I hae killed my fadir deir,
    Mither, mither;
O I hae killed my fadir deir,
    Alas, and wae is me, O!'

'And whatten penance wul ye drie for that,
    Edward, Edward?
And whatten penance wul ye drie for that?
    My deir son, now tell me, O.'

'I'll set my feit in yonder boat,
    Mither, mither;
I'll set my feit in yonder boat,
    And I'll fare ovir the sea, O.'

'And what wul ye doe wi' your towirs and
            your ha,'
        Edward, Edward?
And what wul ye doe wi' your towirs and
            your ha',
    That were sae fair to see, O?'
'I'll let thame stand tul they doun fa',
    Mither, mither;
I'll let thame stand tul they doun fa',
    For here nevir mair maun I be, O.'

'And what wul ye leive to your bairns and
            your wife,
        Edward, Edward?
And what wul ye leive to your bairns and
            your wife,
    When ye gang ovir the sea, O?'
'The warldis room: late thame beg thrae life,   *world's*
    Mither, mither;
The warldis room: late thame beg thrae life;
    For thame nevir mair wul I see, O.'

'And what wul ye leive to your ain mither deir,
        Edward, Edward?
And what wul ye leive to your ain mither deir,
    My deir son, now tell me, O?'
'The curse of hell frae me sall ye beir,
    Mither, mither;
The curse of hell frae me sall ye beir,
    Sic counseils ye gave to me, O!'

Barbara Allan

In Scarlet Town, where I was born,
    There was a fair maid dwellin',
Made every youth cry *Well-a-day!*
    Her name was Barbara Allan.

'Twas in and about the Martinmas time,
  When the green leaves were fallin',
That Sir John Graeme in the West Country
  Fell in love with Barbara Allan.

He sent his man down through the town,
  To the place where she was dwellin';
'O haste and come to my master dear,
  Gin ye be Barbara Allan.'

Oh hooly, hooly raise she up,   *slowly*
  To the place where he was lyin',
And when she drew the curtain by –
  'Young man, I think you're dyin'.'

'O it's I am sick and very very sick,
  And it's a' for Barbara Allan.'
'O the better for me ye's never be,
  Tho' your heart's blood were spillin'!

'O dinna ye mind, young man,' said she,
  'When ye the cups were fillin',
How ye made the healths go round and round,
  And slighted Barbara Allan?'

He turned his face unto the wall,
  And death was with him dealin':
'Adeiu, adieu, my dear friends all,
  Be kind to Barbara Allan!'

Then hooly, hooly raise she up,
  And hooly, hooly left him,
And sighing said she could not stay,
  Since death of life had reft him.

She had not gane a mile but twa
  When she heard the dead-bell knellin';
And every jow the dead-bell geid   *beat, toll*
  Cried 'Wo to Barbara Allan.'

'O mither, mither, make my bed,
  O make it saft and narrow:
Since my love died for me to-day,
  I'se die for him to-morrow.

'Farewell,' she said, 'ye virgins all,
  And shun the fault I fell in:
Henceforth take warning by the fall
  Of cruel Barbara Allan.'

Lord Randal

'O where hae you been, Lord Randal, my son?
And where hae you been, my handsome young man?'
'I hae been at the greenwood; mother, make my bed soon,
For I'm wearied wi' hunting, and fain wad lie down.'

'An wha met ye there, Lord Randal, my son?
And wha met ye there, my handsome young man?'
'O I met wi' my true-love; mother, make my bed soon,
For I'm wearied wi' hunting, and fain wad lie down.'

'And what did she give you, Lord Randal, my son?
And what did she give you, my handsome young man?'
'Eels fried in a pan; mother, make my bed soon,
For I'm wearied wi' hunting, and fain wad lie down.'

'And wha gat your leavins, Lord Randal, my son?
And wha gat your leavins, my handsome young man?'
'My hawks and my hounds; mother, make my bed soon,
For I'm wearied wi' hunting, and fain wad lie down.'

'And what became of them, Lord Randal, my son?
And what became of them, my handsome young man?'
'They stretched their legs out and died; mother, make my bed
     soon,
For I'm wearied wi' hunting, and fain wad lie down.'

'O I fear you are poisoned, Lord Randal, my son!
I fear you are poisoned, my handsome young man!'
'O yes, I am poisoned; mother, make my bed soon,
For I'm sick at the heart, and I fain wad lie down.'

'What d'ye leave to your mother, Lord Randal, my son?
What d'ye leave to your mother, my handsome young man?'
'Four and twenty milk kye; mother, make my bed soon,
For I'm sick at the heart, and I fain wad lie down.'

'What d'ye leave to your sister, Lord Randal, my son?
What d'ye leave to your sister, my handsome young man?'
'My gold and my silver; mother, make my bed soon,
For I'm sick at the heart, and I fain wad lie down.'

'What d'ye leave to your brother, Lord Randal, my son?
What d'ye leave to your brother, my handsome young man?'
'My houses and lands; mother, make my bed soon,
For I'm sick at the heart, and I fain wad lie down.'

'What d'ye leave to your true-love, Lord Randal, my son,
What d'ye leave to your true-love, my handsome young man?'
'I leave her hell and fire; mother, make my bed soon,
For I'm sick at the heart, and I fain wad lie down.'

Sir Patrick Spens

The king sits in Dunfermline toun,
   Drinking the blude-reid wine;
'O whar will I get a guid sailor,
   To sail this ship of mine?'

Up and spak an eldlern knight,
   Sat at the king's right kne;
'Sir Patrick Spens is the best sailor
   That sails upon the sea.'

The king has written a braid letter,
   And signed it with his hand,
And sent it to Sir Patrick Spens,
   Was walking on the sand.

The first line that Sir Patrick read,
   A loud laugh laughed he;
The next line that Sir Patrick read,
   The teir blinded his ee.

'O wha is this has done this deid,
   This ill deid done to me,
To send me out this time o' the yeir,
   To sail upon the sea!

'Mak haste, mak haste, my mirry men all,
   Our guid ship sails the morn.'
'O say na sae, my master deir,
   Fir I feir a deadly storm.

'Late, late yestreen I saw the new moone,
   Wi' the auld moon in his arm,
And I feir, I feir, my deir master,
   That we will come to harm.'

O our Scots nobles wer right laith
   To weet their cork-heil'd schoon;
Bot lang owre a' the play wer play'd,
   Thair hats they swam aboon.

O lang, lang may their ladies sit
    Wi' thair fans into their hand,
Or eir they see Sir Patrick Spens
    Come sailing to the land.

O land, land may the ladies stand,
    Wi' thair gold kems in their hair,
Waiting for thair ain deir lords,
    For they'll see thame na mair.

Haf owre, haf owre to Aberdour,
    It's fifty fadom deip,
And thair lies guid Sir Patrick Spens,
    Wi' the Scots lords at his feit.

Greensleeves

Alas, my love! ye do me wrong
    To cast me off discourteously;
And I have loved you so long,
    Delighting in your company.

Greensleeves was all my joy,
    Greensleeves was my delight;
Greensleeves was my heart of gold,
    And who but my Lady Greensleeves.

I have been ready at your hand,
    To grant whatever you would crave;
I have both waged life and land,
    Your love and good will for to have.
Greensleeves was all my joy, etc.

I bought thee kerchers to thy head,
    That were wrought fine and gallantly,
I kept thee both at board and bed,
    Which cost my purse well favouredly.

I bought thee petticoats of the best,
    The cloth so fine as fine might be;
I gave thee jewels for thy chest,
    And all this cost I spent on thee.

Thy smock of silk, both fair and white,
    With gold embroidered gorgeously;

Thy petticoat of sendal right;
   And thus I bought thee gladly.

Thy girdle of gold so red,
   With pearls bedecked sumptuously;
The like no other lasses had,
   And yet thou would'st not love me.

Thy purse and eke thy gay gilt knives,
   Thy pincase gallant to the eye;
No better wore the burgess wives,
   And yet thou would'st not love me.

Thy crimson stockings all of silk,
   With gold all wrought above the knee;
Thy pumps as white as was the milk,
   And yet thou would'st not love me.

Thy gown was of the grassy green,
   Thy sleeves of satin hanging by,
Which made thee be our harvest queen,
   And yet thou would'st not love me.

Thy garters fringed with the gold,
   And silver aglets hanging by,
Which made thee blithe for to behold.
   And yet thou would'st not love me.

My gayest gelding I thee gave,
   To ride wherever liked thee;
No lady ever was so brave,
   And yet thou would'st not love me.

My men were clothed all in green,
   And they did ever wait on thee;
And this was gallant to be seen,
   And yet thou would'st not love me.

They set thee up, they took thee down,
   They served thee with humility;
Thy foot might not once touch the ground,
   And yet thou would'st not love me.

For every morning when thou rose,
   I sent thee dainties orderly,
To cheer thy stomach from all woes,
   And yet thou would'st not love me.

Thou could'st desire no earthly thing
    But still thou had'st it readily;
Thy music still to play and sing,
    And yet thou would'st not love me.

And who did pay for all this gear
    That thou did'st spend when pleased thee?
Even I that am rejected here,
    And thou disdain'st to love me.

Well, I will pray to God on high,
    That thou my constancy may'st see,
And that yet once before I die,
    Thou wilt vouchsafe to love me.

Greensleeves, now farewell! adieu!
    God I pray to prosper thee;
For I am still thy lover true.
    Come once again and love me.

'There is a lady sweet and kind'

There is a lady sweet and kind,
Was never face so pleased my mind.
I did but see her passing by,
And yet I love her till I die.

Her gesture, motion, and her smiles,
Her wit, her voice my heart beguiles;
Beguiles my heart, I know not why,
And yet I love her till I die.

Cupid is winged and doth range
Her country so my love doth change;
But change she earth, or change she sky,
Yet will I love her till I die.

Thomas Wyatt

'And wilt thou leave me thus?'

And wilt thou leave me thus?
Say nay, say nay, for shame,
To save thee from the blame
Of all my grief and grame.   *sorrow*
And wilt thou leave me thus?
  Say nay, say nay!

And wilt thou leave me thus
That hath loved thee so long,
In wealth and woe among?
And is thy heart so strong
As for to leave me thus?
  Say nay, say nay!

And wilt thou leave me thus
That hath given thee my heart,
Never for to depart,
Neither for pain nor smart;
And wilt thou leave me thus?
  Say nay, say nay!

And wilt thou leave me thus,
And have no more pity,
Of him that loveth thee?
Helas! thy cruelty!
And wilt thou leave me thus!
  Say nay, say nay!

Nicholas Breton

'In the merry month of May'

In the merry month of May,
In a morn by break of day,
Forth I walked by the wood side,
Whereas May was in his pride.
There I spied all alone
Phyllida and Corydon.

Much ado there was, God wot;
He would love and she would not.
She said, never man was true;
He said, none was false to you.
He said, he had loved her long;
She said, love should have no wrong.
Corydon would kiss her then;
She said, maids must kiss no men
Till they did for good and all.
Then she made the shepherd call
All the heavens to witness truth,
Never loved a truer youth.
Thus with many a pretty oath,
Yea and nay, and faith and troth,
Such as silly shepherds use,
When they will not love abuse,
Love, which had been long deluded,
Was with kisses sweet concluded;
And Phyllida with garlands gay
Was made the Lady of the May.

Walter Raleigh

From The Passionate Man's Pilgrimage

Give me my scallop-shell of quiet,
My staff of faith to walk upon,
My scrip of joy, immortal diet,
My bottle of salvation,
My gown of glory, hope's true gage,
And thus I'll take my pilgrimage.

Edmund Spenser

From Prothalamion

Calm was the day, and through the trembling air
Sweet-breathing Zephyrus did softly play
A gentle spirit, that lightly did delay
Hot Titan's beams, which then did glister fair;
When I (whom sullen care,
Through discontent of my long fruitless stay
In prince's court, and expectation vain
Of idle hopes, which still do fly away,
Like empty shadows, did afflict my brain),
Walked forth to ease my pain
Along the shore of silver-streaming Thames;
Whose rutty bank, the which his river hems,
Was painted all with variable flowers,
And all the meads adorned with dainty gems
Fit to deck maidens' bowers.
And crown their paramours
Against the bridal day, which is not long:
  Sweet Thames! run softly, till I end my song.

There, in a meadow, by the river's side,
A flock of nymphs I chanced to espy,
All lovely daughters of the flood thereby,
With goodly greenish locks, all loose untied,
As each had been a bride;
And each one had a little wicker basket,
Made of fine twigs, entrailed curiously,
In which they gathered flowers to fill their flasket,
And with fine fingers cropt full feateously
The tender stalks on high.
Of every sort, which in that meadow grew,
They gathered some; the violet, pallid blue,
The little daisy, that at evening closes,
The virgin lily, and the primrose true,
With store of vermeil roses,
To deck their bridegrooms' posies
Against the bridal day, which was not long:
  Sweet Thames! run softly, till I end my song.

From The Faerie Queene

Eftsoones they heard a most melodious sound,
  Of all that mote delight a daintie eare,
  Such as attonce might not on living ground,
  Save in this Paradise, be heard elsewhere:
  Right hard it was, for wight, which did it heare,
  To read, what manner musicke that mote bee:
  For all that pleasing is to living eare,
  Was there consorted in one harmonee,
Birdes, voices, instruments, windes, waters, all agree.

The joyous birdes shrouded in chearefull shade,
  Their notes unto the voice attempred sweet;
  Th' Angelicall soft trembling voices made
  To th' instruments divine respondence meet:
  The silver sounding instruments did meet
  With the base murmure of the waters fall:
  The waters fall with difference discreet,
  Now soft, now loud, unto the wind did call:
The gentle warbling wind low answered to all.

There, whence that Musick seemed heard to bee,
  Was the faire Witch her selfe now solacing,
  With a new Lover, whom through sorceree
  And witchcraft, she from farre did thither bring:
  There she had him now laid aslombering,
  In secret shade, after long wanton joyes:
  Whilst round about them pleasauntly did sing
  Many faire Ladies, and lascivious boyes,
That ever mixt their song with light licentious toyes.

And all that while, right over him she hong,
  With her false eyes fast fixed in his sight,
  As seeking medicine, whence she was strong,
  Or greedily depasturing delight:
  And oft inclining downe with kisses light,
  For feare of waking him, his lips bedewd,
  And through his humid eyes did sucke his spright,
  Quite molten into lust and pleasure lewd;
Wherewith she sighed soft, as if his case she rewd.

The whiles some one did chaunt this lovely lay;
  Ah see, who so faire thing doest faine to see,
  In springing flowre the image of thy day;

Ah see the Virgin Rose, how sweetly shee
Doth first peepe forth with bashfull modestee,
That fairer seemes, the lesse ye see her may;
Lo see soone after, how more bold and free
Her bared bosome she doth broad display;
Loe see soone after, how she fades, and falles away.

So passeth, in the passing of a day,
  Of mortall life the leafe, the bud, the flowre,
  Ne more doth flourish after first decay,
  That earst was sought to decke both bed and bowre,
  Of many a Ladie, and many a Paramowre:
  Gather therefore the Rose, whilest yet is prime,
  For soone comes age, that will her pride deflowre:
  Gather the Rose of love, whilest yet is time,
Whilest loving thou mayst loved be with equall crime.

Anthony Munday

'Beauty sat bathing by a spring'

Beauty sat bathing by a spring,
  Where fairest shades did hide her.
The winds blew calm, the birds did sing,
  The cool streams ran beside her.
My wanton thoughts enticed mine eye
  To see what was forbidden.
But better memory said 'Fie';
  So vain desire was chidden
                    Hey nonny nonny O!
                    Hey nonny nonny!

Into a slumber then I fell,
  And fond imagination
Seemed to see, but could not tell,
  Her feature or her fashion.
But even as babes in dreams do smile,
  And sometimes fall a-weeping,
So I awaked as wise that while
  As when I fell a-sleeping.

Philip Sidney

'My true love hath my heart, and I have his'

My true love hath my heart, and I have his,
By just exchange, one for the other given.
I hold his dear, and mine he cannot miss:
There never was a better bargain driven.
His heart in me keeps me and him in one,
My heart in him his thoughts and senses guides:
He loves my heart, for once it was his own:
I cherish his, because in me it bides.
His heart his wound received from my sight:
My heart was wounded, with his wounded heart,
For as from me, on him his hurt did light,
So still me thought in me his hurt did smart:
    Both equal hurt, in this change sought our bliss:
    My true love hath my heart and I have his.

Edward Dyer

'My mind to me a kingdom is'

My mind to me a kingdom is;
    Such present joys therein I find
That it excels all other bliss
    That world affords or grows by kind.
Though much I want which most would have,
Yet still my mind forbids to crave.

No princely pomp, no wealthy store,
    No force to win the victory,
No wily wit to salve a sore,
    No shape to feed a loving eye;
To none of these I yield as thrall,
For why, my mind doth serve for all.

I see how plenty suffers oft,
    And hasty climbers soon do fall;
I see that those which are aloft
    Mishap doth threaten most of all.
They get with toil, they keep with fear;
Such cares my mind could never bear.

Content I live, this is my stay,
  I seek no more than may suffice;
I press to bear no haughty sway;
  Look, what I lack my mind supplies.
Lo! thus I triumph like a king,
Content with that my mind doth bring.

Some have too much, yet still do crave;
  I little have, and seek no more.
They are but poor, though much they have,
  And I am rich with little store.
They poor, I rich; they beg, I give;
They lack, I leave; they pine, I live.

I laugh not at another's loss,
  I grudge not at another's gain;
No worldly waves my mind can toss;
  My state at one doth still remain.
I fear no foe, I fawn no friend;
I loathe not life, nor dread my end.

Some weigh their pleasure by their lust,
  Their wisdom by their rage of will;
Their treasure is their only trust,
  A cloaked craft their store of skill.
But all the pleasure that I find
Is to maintain a quiet mind.

My wealth is health and perfect ease,
  My conscience clear my choice defence;
I neither seek by bribes to please,
  Nor by deceit to breed offence.
Thus do I live, thus will I die;
Would all did so as well as I!

Michael Drayton

'Since there's no help, come, let us kiss and part'

Since there's no help, come, let us kiss and part;
Nay, I have done, you get no more of me,
And I am glad, yea glad with all my heart,
That thus so cleanly I my self can free.
Shake hands for ever, cancel all our vows,

And when we meet at any time again,
Be it not seen in either of our brows
That we one jot of former love retain.
Now at the last gasp of love's latest breath,
When, his pulse failing, passion speechless lies,
When faith is kneeling by his bed of death,
And innocence is closing up his eyes,
   Now, if thou would'st, when all have given him over,
   From death to life thou might'st him yet recover.

'Fair stood the wind for France'

Fair stood the wind for France
When we our sails advance,
Nor now to prove our chance
   Longer will tarry;
But putting to the main,
At Caux, the mouth of Seine,
With all his martial train
   Landed King Harry.

And taking many a fort,
Furnished in warlike sort,
Marcheth towards Agincourt
   In happy hour;
Skirmishing day by day
With those that stopped his way,
Where the French general lay
   With all his power.

Which, in his height of pride,
King Henry to deride,
His ransom to provide
   Unto him sending;
Which he neglects the while
As from a nation vile,
Yet with an angry smile
   Their fall portending.

And turning to his men,
Quoth our brave Henry then,
'Though they to one be ten
   Be not amazed:

Yet have we well begun;
Battles so bravely won
Have ever to the sun
    By fame been raised.

'And for myself,' quoth he,
'This my full rest shall be;
England ne'er mourn for me
    Nor more esteem me.
Victor I will remain
Or on this earth lie slain;
Never shall she sustain
    Loss to redeem me.

'Poitiers and Cressy tell,
When most their pride did swell,
Under our swords they fell.
    No less our skill is
Than when our grandsire great,
Claiming the regal seat,
By many a warlike feat
    Lopped the French lilies.'

The Duke of York so dread
The eager vaward led;
With the main Henry sped
    Among his henchmen.
Exeter had the rear,
A braver man not there;
O Lord, how hot they were
    On the false Frenchmen!

They now to fight are gone,
Armour on armour shone,
Drum now to drum did groan,
    To hear was wonder;
That with the cries they make
The very earth did shake.
Trumpet to trumpet spake,
    Thunder to thunder.

Well it thine age became,
O noble Erpingham,
Which didst the signal aim
    To our hid forces!

When from a meadow by,
Like a storm suddenly
The English archery
    Struck the French horses.

With Spanish yew so strong,
Arrows a cloth-yard long
That like to serpents stung,
    Piercing the weather;
None from his fellow starts,
But playing manly parts,
And like true English hearts
    Stuck close together.

When down their bows they threw,
And forth their bilbos drew,
And on the French they flew,
    Not one was tardy;
Arms were from shoulders sent,
Scalps to the teeth were rent,
Down the French peasants went.
    Our men were hardy!

This while our noble king,
His broadsword brandishing,
Down the French host did ding
    As to o'erwhelm it;
And many a deep wound lent,
His arms with blood besprent,
And many a cruel dent
    Bruised his helmet.

Gloster, that duke so good,
Next of the royal blood,
For famous England stood
    With his brave brother;
Clarence, in steel so bright,
Though but a maiden knight,
Yet in that furious fight
    Scarce such another.

Warwick in blood did wade,
Oxford the foe invade,
And cruel slaughter made
    Still as they ran up.
Suffolk his axe did ply,

Beaumont and Willoughby
Bare them right doughtily,
    Ferrers and Fanhope.

Upon Saint Crispin's Day
Fought was this noble fray,
Which fame did not delay
    To England to carry.
O when shall English men
With such acts fill a pen?
Or England breed again
    Such a King Harry?

Christopher Marlowe

From Hero and Leander

It lies not in our power to love, or hate,
For will in us is over-ruled by fate.
When two are stripped, long ere the course begin,
We wish that one should lose, the other win.
And one especially do we affect,
Of two gold ingots like in each respect;
The reason no man knows; let it suffice,
What we behold is censured by our eyes.
Where both deliberate, the love is slight,
Who ever loved, that loved not at first sight?

From Dr Faustus

[Faustus speaks]

Was this the face that launched a thousand ships
And burnt the topless towers of Ilium?
Sweet Helen, make me immortal with a kiss.
Her lips suck forth my soul; see where it flies!
Come, Helen, come, give me my soul again.
Here will I dwell, for Heaven is in these lips,
And all is dross that is not Helena.
I will be Paris and, for love of thee,

Instead of Troy, shall Wertenberg be sacked.
And I will combat with weak Menelaus,
And wear thy colours on my plumed crest.
Yea, I will wound Achilles in the heel,
And then return to Helen for a kiss.
Oh, thou art fairer than the evening air
Clad in the beauty of a thousand stars;
Brighter art thou than flaming Jupiter
When he appeared to hapless Semele;
More lovely than the monarch of the sky
In wanton Arethusa's azured arms.
And none but thou shalt be my paramour.

The Passionate Shepherd to His Love

Come live with me and be my love,
And we will all the pleasures prove
That hills and valleys, dales and fields
And all the craggy mountains yields.

There we will sit upon the rocks,
Seeing the shepherds feed their flocks
By shallow rivers, to whose falls
Melodious birds sing madrigals.

And I will make thee beds of roses
With a thousand fragrant posies,
A cap of flowers and a kirtle
Embroidered all with leaves of myrtle;

A gown made of the finest wool,
Which from our pretty lambs we pull;
Fair lined slippers for the cold,
With buckles of the purest gold;

A belt of straw and ivy buds,
With coral-clasps and amber studs;
And if these pleasures may thee move,
Come live with me, and be my love.

The shepherd swains shall dance and sing
For thy delight each May morning;
If these delights thy mind may move,
Then live with me, and be my love.

Walter Raleigh

The Nymph's Reply to the Shepherd

If all the world and love were young,
And truth in every shepherd's tongue,
These pretty pleasures might me move
To live with thee and be thy love.

Time drives the flocks from field to fold,
When rivers rage and rocks grow cold,
And Philomel becometh dumb;
The rest complains of cares to come.

The flowers do fade, and wanton fields
To wayward winter reckoning yields;
A honey tongue, a heart of gall,
Is fancy's spring but sorrow's fall.

Thy gowns, thy shoes, thy beds of roses,
Thy cap, thy kirtle, and thy posies,
Soon break, soon wither, soon forgotten:
In folly ripe, in reason rotten.

Thy belt of straw and ivy buds,
Thy coral clasps and amber studs,
All these in me no means can move,
To come to thee and be thy love.

But could youth last and love still breed,
Had joys no date nor age no heed,
Then these delights my mind might move
To live with thee and be thy love.

William Shakespeare

From The Passionate Pilgrim

Crabbed age and youth cannot live together:
Youth is full of pleasance, age is full of care;
Youth is like summer morn, age like winter weather;
Youth like summer brave, age like winter bare.
Youth is full of sport, age's breath is short;

Youth is nimble, age is lame;
Youth is hot and bold, age is weak and cold;
Youth is wild, and age is tame.
Age, I do abhor thee; youth, I do adore thee.
O, my love, my love is young!
Age I do defy thee: O, sweet shepherd, hie thee,
For methinks thou stayest too long.

From The Sonnets

[1]

Shall I compare thee to a summer's day?
Thou art more lovely and more temperate:
Rough winds do shake the darling buds of May,
And summer's lease hath all too short a date:
Sometime too hot the eye of heaven shines,
And often is his gold complexion dimmed;
And every fair from fair sometime declines,
By chance or nature's changing course untrimmed;
But thy eternal summer shall not fade,
Nor lose possession of that fair thou owest;
Nor shall death brag thou wander'st in his shade,
When in eternal lines to time thou growest:
So long as men can breathe, or eyes can see,
So long lives this, and this gives life to thee.

[2]

When to the sessions of sweet silent thought
I summon up remembrance of things past,
I sigh the lack of many a thing I sought,
And with old woes new wail my dear time's waste:
Then can I drown an eye, unused to flow,
For precious friends hid in death's dateless night,
And weep afresh love's long since cancelled woe,
And moan the expense of many a vanished sight:
Then can I grieve at grievances foregone,
And heavily from woe to woe tell o'er
The sad account of fore-bemoaned moan,
Which I new pay as if not paid before.
But if the while I think on thee, dear friend,
All losses are restored and sorrows end.

[3]

Full many a glorious morning have I seen
Flatter the mountain tops with sovereign eye,
Kissing with golden face the meadows green,
Gilding pale streams with heavenly alchemy;
Anon permit the basest clouds to ride
With ugly rack on his celestial face,
And from the forlorn world his visage hide,
Stealing unseen to west with this disgrace:
Even so my son one early morn did shine
With all-triumphant splendour on my brow;
But, out, alack! he was but one hour mine,
The region cloud hath masked him from me now.
  Yet him for this my love no whit disdaineth;
  Suns of the world may stain when heaven's sun staineth.

[4]

Farewell! thou art too dear for my possessing,
And like enough thou knowest thy estimate:
The charter of thy worth gives thee releasing;
My bonds in thee are all determinate.
For how do I hold thee but by thy granting?
And for that riches where is my deserving?
The cause of this fair gift in me is wanting,
And so my patent back again is swerving.
Thyself thou gavest, thy own worth then not knowing,
Or me, to whom thou gavest it, else mistaking;
So thy great gift, upon misprision growing,
Comes home again, on better judgement making.
  Thus have I had thee, as a dream doth flatter,
  In sleep a king, but waking no such matter.

[5]

When in the chronicle of wasted time
I see descriptions of the fairest wights,
And beauty making beautiful old rhyme
In praise of ladies dead and lovely knights,
Then, in the blazon of sweet beauty's best,
Of hand, of foot, of lip, of eye, of brow,
I see their antique pen would have expressed
Even such a beauty as you master now.
So all their praises are but prophecies

Of this our time, all you prefiguring;
And, for they looked but with divining eyes,
They had not skill enough your worth to sing:
    For we, which now behold these present days,
    Have eyes to wonder, but lack tongues to praise.

[6]

Let me not to the marriage of true minds
Admit impediments. Love is not love
Which alters when it alteration finds,
Or bends with the remover to remove:
O, no! it is an ever-fixed mark,
That looks on tempests and is never shaken;
It is the star to every wandering barque,
Whose worth's unknown, although his height be taken.
Love's not time's fool, though rosy lips and cheeks
Within his bending sickle's compass come;
Love alters not with his brief hours and weeks,
But bears it out even to the edge of doom.
    If this be error and upon me proved,
    I never writ, nor no man ever loved.

From Richard III

[Richard speaks]

Now is the winter of our discontent
Made glorious summer by this sun of York;
And all the clouds that loured upon our house
In the deep bosom of the ocean buried.
Now are our brows bound with victorious wreaths;
Our bruised arms hung up for monuments;
Our stern alarums changed to merry meetings,
Our dreadful marches to delightful measures.
Grim-visaged war hath smoothed his wrinkled front;
And now – instead of mounting barbed steeds,
To fright the souls of fearful adversaries—
He capers nimbly in a lady's chamber
To the lascivious pleasing of a lute.

From The Two Gentlemen of Verona

[*Song*]

Who is Silvia? what is she,
    That all our swains commend her?
Holy, fair, and wise is she;
    The heaven such grace did lend her,
That she might admired be.

Is she kind as she is fair—
    For beauty lives with kindness?
Love doth to her eyes repair,
    To help him of his blindness;
And, being helped, inhabits there.

Then to Silvia let us sing,
    That Silvia is excelling;
She excels each mortal thing
    Upon the dull earth dwelling.
To her let us garlands bring.

From Romeo and Juliet

[*Romeo and Juliet speak*]

Romeo: He jests at scars that never felt a wound.

Enter Juliet *above, at a window*

But soft! What light through yonder window breaks?
It is the east, and Juliet is the sun.
Arise, fair sun, and kill the envious moon,
Who is already sick and pale with grief
That thou her maid art far more fair than she.
Be not her maid, since she is envious.
Her vestal livery is but sick and green,
And none but fools do wear it; cast it off.
It is my lady, O it is my love;
O that she knew she were!
She speaks, yet she says nothing. What of that?
Her eye discourses; I will answer it.
I am too bold; 'tis not to me she speaks.
Two of the fairest stars in all the heaven,

Having some business, do entreat her eyes
To twinkle in their spheres till they return.
What if her eyes were there, they in her head?
The brightness of her cheek would shame those stars
As daylight doth a lamp; her eyes in heaven
Would through the airy region stream so bright
That birds would sing and think it were not night.
See how she leans her cheek upon her hand!
O that I were a glove upon that hand,
That I might touch that cheek.

Juliet: Ay me!

Romeo: She speaks.
Oh speak again, bright angel, for thou art
As glorious to this night, being o'er my head,
As is a winged messenger of heaven
Unto the white-upturned wondering eyes
Of mortals that fall back to gaze on him
When he bestrides the lazy-pacing clouds
And sails upon the bosom of the air.

Juliet: O Romeo, Romeo! Wherefore art thou Romeo?
Deny thy father and refuse thy name;
Or, if thou wilt not, be but sworn my love,
And I'll no longer be a Capulet.

Romeo: Shall I hear more, or shall I speak at this?

Juliet: 'Tis but thy name that is my enemy;
Thou art thyself, though not a Montague.
What's Montague? It is nor hand nor foot
Nor arm nor face, nor any other part
Belonging to a man. O be some other name!
What's in a name? That which we call a rose
By any other name would smell as sweet.
So Romeo would, were he not Romeo called,
Retain that dear perfection which he owes
Without that title. Romeo, doff thy name;
And for thy name, which is no part of thee,
Take all myself.

Romeo (aloud): I take thee at thy word:
Call me but love, and I'll be new baptised;
Henceforth I never will be Romeo.

[Juliet speaks]

Gallop apace, you fiery-footed steeds,
Towards Phoebus' lodging! Such a waggoner
As Phaethon would whip you to the west
And bring in cloudy night immediately.
Spread thy close curtain, love-performing night,
That runaways' eyes may wink, and Romeo
Leap to these arms untalked of and unseen.
Lovers can see to do their amorous rites
By their own beauties, or if love be blind
It best agrees with the night. Come, civil night,
Thou sober-suited matron all in black,
And learn me how to lose a winning match,
Played for a pair of stainless maidenhoods.
Hood my unmanned blood, bating in my cheeks,
With thy black mantle, till strange love, grown bold,
Think true love acted simple modesty.
Come, night! Come, Romeo! Come, thou day in night;
For thou wilt lie upon the wings of night
Whiter than new snow on a raven's back.
Come, gentle night! Come, loving black-browed night!
Give me my Romeo: and when he shall die,
Take him and cut him out in little stars,
And he will make the face of heaven so fine
That all the world will be in love with night
And pay no worship to the garish sun.
O, I have bought the mansion of a love,
But not possessed it; and though I am sold,
Not yet enjoyed. So tedious is the day
As is the night before some festival
To an impatient child that hath new robes
And may not wear them.

From A Midsummer Night's Dream

[Theseus speaks]

The lunatic, the lover, and the poet
Are of imagination all compact.
One sees more devils than vast hell can hold—

That is, the madman. The lover, all as frantic,
Sees Helen's beauty in a brow of Egypt.
The poet's eye, in a fine frenzy rolling,
Doth glance from heaven to earth, from earth to heaven;
And, as imagination bodies forth
The forms of things unknown, the poet's pen
Turns them to shapes, and gives to airy nothing
A local habitation and a name.
Such tricks hath strong imagination,
That, if it would but apprehend some joy,
It comprehends some bringer of that joy;
Or in the night, imagining some fear,
How easy is a bush supposed a bear!

From Richard II

[John of Gaunt speaks]

This royal throne of kings, this sceptred isle,
This earth of majesty, this seat of Mars,
This other Eden, demi-Paradise,
This fortress built by Nature for herself
Against infection and the hand of war;
This happy breed of men, this little world;
This precious stone set in the silver sea,
Which serves it in the office of a wall,
Or as a moat defensive to a house,
Against the envy of less happier lands;
This blessed plot, this earth, this realm, this England,
This nurse, this teeming womb of royal kings,
Feared by their breed and famous by their birth,
Renowned for their deeds as far from home—
For Christian service, and true chivalry—
As is the sepulchre, in stubborn Jewry,
Of the world's ransom, blessed Mary's Son;
This land of such dear souls, this dear dear land,
Dear for her reputation through the world,
Is now leased out – I die pronouncing it—
Like to a tenement or pelting farm:
England, bound in with the triumphant sea,
Whose rocky shore beats back the envious siege

Of watery Neptune, is now bound in with shame,
With inky blots, and rotten parchment bonds:
That England, that was wont to conquer others,
Hath made a shameful conquest of itself.

From The Merchant of Venice

[Song]

Tell me where is fancy bred,
Or in the heart or in the head?
How begot, how nourished?
    Reply, reply.
It is engendered in the eyes,
With gazing fed; and fancy dies
In the cradle where it lies.
    Let us all ring fancy's knell;
    I'll begin it: Ding, dong, bell.
Ding, dong, bell.

[Portia speaks]

The quality of mercy is not strained:
It droppeth as the gentle rain from heaven
Upon the place beneath. It is twice blessed—
It blesseth him that gives, and him that takes:
'Tis mightiest in the mightiest – it becomes
The throned monarch better than his crown;
His sceptre shows the force of temporal power,
The attribute to awe and majesty,
Wherein doth sit the dread and fear of kings;
But mercy is above this sceptred sway—
It is enthroned in the hearts of kings,
It is an attribute to God himself;
And earthly power doth then show likest God's
When mercy seasons justice. Therefore, Jew,
Though justice be thy plea, consider this—
That, in the course of justice, none of us
Should see salvation: we do pray for mercy;
And that same prayer doth teach us all to render
The deeds of mercy.

From Henry V

[Henry speaks]

[1]

Once more unto the breach, dear friends, once more;
Or close the wall up with our English dead!
In peace there's nothing so becomes a man
As modest stillness, and humility:
But when the blast of war blows in our ears,
Then imitate the action of the tiger;
Stiffen the sinews, summon up the blood,
Disguise fair nature with hard-favoured rage;
Then lend the eye a terrible aspect; .
Let it pry through the portage of the head
Like the brass cannon; let the brow o'erwhelm it,
As fearfully as doth a galled rock
O'erhang and jutty his confounded base,
Swilled with the wild and wasteful ocean.
Now set the teeth, and stretch the nostril wide;
Hold hard the breath, and bend up every spirit
To his full height! On, on, you noble English,
Whose blood is fet from fathers of war-proof—
Fathers that, like so many Alexanders,
Have in these parts from morn till even fought,
And sheathed their swords for lack of argument—
Dishonour not your mothers; now attest
That those whom you called fathers did beget you!
Be copy now to men of grosser blood,
And teach them how to war! And you, good yeomen,
Whose limbs were made in England, show us here
The mettle of your pasture; let us swear
That you are worth your breeding, which I doubt not,
For there is none of you so mean and base,
That hath not noble lustre in your eyes.
I see you stand like greyhounds in the slips,
Straining upon the start. The game's afoot:
Follow your spirit; and upon this charge,
Cry, 'God for Harry, England, and Saint George!'

[2]

This day is called the feast of Crispian:
He that outlives this day, and comes safe home,
Will stand a tip-toe when this day is named,
And rouse him at the name of Crispian.
He that shall live this day, and see old age,
Will yearly on the vigil feast his neighbours,
And say, 'To-morrow is Saint Crispian:'
Then will he strip his sleeve and show his scars,
And say, 'These wounds I had on Crispin's day.'
Old men forget; yet all shall be forgot,
But he'll remember with advantages
What feats he did that day. Then shall our names,
Familiar in his mouth as household words—
Harry the King, Bedford and Exeter,
Warwick and Talbot, Salisbury and Gloster—
Be in their flowing cups freshly remembered.
This story shall the good man teach his son;
And Crispin Crispian shall ne'er go by,
From this day to the ending of the world,
But we in it shall be remembered—
We few, we happy few, we band of brothers;
For he today that sheds his blood with me
Shall be my brother; be he ne'er so vile,
This day shall gentle his condition:
And gentlemen in England now a-bed
Shall think themselves accursed they were not here;
And hold their manhoods cheap whiles any speaks
That fought with us upon Saint Crispin's day.

From As You Like It

[Jaques speaks]

                    All the world's a stage,
And all the men and women merely players;
They have their exits and their entrances;
And one man in his time plays many parts,
His acts being seven ages. At first the infant,
Mewling and puking in the nurse's arms.
Then the whining schoolboy, with his satchel
And shining morning face, creeping like a snail

Unwillingly to school. And then the lover,
Sighing like furnace, with a woeful ballad
Made to his mistress' eyebrow. Then the soldier,
Full of strange oaths, and bearded like the pard,
Jealous in honour, sudden and quick in quarrel,
Seeking the bubble reputation
Even in the cannon's mouth. And then the justice,
In fair round belly with good capon lined,
With eyes severe and beard of formal cut,
Full of wise saws and modern instances;
And so he plays his part. The sixth age shifts
Into the lean and slippered pantaloon,
With spectacles on nose and pouch on side;
His youthful hose, well saved, a world too wide
For his shrunk shank; and his big manly voice,
Turning again toward childish treble, pipes
And whistles in his sound. Last scene of all,
That ends this strange eventful history,
Is second childishness, and mere oblivion,
Sans teeth, sans eyes, sans taste, sans everything.

[Songs]

[1]

Under the greenwood tree
    Who loves to lie with me,
And turn his merry note
    Unto the sweet bird's throat,
Come hither, come hither, come hither:
    Here shall he see
    No enemy
But winter and rough weather.

Who doth ambition shun
    And loves to live i' th' sun,
Seeking the food he eats
    And pleased with what he gets,
Come hither, come hither, etc.

[2]

Blow, blow, thou winter wind,
Thou art not so unkind
    As man's ingratitude;
Thy tooth is not so keen,
Because thou art not seen,
    Although thy breath be rude.
Heigh-ho! Sing, heigh-ho! unto the green holly;
Most friendship is feigning, most loving mere folly.
    Then, heigh-ho, the holly!
        This life is most jolly.

Freeze, freeze, thou bitter sky,
That dost not bite so nigh
    As benefits forgot;
Though thou the waters warp,
Thy sting is not so sharp,
    As friend remembered not.
Heigh-ho! Sing, heigh-ho! etc.

[3]

It was a lover and his lass,
    With a hey, and a ho, and a hey nonino,
That o'er the green cornfield did pass
    In spring time, the only pretty ring-time,
When birds do sing, hey ding a ding, ding:
    Sweet lovers love the spring.

Between the acres of the rye,
    With a hey, and a ho, and a hey nonino,
These pretty countryfolks would lie,
    In spring time, etc.

This carol they began that hour,
    With a hey, and a ho, and a hey nonino,
How that a life was but a flower

And therefore take the present time,
    With a hey, and a ho, and a hey nonino;
For love is crowned with the prime.

From Julius Caesar

[*Antony speaks*]

[1]

O, pardon me, thou bleeding piece of earth,
That I am meek and gentle with these butchers!
Thou art the ruins of the noblest man
That ever lived in the tide of times.
Woe to the hand that shed this costly blood!
Over thy wounds now do I prophesy—
Which, like dumb mouths, do ope their ruby lips,
To beg the voice and utterance of my tongue—
A curse shall light upon the limbs of men;
Domestic fury and fierce civil strife
Shall cumber all the parts of Italy;
Blood and destruction shall be so in use,
And dreadful objects so familiar,
That mothers shall but smile when they behold
Their infants quartered with the hands of war;
All pity choked with custom of fell deeds:
And Caesar's spirit, ranging for revenge,
With Ate by his side come hot from hell,
Shall in these confines with a monarch's voice
Cry 'Havoc', and let slip the dogs of war;
That this foul deed shall smell above the earth
With carrion men, groaning for burial.

[2]

Friends, Romans, countrymen, lend me your ears;
I come to bury Caesar, not to praise him.
The evil that men do lives after them;
The good is oft interred with their bones;
So let it be with Caesar. The noble Brutus
Hath told you Caesar was ambitious:
If it were so, it was a grievous fault;
And grievously hath Caesar answered it.
Here, under leave of Brutus and the rest—
For Brutus is an honourable man;
So are they all, all honourable men—
Come I to speak in Caesar's funeral.
He was my friend, faithful and just to me:

But Brutus says he was ambitious;
And Brutus is an honourable man.
He hath brought many captives home to Rome,
Whose ransoms did the general coffers fill:
Did this in Caesar seem ambitious?
When that the poor have cried, Caesar hath wept:
Ambition should be made of sterner stuff:
Yet Brutus says he was ambitious;
And Brutus is an honourable man.
You all did see, that on the Lupercal
I thrice presented him a kingly crown,
Which he did thrice refuse: was this ambition?
Yet Brutus says he was ambitious;
And, sure, he is an honourable man.
I speak not to disprove what Brutus spoke,
But here I am to speak what I do know.
You all did love him once – not without cause:
What cause withholds you, then, to mourn for him?
O judgment, thou art fled to brutish beasts,
And men have lost their reason! Bear with me;
My heart is in the coffin there with Caesar,
And I must pause till it come back to me.

. . .

If you have tears, prepare to shed them now.
You all do know this mantle: I remember
The first time ever Caesar put it on;
'Twas on a summer's evening, in his tent,
That day he overcame the Nervii.
Look, in this place ran Cassius' dagger through:
See what a rent the envious Casca made:
Through this the well-beloved Brutus stabbed;
And as he plucked his cursed steel away,

Mark how the blood of Caesar followed it,
As rushing out of doors, to be resolved
If Brutus so unkindly knocked, or no;
For Brutus, as you know, was Caesar's angel:
Judge, O you gods, how dearly Caesar loved him!
This was the most unkindest cut of all;
For when the noble Caesar saw him stab,
Ingratitude, more strong than traitors' arms,
Quite vanquished him: then burst his mighty heart;
And, in his mantle muffling up his face,
Even at the base of Pompey's statue,
Which all the while ran blood, great Caesar fell.
O, what a fall was there, my countrymen!
Then I, and you, and all of us fell down,
Whilst bloody treason flourished over us.
O, now you weep; and, I perceive, you feel
The dint of pity: these are gracious drops.
Kind souls, what, weep you when you but behold
Our Caesar's vesture wounded? Look you here,
Here is himself, marred, as you see, with traitors.

From Hamlet

[Polonius speaks]

Yet here, Laertes! aboard, aboard, for shame!
The wind sits in the shoulder of your sail,
And you are stayed for. There – my blessing with thee!
And these few precepts in thy memory
Look thou character. Give thy thoughts no tongue,
Nor any unproportioned thought his act.
Be thou familiar, but by no means vulgar.
Those friends thou hast, and their adoption tried,
Grapple them to thy soul with hoops of steel;
But do not dull thy palm with entertainment
Of each new-hatched unfledged comrade. Beware
Of entrance to a quarrel; but being in,
Bear 't that the opposed may beware of thee.
Give every man thine ear, but few thy voice:
Take each man's censure, but reserve thy judgment.
Costly thy habit as thy purse can buy,
But not expressed in fancy; rich, not gaudy:

For the apparel oft proclaims the man;
And they in France of the best rank and station
Or of a most select and generous, chief in that.
Neither a borrower nor a lender be:
For loan oft loses both itself and friend;
And borrowing dulls the edge of husbandry.
This above all – to thine own self be true;
And it must follow, as the night the day,
Thou canst not then be false to any man.
Farewell! my blessing season this in thee!

[*Hamlet speaks*]

To be, or not to be – that is the question:
Whether 'tis nobler in the mind to suffer
The slings and arrows of outrageous fortune,
Or to take arms against a sea of troubles,
And by opposing end them. To die; to sleep,
No more; and by a sleep to say we end
The heartache, and the thousand natural shocks
That flesh is heir to. 'Tis a consummation
Devoutly to be wished, to die, to sleep;
To sleep! perchance to dream: ay, there's the rub;
For in that sleep of death what dreams may come,
When we have shuffled off this mortal coil,
Must give us pause. There's the respect
That makes calamity of so long life;
For who would bear the whips and scorns of time,
The oppressor's wrong, the proud man's contumely,
The pangs of despised love, the law's delay,
The insolence of office, and the spurns
That patient merit of the unworthy takes,
When he himself might his quietus make
With a bare bodkin? Who would fardels bear,
To grunt and sweat under a weary life,
But that the dread of something after death—
The undiscovered country, from whose bourn
No traveller returns – puzzles the will,
And makes us rather bear those ills we have
Than fly to others that we know not of?
Thus conscience does make cowards of us all;
And thus the native hue of resolution

Is sicklied o'er with the pale cast of thought;
And enterprises of great pith and moment,
With this regard, their currents turn awry
And lose the name of action.

[*Ophelia's song*]

[1]

How should I your true love know
    From another one?
By his cockle hat and staff
    And his sandal shoon.

He is dead and gone, lady,
    He is dead and gone;
At his head a grass-green turf,
    At his heels a stone.

White his shroud as the mountain snow,
    Larded with sweet flowers;
Which bewept to the grave did go
    With true-love showers.

[2]

To-morrow is Saint Valentine's day,
    All in the morning betime,
And I a maid at your window,
    To be your Valentine.
Then up he rose and donned his clothes,
    And dupped the chamber door;
Let in the maid, that out a maid
    Never departed more.

By Gis and by Saint Charity,
    Alack, and fie for shame!
Young men will do 't, if they come to 't;
    By cock, they are to blame.
Quoth she, before you tumbled me,
    You promised me to wed.
So would I ha' done, by yonder sun,
    An' thou had'st not come to my bed.

From Twelfth Night

[*Orsino speaks*]

If music be the food of love, play on;
Give me excess of it, that, surfeiting,
The appetite may sicken, and so die.
That strain again – it had a dying fall:
O, it came o'er my ear like the sweet sound
That breathes upon a bank of violets,
Stealing and giving odour! Enough; no more.
'Tis not so sweet now as it was before.
O spirit of love, how quick and fresh art thou!
That, notwithstanding thy capacity
Receiveth as the sea, nought enters there,
Of what validity and pitch soe'er,
But falls into abatement and low price,
Even in a minute! So full of shapes is fancy,
That it alone is high-fantastical.

[*Songs*]

[1]

O mistress mine, where are you roaming?
O, stay and hear; your true love's coming,
    That can sing both high and low.
Trip no further, pretty sweeting;
Journeys end in lovers' meeting.
    Every wise man's son doth know.

What is love? 'Tis not hereafter;
Present mirth hath present laughter;
    What's to come is still unsure.
In delay there lies no plenty;
Then come kiss me, sweet-and-twenty,
    Youth's a stuff will not endure.

[2]

When that I was and a little tiny boy,
    With a hey, ho, the wind and the rain,
A foolish thing was but a toy,
    For the rain it raineth every day.

But when I came to man's estate,
    With a hey, ho, the wind and the rain,
'Gainst knaves and thieves men shut their gate,
    For the rain it raineth every day.

But when I came, alas! to wive,
    With a hey, ho, the wind and the rain,
By swaggering could I never thrive,
    For the rain it raineth every day.

But when I came unto my beds,
    With a hey, ho, the wind and the rain,
With toss-pots still had drunken heads,
    For the rain it raineth every day.

A great while ago the world begun,
    With a hey, ho, the wind and rain,
But that's all one, our play is done,
    And we'll strive to please you every day.

From Othello

[Desdemona's Song, derived from an old ballad]

The poor soul sat sighing by sycamore tree,
    Sing all a green willow;
Her hand on her bosom, her head on her knee,
    Sing willow, willow, willow:
The fresh streams ran by her, and murmured her moans;
    Sing willow, willow, willow:
Her salt tears fell from her, and softened the stones;
    Sing willow, willow, willow:
Sing all a green willow must be my garland.
    Let nobody blame him; his scorn I approve,
I called my love false love; but what said he then?
    Sing willow, willow, willow:
If I court moe women, you'll couch with moe men.

From Macbeth

[*Lady Macbeth speaks*]

                        The raven himself is hoarse
That croaks the fatal entrance of Duncan
Under my battlements. Come, you spirits
That tend on mortal thoughts, unsex me here!
And fill me, from the crown to the toe, top-full
Of direst cruelty! make thick my blood,
Stop up the access and passage to remorse,
That no compunctious visitings of nature
Shake my fell purpose, nor keep peace between
The effect and it! Come to my woman's breasts,
And take my milk for gall, you murdering ministers,
Wherever, in your sightless substances,
You wait on nature's mischief! Come, thick night,
And pall thee in the dunnest smoke of hell,
That my keen knife see not the wound it makes,
Nor heaven peep through the blanket of the dark,
To cry 'Hold, hold!'

[*Macbeth speaks*]

[1]

If 'twere done when 'tis done, then 'twere well
It were done quickly: if the assassination
Could trammel up the consequence and catch,
With his surcease, success; that but this blow
Might be the be-all and end-all here,
But here, upon this bank and shoal of time,
We'ld jump the life to come. But in these cases
We still have judgment here; that we but teach
Bloody instructions, which, being taught, return
To plague the inventor. This even-handed justice
Commends the ingredients of our poisoned chalice
To our own lips. He's here in double trust:
First, as I am his kinsman and his subject,
Strong both against the deed, then, as his host,
Who should against his murderer shut the door,
Not bear the knife myself. Besides, this Duncan
Hath borne his faculties so meek, hath been
So clear in his great office, that his virtues

Will plead like angels, trumpet-tongued, against
The deep damnation of his taking-off;
And pity, like a naked new-born babe,
Striding the blast, or heaven's cherubin, horses
Upon the sightless couriers of the air,
Shall blow the horrid deed in every eye,
That tears shall drown the wind. I have no spur
To prick the sides of my intent, but only
Vaulting ambition, which o'erleaps itself,
And falls on the other.

[2]

Is this a dagger which I see before me,
The handle toward my hand? Come, let me clutch thee—
I have thee not, and yet I see thee still.
Art thou not, fatal vision, sensible
To feeling as to sight? Or art thou but
A dagger of the mind, a false creation,
Proceeding from the heat-oppressed brain?
I see thee yet, in form as palpable
As this which now I draw.
Thou marshall'st me the way that I was going;
And such an instrument I was to use.
Mine eyes are made the fools o' the other sense,
Or else worth all the rest: I see thee still;
And on thy blade and dudgeon gouts of blood,
Which was not so before. There's no such thing:
It is the bloody business which informs
Thus to mine eyes. Now o'er the one half-world
Nature seems dead, and wicked dreams abuse
The curtained sleep; now witchcraft celebrates
Pale Hecate's offerings; and withered murder,
Alarumed by his sentinel, the wolf,
Whose howl's his watch, thus with his stealthy pace,
With Tarquin's ravishing strides, towards his design
Moves like a ghost. Thou sure and firm-set earth,
Hear not my steps, which way they walk, for fear
Thy very stones prate of my whereabout,
And take the present horror from the time,
Which now suits with it. Whiles I threat, he lives:
Words to the heat of deeds too cold breath gives.
I go, and it is done; the bell invites me.

Hear it not, Duncan, for it is a knell
That summons thee to heaven, or to hell.

[3]

To-morrow, and to-morrow, and to-morrow,
Creeps in this petty pace from day to day,
To the last syllable of recorded time;
And all our yesterdays have lighted fools
The way to dusty death. Out, out, brief candle,
Life's but a walking shadow, a poor player,
That struts and frets his hour upon the stage,
And then is heard no more: it is a tale
Told by an idiot, full of sound and fury,
Signifying nothing.

From Antony and Cleopatra

[Enobarbus speaks]

The barge she sat in, like a burnished throne,
Burned on the water: the poop was beaten gold;
Purple the sails, and so perfumed that
The winds were lovesick with them; the oars were silver,
Which to the tune of flutes kept stroke, and made
The water which they beat to follow faster,
As amorous of their strokes. For her own person,
It beggared all description: she did lie
In her pavilion – cloth-of-gold of tissue—
O'er-picturing that Venus where we see
The fancy outwork nature: on each side her
Stood pretty dimpled boys, like smiling Cupids,
With divers-coloured fans, whose wind did seem
To glow the delicate cheeks which they did cool,
And what they undid did.

. . .

Age cannot wither her, nor custome stale
Her infinite variety: other women cloy
The appetites they feed; but she makes hungry
Where most she satisfies: for vilest things
Become themselves in her, that the holy priests
Bless her when she is riggish.

From Cymbeline

[*Songs*]

[1]

Hark, hark! the lark at heaven's gate sings,
  And Phoebus 'gins arise,
His steeds to water at those springs
  On chaliced flowers that lies;
And winking Mary-buds begin
  To ope their golden eyes;
With every thing that pretty bin,
  My lady sweet, arise:
    Arise, arise!

[2]

Fear no more the heat o' the sun,
  Nor the furious winter's rages;
Thou thy worldly task hast done,
  Home art gone, and ta'en thy wages:
Golden lads and girls all must,
As chimney-sweepers, come to dust.

Fear no more the frown of the great,
  Thou art past the tyrant's stroke.
Care no more to clothe and eat;
  To thee the reed is as the oak:
The sceptre, learning, physic, must
All follow this, and come to dust.

Fear no more the lightning-flash;
  Nor the all-dreaded thunder-stone;
Fear not slander, censure rash;
  Thou hast finished joy and moan:
All lovers young, all lovers must
Consign to thee, and come to dust.

No exorciser harm thee!
Nor no witchcraft charm thee!
Ghost unlaid forbear thee!
Nothing ill come near thee!
Quiet consummation have;
And renowned be thy grave!

From The Tempest

[*Ariel's Songs*]

[1]

Come unto these yellow sands,
    And then take hands:
Courtsied when you have, and kissed—
    The wild waves whist—
Foot it featly here and there;
And, sweet sprites, the burden bear.
                    Hark, hark!
                        Bow wow.
    The watch dogs bark:
                        Bow wow.
    Hark, hark! I hear
The strain of strutting chanticleer
    Cry, 'Cock-a-diddle-dow'.

[2]

Full fathom five thy father lies;
    Of his bones are coral made;
Those are pearls that were his eyes.
    Nothing of him that doth fade
But doth suffer a sea-change.
Into something rich and strange.
Sea-nymphs hourly ring his knell:
                            Ding-dong.
Hark! now I hear them – Ding-dong, bell.

[3]

Where the bee sucks, there suck I:
In a cowslip's bell I lie;
There I couch when owls do cry.
On a bat's back I do fly
After summer merrily.
Merrily, merrily shall I live now
Under the blossom that hangs on the bough.

[*Prospero speaks*]

You do look, my son, in a moved sort,
As if you were dismayed: be cheerful, sir.
Our revels now are ended. These our actors,
As I foretold you, were all spirits, and
Are melted into air, into thin air:
And, like the baseless fabric of this vision,
The cloud-capped towers, the gorgeous palaces,
The solemn temples, the great globe itself,
Yea, all which it inherit, shall dissolve,
And, like this insubstantial pageant faded,
Leave not a rack behind. We are such stuff
As dreams are made on; and our little life
Is rounded with a sleep.

Thomas Campion

'There is a garden in her face'

There is a garden in her face
  Where roses and white lilies grow;
A heavenly paradise is that place,
  Wherein all pleasant fruits do flow:
    There cherries grow which none may buy
    Till 'Cherry ripe' themselves do cry.

Those cherries fairly do enclose
  Of orient pearls a double row,
Which when her lovely laughter shows,
  They look like rose-buds filled with snow.
    Yet them nor peer nor prince can buy
    Till 'Cherry ripe' themselves do cry.

Her eyes like angels watch them still;
  Her brows like bended bows do stand,
Threatening with piercing frowns to kill
  All that attempt with eye or hand
    Those sacred cherries to come nigh,
    Till 'Cherry ripe' themselves do cry.

Henry Wotton

The Character of a Happy Life

How happy is he born and taught
That serveth not another's will;
Whose armour is his honest thought,
And simple truth his utmost skill!

Whose passions not his masters are;
Whose soul is still prepared for death,
Untied unto the world by care
Of public fame or private breath.

Who envies none that chance doth raise,
Nor vice hath never understood;
How deepest wounds are given by praise;
Nor rules of state, but rules of good.

Who hath his life from rumours freed;
Whose conscience is his strong retreat;
Whose state can neither flatterers feed,
Nor ruin make oppressors great.

Who God doth late and early pray
More of His grace than gifts to lend;
And entertains the harmless day
With a religious book or friend.

This man is freed from servile bands,
Of hope to rise or fear to fall:
Lord of himself, though not of lands,
And having nothing, yet hath all.

Ben Jonson

From Cynthia's Revels

[Song]

Queen, and Huntress, chaste, and fair,
Now the Sun is laid to sleep,
Seated, in thy silver chair,

State in wonted manner keep:
    Hesperus entreats thy light,
    Goddess, excellently bright.

Earth, let not thy envious shade
Dare itself to interpose;
Cynthia's shining orb was made
Heaven to clear, when day did close:
    Bless us then with wished sight,
    Goddess, excellently bright.

Lay thy bow of pearl apart,
And thy crystal-shining quiver;
Give unto the flying hart
Space to breathe, how short soever:
    Thou that mak'st a day of night,
    Goddess, excellently bright.

To Celia

Drink to me only with thine eyes,
    And I will pledge with mine;
Or leave a kiss but in the cup
    And I'll not look for wine.
The thirst that from the soul doth rise
    Doth ask a drink divine;
But might I of Jove's nectar sup,
    I would not change for thine.

I sent thee late a rosy wreath,
    Not so much honouring thee
As giving it a hope that there
    It could not withered be;
But thou thereon didst only breathe,
    And sent'st it back to me;
Since when it grows, and smells, I swear,
    Not of itself but thee!

From The Silent Woman

[Song]

Still to be neat, still to be dressed,
As you were going to a feast;
Still to be powdered, still perfumed:
Lady, it is to be presumed,
Though art's hid causes are not found,
All is not sweet, all is not sound.

Give me a look, give me a face,
That makes simplicity a grace;
Robes loosely flowing, hair as free:
Such sweet neglect more taketh me,
Than all the adulteries of art.
They strike mine eyes, but not my heart.

John Donne

Song

Go, and catch a falling star,
　Get with child a mandrake root,
Tell me where all past years are,
　Or who cleft the Devil's foot,
Teach me to hear mermaids singing,
Or to keep off envy's stinging,
　　　And find
　　　What wind
Serves to advance an honest mind.

If thou beest born to strange sights,
　Things invisible to see,
Ride ten thousand days and nights,
　Till age snow white hairs on thee,
Thou, when thou returnest, wilt tell me,
All strange wonders that befell thee,
　　　And swear,
　　　No where
Lives a woman true, and fair.

If thou findest one, let me know,
   Such a pilgrimage were sweet;
Yet do not, I would not go,
   Though at next door we might meet,
Though she were true, when you met her,
And last, till you write your letter,
     Yet she
     Will be
False, ere I come, to two or three.

The Sun Rising

   Busy old fool, unruly sun,
    Why dost thou thus,
Through windows, and through curtains, call on us?
Must to thy motions lovers' seasons run?
    Saucy pedantic wretch, go chide
    Late schoolboys and sour prentices,
  Go tell court-huntsmen, that the King will ride,
  Call country ants to harvest offices;
Love, all alike, no season knows, nor clime,
Nor hours, days, months, which are the rags of time.

    Thy beams, so reverend, and strong
    Why shouldst thou think?
I could eclipse and cloud them with a wink,
But that I would not lose her sight so long:
    If her eyes have not blinded thine,
    Look, and to-morrow late, tell me,
  Whether both the Indias of spice and mine
  Be where thou left'st them, or lie here with me.
Ask for those kings whom thou saw'st yesterday,
And thou shalt hear, 'All here in one bed lay.'

    She is all states, and all princes, I,
    Nothing else is.
Princes do but play us; compared to this,
All honour's mimic; all wealth alchemy.
    Thou, sun, art half as happy as we,
    In that the world's contracted thus;
  Thine age asks ease, and since thy duties be
  To warm the world, that's done in warming us.
Shine here to us, and thou art everywhere;
This bed thy centre is, these walls, thy sphere.

'Batter my heart, three-personed God; for you'

Batter my heart, three-personed God; for you
As yet but knock, breathe, shine, and seek to mend;
That I may rise, and stand, o'erthrow me, and bend
Your force, to break, blow, burn and make me new.
I, like an usurped town, to another due,
Labour to admit you, but oh, to no end,
Reason your viceroy in me, me should defend,
But is captived, and proves weak or untrue.
Yet dearly I love you, and would be loved fain,
But am betrothed unto your enemy:
Divorce me, untie, or break that knot again,
Take me to you, imprison me, for I
Except you enthrall me, never shall be free,
Nor ever chaste, except you ravish me.

'Death, be not proud, though some have called thee'

Death, be not proud, though some have called thee
Mighty and dreadful, for thou art not so;
For those, whom thou think'st thou dost overthrow,
Die not, poor death, nor yet canst thou kill me.
From rest and sleep, which but thy pictures be,
Much pleasure, then from thee, much more must flow,
And soonest our best men with thee do go,
Rest of their bones, and soul's delivery.
Thou art slave to fate, chance, kings, and desperate men,
And dost with poison, war, and sickness dwell,
And poppy, or charms can make us sleep as well,
And better than thy stroke; why swell'st thou then?
One short sleep past, we wake eternally,
And death shall be no more; death, thou shalt die.

Robert Herrick

Delight in Disorder

A sweet disorder in the dress
Kindles in clothes a wantonness:
A lawn about the shoulders thrown
Into a fine distraction:
An erring lace which here and there
Enthralls the crimson stomacher:
A cuff neglectful, and thereby
Ribands to flow confusedly:
A winning wave (deserving note)
In the tempestuous petticoat:
A careless shoe-string, in whose tie
I see a wild civility:
Do more bewitch me, than when art
Is too precise in every part.

To the Virgins, to Make Much of Time

Gather ye rosebuds, while ye may,
   Old Time is still a-flying:
And this same flower that smiles to-day
   To-morrow will be dying.

The glorious lamp of heaven, the sun,
   The higher he's a-getting,
The sooner will his race be run,
   And nearer he's to setting.

That age is best which is the first,
   When youth and blood are warmer;
But being spent, the worse, and worst
   Times still succeed the former.

Then be not coy, but use your time,
   And, while ye may go marry:
For having lost but once your prime
   You may for ever tarry.

To Daffodils

Fair daffodils, we weep to see
   You haste away so soon;
As yet the early-rising sun
   Has not attained his noon.
     Stay, stay,
    Until the hasting day
     Has run
   But to the evensong;
And having prayed together, we
   Will go with you along.

We have short time to stay, as you,
   We have as short a spring;
As quick a growth to meet decay,
   As you, or anything.
     We die,
   As hours do, and dry
     Away,
   Like to the summer's rain;
Or as the pearls of morning's dew,
   Ne'er to be found again.

Night-Piece, to Julia

Her eyes the glow-worm lend thee,
The shooting stars attend thee;
    And the elves also,
    Whose little eyes glow
Like the sparks of fire, befriend thee.

No Will-o'-the-Wisp mislight thee,
Nor snake or slow-worm bite thee;
    But on, on thy way
    Not making a stay,
Since ghost there's none to affright thee.

Let not the dark thee cumber:
What though the moon does slumber?
    The stars of the night
    Will lend thee their light
Like tapers clear without number.

Then, Julia, let me woo thee,
Thus, thus to come unto me;
   And when I shall meet
   Thy silvery feet
My soul I'll pour into thee.

Upon Julia's Clothes

When as in silks my Julia goes,
Then, then (methinks) how sweetly flows
That liquefaction of her clothes.

Next, when I cast mine eyes and see
That brave vibration each way free;
O how that glittering taketh me!

Cherry-Ripe

Cherry ripe, ripe, ripe, I cry,
Full and fair ones; come and buy:
If so be you ask me where
They do grow, I answer: 'There
Where my Julia's lips do smile;
There's the land, or cherry-isle:
Whose plantations fully show
All the year, where cherries grow.'

George Herbert

Virtue

Sweet day, so cool, so calm, so bright,
The bridal of the earth and sky:
The dew shall weep thy fall to night;
    For thou must die.

Sweet rose, whose hue angry and brave
Bids the rash gazer wipe his eye:
Thy root is ever in its grave,
                    And thou must die.

Sweet spring, full of sweet days and roses,
A box where sweets compacted lie;
My music shows ye have your closes,
                    And all must die.

Only a sweet and virtuous soul,
Like seasoned timber, never gives;
But though the whole world turn to coal,
                    Then chiefly lives.

The Collar

I struck the board, and cried, No more.
              I will abroad.
      What? shall I ever sigh and pine?
My lines and life are free; free as the road,
        Loose as the wind, as large as store.
              Shall I be still in suit?
      Have I no harvest but a thorn
      To let me blood, and not restore
      What I have lost with cordial fruit?
              Sure there was wine
Before my sighs did dry it: there was corn
        Before my tears did drown it.
      Is the year only lost to me?
              Have I no bays to crown it?
No flowers, no garlands gay? all blasted?
              All wasted?
      Not so, my heart: but there is fruit,
              And thou hast hands.
      Recover all thy sigh-blown age
On double pleasures: leave thy cold dispute
Of what is fit, and not. Forsake thy cage,
              Thy rope of sands,
Which petty thoughts have made, and made to thee
        Good cable, to enforce and draw,
              And be thy law,

While thou didst wink and wouldst not see.
Away; take heed:
I will abroad.
Call in thy death's head there: tie up thy fears.
He that forbears
To suit and serve his need,
Deserves his load.
But as I raved and grew more fierce and wild
At every word,
Me thought I heard one calling, *Child!*
And I replied, *My Lord.*

The Pulley

When God at first made man,
Having a glass of blessings standing by;
Let us (said he) pour on him all we can:
Let the world's riches, which dispersed lie,
Contract into a span.

So strength first made a way;
Then beauty flowed, then wisdom, honour, pleasure:
When almost all was out, God made a stay,
Perceiving that alone of all his treasure
Rest in the bottom lay.

For if I should (said he)
Bestow this jewel also on my creature,
He would adore my gifts in stead of me,
And rest in nature, not the God of nature:
So both should losers be.

Yet let him keep the rest,
But keep them with repining restlessness:
Let him be rich and weary, that at least,
If goodness lead him not, yet weariness
May toss him to my breast.

Anonymous

'If all the world were paper'

If all the world were paper,
    And all the sea were ink,
And all the trees were bread and cheese,
    How should we do for drink?

If all the world were sand-o,
    Oh, then what should we lack-o?
If, as they say, there were no clay,
    How should we take tobacco?

If all our vessels ran-a,
    If none but had a crack-a;
If Spanish apes ate all the grapes,
    How should we do for sack-a?

If friars had no bald pates,
    Nor nuns had no dark cloisters;
If all the seas were beans and peas,
    How should we do for oysters?

If there had been no projects,
    Nor none that did great wrongs;
If fiddlers shall turn players all,
    How should we do for songs?

If all things were eternal,
    And nothing their end bringing;
If this should be, then how should we
    Here make an end of singing?

James Shirley

'The glories of our blood and state'

The glories of our blood and state
  Are shadows, not substantial things;
There is no armour against fate.
  Death lays his icy hand on kings;
    Sceptre and crown
    Must tumble down,
And in the dust be equal made
With the poor crooked scythe and spade.

Some men with swords may reap the field,
  And plant fresh laurels where they kill;
But their strong nerves at last must yield.
  They tame but one another still;
    Early or late
    They stoop to fate,
And must give up their murmuring breath
When they, pale captives, creep to death.

The garlands wither on your brow;
  Then boast no more your mighty deeds.
Upon death's purple altar now,
  See, where the victor-victim bleeds.
    Your heads must come
    To the cold tomb:
Only the actions of the just
Smell sweet, and blossom in their dust.

Edmund Waller

'Go, lovely rose!'

Go, lovely rose!
Tell her that wastes her time, and me,
  That now she knows,
When I resemble her to thee,
How sweet and fair she seems to be.

Tell her that's young,
And shuns to have her graces spied
That, hadst thou sprung
In deserts where no men abide,
Thou must have uncommended died.

Small is the worth
Of beauty from the light retired:
Bid her come forth,
Suffer her self to be desired
And not blush so to be admired.

Then die! That she
The common fate of all things rare
May read in thee
How small a part of time they share,
That are so wondrous sweet, and fair!

John Milton

Lycidas

In this Monody the Author bewails a learned Friend, unfortunately drowned in his passage from Chester on the Irish Seas, 1637; and, by occasion, foretells the ruin of our corrupted clergy, then in their height.

Yet once more, O ye laurels, and once more,
Ye myrtles brown, with ivy never-sear,
I come to pluck your berries harsh and crude,
And with forced fingers rude
Shatter your leaves before the mellowing year.
Bitter constraint and sad occasion dear
Compels me to disturb your season due;
For Lycidas, is dead, dead ere his prime,
Young Lycidas, and hath not left his peer.
Who would not sing for Lycidas? He knew
Himself to sing, and build the lofty rhyme.
He must not flote upon his watery bier
Unwept, and welter to the parching wind,
Without the meed of some melodious tear.
Begin then, Sisters of the sacred well,
That from beneath the seat of Jove doth spring,

Begin, and somewhat loudly sweep the string.
Hence with denial vain, and coy excuse:
So may some gentle muse
With lucky words favour my destined urn,
And as he passes turn,
And bid fair peace be to my sable shroud!
For we were nursed upon the self-same hill,
Fed the same flock, by fountain, shade, and rill.

    Together both, ere the high lawns appeared
Under the opening eyelids of the morn,
We drove a-field, and both together heard
What time the gray-fly winds her sultry horn,
Battening our flocks with the fresh dews of night,
Oft till the star that rose, at evening, bright
Toward heaven's descent had sloped his westering wheel.
Meanwhile the rural ditties were not mute;
Tempered to the oaten flute
Rough Satyrs danced, and Fauns with cloven heel
from the glad sound would not be absent long;
And old Damœtas loved to hear our song.

    But, O the heavy change, now thou art gone,
Now thou art gone and never must return!
Thee, Shepherd, thee the woods, and desert caves,
With wild thyme and the gadding vine o'ergrown,
And all their echoes, mourn.
The willows, and the hazel corpses green,
Shall now no more be seen,
Fanning their joyous leaves to thy soft lays.
As killing as the canker to the rose,
Or taint-worm to the weanling herds that graze,
Or frost to flowers, that their gay wardrobe wear,
When first the white-thorn blows;
Such, Lycidas, thy loss to shepherd's ear.

    Where were ye, Nymphs, when the remorseless deep
Closed o'er the head of your loved Lycidas?
For neither were ye playing on the steep
Where your old bards, the famous Druids, lie,
Nor on the shaggy top of Mona high,
Nor yet where Deva spreads her wizard stream.
Ay me! I fondly dream!
Had ye been there — for what could that have done?
What could the Muse herself that Orpheus bore,
The Muse herself for her enchanting son,

Whom universal nature did lament,
When by the rout that made the hideous roar,
His gory visage down the stream was sent,
Down the swift Hebrus to the Lesbian shore?
    Alas! what boots it with uncessant care
To tend the homely slighted shepherd's trade,
And strictly meditate the thankless Muse?
Were it not better done as others use,
To sport with Amaryllis in the shade,
Or with the tangles of Neæra's hair?
Fame is the spur that the clear spirit doth raise
(That last infirmity of noble mind)
To scorn delights, and live laborious days;
But the fair guerdon when we hope to find,
And think to burst out into sudden blaze,
Come the blind Fury with the abhorred shears,
And slits the thin-spun life. But not the praise,
Phœbus replied, and touched my trembling ears:
Fame is no plant that grows on mortal soil,
Nor in the glistering foil
Set off to the world, nor in broad rumour lies,
But lives and spreads aloft by those pure eyes
And perfect witness of all-Judging Jove;
As he pronounces lastly on each deed,
Of so much fame in Heaven expect thy meed.
    O fountain Arethuse, and thou honoured flood,
Smooth-sliding Mincius, crowned with vocal reeds,
That strain I heard was of a higher mood.
But now my oat proceeds,
And listens to the Herald of the Sea,
That came in Neptune's plea.
He asked the waves, and asked the felon winds,
What hard mishap hath doomed this gentle swain?
And questioned every gust of rugged wings
That blows from off each beaked promontory.
They knew not of his story;
And sage Hippotades their answer brings,
That not a blast was from his dungeon strayed;
The air was calm, and on the level brine
Sleek Panope with all her sisters played.
It was that fatal and perfidious bark,
Built in the eclipse, and rigged with curses dark,
That sunk so low that sacred head of thine.

Next Camus, reverend sire, went footing slow,
His mantle hairy, and his bonnet sedge,
Inwrought with figures dim, and on the edge
Like to that sanguine flower inscribed with woe.
Ah! who hath reft (quoth he) my dearest pledge?
Last came, and last did go,
The Pilot of the Galilean Lake;
Two massy keys he bore of metals twain,
(The golden opes, the iron shuts amain).
He shook his mitred locks, and stern bespake
How well could I have spared for thee, young swain,
Enow of such as for their bellies' sake,
Creep and intrude, and climb into the fold!
Of other care they little reckoning make
Than how to scramble at the shearers' feast,
And shove away the worthy bidden guest.
Blind mouths! that scarce themselves know how to hold
A sheephook, or have learned ought else the least
That to the faithful herdman's art belongs!
What recks it them? What need they? They are sped;
And when they list, their lean and flashy songs
Grate on their scrannel pipes of wretched straw;
The hungry sheep look up, and are not fed,
But swollen with wind, and the rank mist they draw,
Rot inwardly, and foul contagion spread:
Besides what the grim wolf with privy paw
Daily devours apace, and nothing said,
But that two-handed engine at the door,
Stands ready to smite once, and smite no more.
Return, Alpheus, the dread voice is past,
That shrunk thy streams; return Sicilian Muse,
And call the vales, and bid them hither cast
Their bells, and flowerets of a thousand hues.
Ye valleys low where the mild whispers use,
Of shades and wanton winds, and gushing brooks,
On whose fresh lap the swart star sparely looks,
Throw hither all your quaint enamelled eyes,
That on the green turf suck the honeyed showers,
And purple all the ground with vernal flowers.
Bring the rathe primrose that forsaken dies,
The tufted crow-toe, and pale jessamine,
The white pink, and the pansy freaked with jet,
The glowing violet,

The musk-rose, and the well-attired woodbine,
With cowslips wan that hang the pensive head,
And every flower that sad embroidery wears;
Bid amaranthus all his beauty shed,
And daffadillies fill their cups with tears,
To strew the laureate hearse where Lycid lies.
For so, to interpose a little ease,
Let our frail thoughts dally with false surmise.
Ay me! whilst thee the shores and sounding seas
Wash far away, where'er thy bones are hurled;
Whether beyond the stormy Hebrides,
Where thou perhaps under the whelming tide
Visitest the bottom of the monstrous world;
Or whether thou, or to moist vows denied,
Sleepest by the fable of Bellerus old,
Where the great Vision of the guarded mount
Looks toward Namancos and Bayona's hold.
Look homeward Angel now, and melt with ruth:
And, O ye dolphins, waft the hapless youth.
    Weep no more, woeful shepherds, weep no more,
For Lycidas, your sorrow, is not dead,
Sunk though he be beneath the watery floor,
So sinks the day-star in the ocean bed,
And yet anon repairs his drooping head,
And tricks his beams, and with new-spangled ore
Flames in the forehead of the morning sky:
So Lycidas sunk low, but mounted high,
Through the dear might of him that walked the waves,
Where other groves, and other streams along,
With nectar pure his oozy locks he laves,
And hears the unexpressive nuptial song,
In the blest kingdoms meek of joy and love.
There entertain him all the saints above,
In solemn troops, and sweet societies
That sing, and singing in their glory move,
And wipe the tears for ever from his eyes.
Now Lycidas, the shepherds weep no more;
Henceforth thou art the Genius of the shore,
In thy large recompense, and shalt be good
To all that wander in that perilous flood.
    Thus sang the uncouth swain to the oaks and rills,
While the still morn went out with sandals grey:
He touched the tender stops of various quills,

With eager thought warbling his Doric lay:
And now the sun had stretched out all the hills,
And now was dropped into the western bay.
At last he rose, and twitched his mantle blue:
To-morrow to fresh woods, and pastures new.

Sonnet [on His Blindness]

When I consider how my light is spent,
  Ere half my days in this dark world and wide,
  And that one talent which is death to hide
Lodged with me useless, though my soul more bent
To serve therewith my maker, and present
  My true account, lest he returning chide;
  'Doth God exact day-labour, light denied?'
I fondly ask. But patience, to prevent
That murmur, soon replies, 'God doth not need
  Either man's work or his own gifts. Who best
  Bear his mild yoke, they serve him best. His state
Is kingly: thousands at his bidding speed
  And post o'er land and ocean without rest;
  They also serve who only stand and wait.'

From Paradise Lost: Book I

Of man's first disobedience, and the fruit
Of that forbidden tree, whose mortal taste
Brought death into the world, and all our woe,
With loss of Eden, till one greater Man
Restore us, and regain the blissful seat,
Sing, Heavenly Muse, that, on the secret top
Of Oreb, or of Sinai, didst inspire
That shepherd who first taught the chosen seed
In the beginning how the heavens and earth
Rose out of Chaos: or, if Sion Hill
Delight thee more, and Siloa's brook that flowed
Fast by the oracle of God, I thence
Invoke thy aid to my adventurous song,
That with no middle flight intends to soar

Above the Aonian mount, while it pursues
Things unattempted yet in prose or rhyme.
And chiefly Thou, O Spirit, that dost prefer
Before all temples the upright heart and pure,
Instruct me, for Thou knowest; Thou from the first
Wast present, and, with mighty wings outspread,
Dove-like sat'st brooding on the vast Abyss,
And madest it pregnant: what in me is dark
Illumine, what is low raise and support;
That, to the height of this great argument,
I may assert Eternal Providence,
And justify the ways of God to men.

From Paradise Lost: Book XII

High in front advanced,
The brandished sword of God before them blazed,
Fierce as a comet; which with torrid heat,
And vapour as the Libyan air adust,
Began to parch that temperate clime; whereat
In either hand the hastening Angel caught
Our lingering parents, and to the eastern gate
Led them direct, and down the cliff as fast
To the subjected plain – then disappeared.
They, looking back, all the eastern side beheld
Of Paradise, so late their happy seat,
Waved over by that flaming brand; the gate
With dreadful faces thronged and fiery arms.
Some natural tears they dropped, but wiped them soon;
The world was all before them, where to choose
Their place of rest, and Providence their guide.
They, hand in hand, with wandering steps and slow,
Through Eden took their solitary way.

John Suckling

'Why so pale and wan, fond lover?'

Why so pale and wan, fond lover?
    Prithee, why so pale?
Will, when looking well can't move her.
    Looking ill prevail?
    Prithee, why so pale?

Why so dull and mute, young sinner?
    Prithee, why so mute?
Will, when speaking well can't win her,
    Saying nothing do 't?
    Prithee, why so mute?

Quit, quit, for shame! This will not move;
    This cannot take her.
If of herself she will not love,
    Nothing can make her:
    The devil take her!

'Out upon it, I have loved'

Out upon it, I have loved
    Three whole days together;
And am like to love three more,
    If it prove fair weather.

Time shall moult away his wings
    Ere he shall discover
In the whole wide world again
    Such a constant lover.

But the spite on 't is, no praise
    Is due at all to me;
Love with me had made no stays,
    Had it any been but she.

Had it any been but she,
    And that very face,
There had been at least ere this
    A dozen dozen in her place.

James Graham, Marquis of Montrose

To His Mistress

My dear and only love, I pray
  This noble world of thee,
Be governed by no other sway
  But purest monarchy.
For if confusion have a part,
  Which virtuous souls abhor,
And hold a synod in thy heart,
  I'll never love thee more.

Like Alexander I will reign,
  And I will reign alone,
My thoughts shall evermore disdain
  A rival on my throne.
He either fears his fate too much,
  Or his deserts are small,
That puts it not unto the touch,
  To win or lose it all.

But I must rule, and govern still,
  And always give the law,
And have each subject at my will,
  And all to stand in awe.
But 'gainst my battery if I find
  Thou shun'st the prize so sore,
As that thou set'st me up a blind,
  I'll never love thee more.

Or in the empire of thy heart,
  Where I should solely be,
Another do pretend a part,
  And dares to vie with me,
Or if committees thou erect,
  And goes on such a score,
I'll sing and laugh at thy neglect,
  And never love thee more.

But if thou wilt be constant then,
    And faithful of thy word,
I'll make thee glorious by my pen,
    And famous by my sword.
I'll serve thee in such noble ways
    Was never heard before:
I'll crown and deck thee all with bays,
    And love thee evermore.

Richard Lovelace

To Lucasta, Going to the Wars

Tell me not (Sweet) I am unkind,
    That from the nunnery
Of thy chaste breasts, and quiet mind,
    To war and arms I fly,

True; a new mistress now I chase,
    The first foe in the field;
And with a stronger faith embrace
    A sword, a horse, a shield.

Yet this inconstancy is such,
    As you too shall adore;
I could not love thee (dear) so much,
    Loved I not honour more.

To Althea, from Prison

When love with unconfined wings
    Hovers within my gates;
And my divine Althea brings
    To whisper at the grates:
When I lie tangled in her hair,
    And fettered to her eye;
The birds that wanton in the air,
    Know no such liberty.

When flowing cups run swiftly round
   With no allaying Thames,
Our careless heads with roses bound,
   Our hearts with loyal flames;
When thirsty grief in wine we steep,
   When healths and draughts go free,
Fishes that tipple in the deep,
   Know no such liberty.

When (like committed linnets) I
   With shriller throat shall sing
The sweetness, mercy, majesty,
   And glories of my King;
When I shall voice aloud, how good
   He is, how great should be;
Enlarged winds that curl the flood,
   Know no such liberty.

Stone walls do not a prison make,
   Nor iron bars a cage;
Minds innocent and quiet take
   That for an hermitage;
If I have freedom in my love,
   And in my soul am free;
Angels alone that soar above,
   Enjoy such liberty.

Andrew Marvell

To His Coy Mistress

Had we but world enough, and time,
This coyness, lady, were no crime.
We would sit down, and think which way
To walk, and pass our long love's day.
Thou by the Indian Ganges' side
Should'st rubies find: I by the tide
Of Humber would complain. I would
Love you ten years before the Flood;
And you should if you please refuse
Till the Conversion of the Jews.
My vegetable love should grow
Vaster than empires, and more slow.

An hundred years should go to praise
Thine eyes, and on thy forehead gaze;
Two hundred to adore each breast;
But thirty thousand to the rest;
An age at least to every part,
And the last age should show your heart.
For lady you deserve this state;
Nor would I love at lower rate.

   But at my back I always hear
Time's winged chariot hurrying near;
And yonder all before us lie
Deserts of vast eternity.
Thy beauty shall no more be found,
Nor, in thy marble vault, shall sound
My echoing song: then worms shall try
That long preserved virginity:
And your quaint honour turn to dust,
And into ashes all my lust.
The grave's a fine and private place,
But none I think do there embrace.

   Now therefore, while the youthful hue
Sits on thy skin like morning dew,
And while thy willing soul transpires
At every pore with instant fires,
Now let us sport us while we may;
And now, like amorous birds of prey,
Rather at once our time devour,
Than languish in his slow-chapped power.
Let us roll all our strength, and all
Our sweetness, up into one ball:
And tear our pleasures with rough strife,
Thorough the iron gates of life.
Thus, though we cannot make our sun
Stand still, yet we will make him run.

Henry Vaughan

Peace

My soul, there is a country
  Far beyond the stars,
Where stands a winged sentry
  All skilful in the wars:
There, above noise and danger,
  Sweet peace sits crowned with smiles,
And one born in a manger
  Commands the beauteous files.
He is thy gracious friend,
  And – O my soul, awake!—
Did in pure love descend
  To die here for thy sake.
If thou canst get but thither,
  There grows the flower of peace,
The rose that cannot wither,
  Thy fortress, and thy ease.
Leave then thy foolish ranges;
  For none can thee secure
But One who never changes—
  Thy God, thy life, thy cure.

John Bunyan

From The Pilgrim's Progress

[Songs]

[1]

He that is down, needs fear no fall,
He that is low, no pride:
He that is humble, ever shall
Have God to be his guide.

I am content with what I have,
Little be it, or much:
And, Lord, contentment still I crave,
Because thou savest such.

Fullness to such a burden is
That go on pilgrimage:
Here little, and hereafter bliss,
Is best from age to age.

[2]

Who would true valour see,
Let him come hither;
One here will constant be,
Come wind, come weather.
There's no discouragement,
Shall make him once relent,
His first avowed intent,
To be a pilgrim.

Who so beset him round,
With dismal stories,
Do but themselves confound;
His strength the more is.
No lion can him fright,
He'll with a giant fight,
But he will have a right,
To be a pilgrim.

Hobgoblin, nor foul fiend,
Can daunt his spirit:
He knows, he at the end,
Shall life inherit.
Then fancies fly away,
He'll fear not what men say,
He'll labour night and day,
To be a pilgrim.

John Dryden

From Absalom and Achitophel

In pious times ere priest-craft did begin,
Before polygamy was made a sin;
When man on many multiplied his kind,
Ere one to one was, cursedly, confined;
When nature prompted and no law denied
Promiscuous use of concubine and bride;
Then Israel's[1] monarch, after Heaven's own heart,
His vigorous warmth did, variously, impart
To wives and slaves; and, wide as his command,
Scattered his Maker's image through the land.
Michal,[2] of royal blood, the crown did wear;
A soil ungrateful to the tiller's care.
Not so the rest; for several mothers bore
To God-like David[3] several sons before.
But since like slaves his bed they did ascend,
No true succession could their seed attend.
Of all this numerous progeny was none
So beautiful, so brave as Absalom.[4]
Whether, inspired by some diviner lust,
His father got him with a greater gust;
Or that his conscious destiny made way
By manly beauty to imperial sway.
Early in foreign fields he won renown,
With kings and state allied to Israel's crown.
In peace the thoughts of war he could remove,
And seemed as he were only born for love.
Whate'er he did was done with so much ease,
In him alone 'twas natural to please:
His motions all accompanied with grace,
And Paradise was opened in his face.

---

[1] Israel] England
[2] Michal] the Queen
[3] David] King Charles II
[4] Absalom] Monmouth

Isaac Watts

Against Idleness and Mischief

How doth the little busy bee
   Improve each shining hour,
And gather honey all the day
   From every opening flower!

How skilfully she builds her cell!
   How neat she spreads the wax!
And labours hard to store it well
   With the sweet food she makes.

In works of labour or of skill
   I would be busy too:
For Satan finds some mischief still
   For idle hands to do.

In books, or work, or healthful play,
   Let my first years be past,
That I may give for every day
   Some good account at last.

The Sluggard

'Tis the voice of the sluggard; I heard him complain,
'You have waked me too soon, I must slumber again.'
As the door on its hinges, so he on his bed,
Turns his sides and his shoulders and his heavy head.

'A little more sleep, and a little more slumber;'
Thus he wastes half his days and his hours without number;
And when he gets up, he sits folding his hands,
Or walks about sauntering, or trifling he stands.

I passed by his garden, and saw the wild brier,
The thorn and the thistle grow broader and higher;
The clothes that hang on him are turning to rags;
And his money still wastes, till he starves or he begs.

I made him a visit, still hoping to find
He had took better care for improving his mind:

He told me his dreams, talked of eating and drinking;
But he scarce reads his Bible, and never loves thinking

Said I then to my heart, 'Here's a lesson for me;'
That man's but a picture of what I might be:
But thanks to my friends for their care in my breeding,
Who taught me betimes to love working and reading.

John Gay

From The Beggar's Opera

[Song]

Macheath   Were I laid on Greenland's coast,
        And in my arms embraced my lass,
    Warm amidst eternal frost,
        Too soon the half-year's night would pass.

Polly   Were I sold on Indian soil,
        Soon as the burning day was closed,
    I could mock the sultry toil,
        When on my charmer's breast reposed.

Macheath   And I would love you all the day,
Polly   Every night would kiss and play;
Macheath   If with me you'd fondly stray
Polly   Over the hills and far away.

From Acis and Galatea

[Song]

O ruddier than the cherry,
O sweeter than the berry,
    O nymph more bright
    Than moonshine night,
Like kidlings blithe and merry.
Ripe as the melting cluster,
No lily has such lustre,
    Yet hard to tame,
    As raging flame,
And fierce as storms that bluster.

Alexander Pope

Ode on Solitude

Happy the man, whose wish and care
  A few paternal acres bound,
Content to breathe his native air,
                    In his own ground.
Whose herds with milk, whose fields with bread,
  Whose flocks supply him with attire,
Whose trees in summer yield him shade,
                    In winter fire.
Blessed, who can unconcernedly find
  Hours, days, and years slide soft away,
In health of body, peace of mind,
                    Quiet by day,
Sound sleep by night; study and ease,
  Together mixed; sweet recreation;
And innocence, which most does please
                    With meditation.
Thus let me live, unseen, unknown,
  Thus unlamented let me die,
Steal from the world, and not a stone
                    Tell where I lie.

From An Essay on Criticism

A little learning is a dangerous thing;
Drink deep, or taste not the Pierian spring:
There shallow draughts intoxicate the brain,
And drinking largely sobers us again.
Fired at first sight with what the Muse imparts,
In fearless youth we tempt the heights of arts,
While from the bounded level of our mind,
Short views we take, nor see the lengths behind;
But more advanced, behold with strange surprise
New distant scenes of endless science rise!
So pleased at first the towering Alps we try,
Mount o'er the vales, and seem to tread the sky,
The eternal snows appear already past,

And the first clouds and mountains seem the last:
But those attained, we tremble to survey
The growing labours of the lengthened way,
The increasing prospect tires our wandering eyes,
Hills peep o'er hills, and Alps on Alps arise!

From The Rape of the Lock

Close by those meads, for ever crowned with flowers,
Where Thames with pride surveys his rising towers,
There stands a structure of majestic frame,
Which from the neighbouring Hampton takes its name.
Here Britain's statesmen oft the fall foredoom
Of foreign tyrants, and of nymphs at home;
Here thou, great Anna! whom three realms obey,
Dost sometimes counsel take – and sometimes tay.
    Hither the heroes and the nymphs resort,
To taste a while the pleasures of a court;
In various talk the instructive hours they past,
Who gave the ball, or paid the visit last:
One speaks the glory of the British Queen,
And one describes a charming Indian screen;
A third interprets motions, looks, and eyes;
At every word a reputation dies.
Snuff, or the fan, supply each pause of chat,
With singing, laughing, ogling, and all that.
    Meanwhile, declining from the noon of day,
The sun obliquely shoots his burning ray;
The hungry judges soon the sentence sign,
And wretches hang that jury-men may dine;
The merchant from the Exchange returns in peace,
And the long labours of the toilet cease.

From An Essay on Man

    Hope dumbly then: with trembling pinions soar;
Wait the great teacher, Death, and God adore!
What future bliss, he gives not thee to know,
But gives that hope to be thy blessing now.

Hope springs eternal in the human breast:
Man never is, but always to be, blest.
The soul uneasy, and confined from home,
Rests and expatiates in a life to come.

. . .

Know then thyself, presume not God to scan;
The proper study of mankind is man.
Placed on this isthmus of a middle state,
A being darkly wise, and rudely great:
With too much knowledge for the sceptic side,
With too much weakness for the stoic's pride,
He hangs between; in doubt to act, or rest;
In doubt to deem himself a god, or beast;
In doubt his mind or body to prefer;
Born but to die, and reasoning but to err;
Alike in ignorance, his reason such,
Whether he thinks too little, or too much:
Chaos of thought and passion, all confused;
Still by himself abused, or dis-abused;
Created half to rise, and half to fall;
Great lord of all things, yet a prey to all;
Sole judge of truth, in endless error hurled:
The glory, jest, and riddle of the world!

Henry Carey

'Of all the girls that are so smart'

Of all the girls that are so smart
    There's none like pretty Sally;
She is the darling of my heart,
    And lives in our alley.
There is no lady in the land
    Is half so sweet as Sally;
She is the darling of my heart,
    And lives in our alley.

Her father he makes cabbage nets,
    And through the streets does cry 'em;
Her mother she sells laces long
    To such as please to buy 'em:
But sure such folks could ne'er beget
    So sweet a girl as Sally!

She is the darling of my heart,
    And lives in our alley.

When she is by, I leave my work,
    I love her so sincerely;
My master comes like any Turk,
    And bangs me most severely:
But let him bang his bellyful,
    I'll bear it all for Sally;
She is the darling of my heart,
    And lives in our alley.

Of all the days are in the week
    I dearly love but one day,
And that's the day that comes betwixt
    A Saturday and Monday;
For then I'm drest all in my best
    To walk abroad with Sally;
She is the darling of my heart
    And lives in our alley.

My master carries me to church,
    And often am I blamed
Because I leave him in the lurch
    As soon as text is named;
I leave the church in sermon time
    And slink away to Sally;
She is the darling of my heart,
    And lives in our alley.

When Christmas comes about again,
    O, then I shall have money;
I'll hoard it up, and box and all,
    I'll give it to my honey:
I would it were ten thousand pound,
    I'd give it all to Sally;
She is the darling of my heart,
    And lives in our alley.

My master and the neighbours all,
    Make game of me and Sally,
And, but for her, I'd better be
    A slave and row a galley;
But when my seven long years are out,
    O, then I'll marry Sally;
O, then we'll wed, and then we'll bed—
    But not in our alley!

Anonymous

The Vicar of Bray

In good King Charles's golden days,
　　When loyalty no harm meant,
A zealous high-church man was I,
　　And so I gained preferment.
Unto my flock I daily preached,
　　Kings are by God appointed,
And damned are those who dare resist,
　　Or touch the Lord's anointed.
　　　　And this is law, I will maintain
　　　　Unto my dying day, sir;
　　　　That whatsoever king shall reign,
　　　　I will be Vicar of Bray, sir!

When royal James possessed the crown,
　　And popery grew in fashion;
The penal law I hooted down,
　　And read the Declaration:
The Church of Rome I found would fit
　　Full well my constitution,
And I had been a Jesuit,
　　But for the Revolution.
　　　　And this is law, etc.

When William our deliverer came,
　　To heal the nation's grievance,
I turned the cat in pan again,
　　And swore to him allegiance:
Old principles I did revoke,
　　Set conscience at a distance,
Passive obedience is a joke,
　　A jest is non-resistance.

When glorious Ann became our queen,
　　The Church of England's glory,
Another face of things was seen,
　　And I became a Tory:
Occasional conformists base,
　　I damned, and moderation,
And thought the Church in danger was,
　　From such prevarication.

When George in pudding time came o'er,
   And moderate men looked big, sir,
My principles I changed once more,
   And so became a Whig, sir:
And thus preferment I procured,
   From our faith's great defender,
And almost every day abjured
   The Pope, and the Pretender.

The illustrious House of Hanover,
   And Protestant Succession,
To these I lustily will swear,
   Whilst they can keep possession:
For in my faith and loyalty,
   I never more will falter,
But George my lawful king shall be,
   Except the times should alter.

James Thomson

Rule Britannia

When Britain first, at heaven's command,
   Arose from out the azure main;
This was the charter of the land,
   And guardian angels sung this strain:
     'Rule, Britannia, rule the waves;
     Britons never will be slaves.'

The nations, not so blest as thee,
   Must, in their turns, to tyrants fall;
While thou shalt flourish great and free,
   The dread and envy of them all.
     Rule, Britannia, etc.

Still more majestic shalt thou rise,
   More dreadful, from each foreign stroke;
As the loud blast that tears the skies,
   Serves but to root thy native oak.

Thee haughty tyrants ne'er shall tame:
   All their attempts to bend thee down,
Will but arouse thy generous flame;
   But work their woe, and thy renown.

To thee belongs the rural reign;
   Thy cities shall with commerce shine;
All thine shall be the subject main,
   And every shore it circles thine.

The muses, still with freedom found,
   Shall to thy happy coast repair:
Blest isle! with matchless beauty crowned,
   And manly hearts to guard the fair.

Anonymous

God Save the King

God save great George our King,
Long live our noble King,
   God save the King.
Send him victorious,
Happy and glorious,
Long to reign over us,
   God save the King.

O Lord our God arise,
Scatter his enemies,
   And make them fall:
Confound their politics,
Frustrate their knavish tricks,
On him our hopes we fix,
   God save us all.

Thy choicest gifts in store,
On him be pleased to pour,
   Long may he reign.
May he defend our laws,
And ever give us cause,
To sing with heart and voice,
   God save the King.

Lord grant that Marshal Wade
May by thy mighty aid
   Victory bring.
May he sedition hush,
And like a torrent rush,
Rebellious Scots to crush,
   God save the King.

Thomas Gray

Elegy Written in a Country Churchyard

The curfew tolls the knell of parting day,
   The lowing herd wind slowly o'er the lea,
The plowman homeward plods his weary way,
   And leaves the world to darkness and to me.

Now fades the glimmering landscape on the sight,
   And all the air a solemn stillness holds,
Save where the beetle wheels his droning flight,
   And drowsy tinklings lull the distant folds;

Save that from yonder ivy-mantled tower
   The moping owl does to the moon complain
Of such as, wandering near her secret bower,
   Molest her ancient solitary reign.

Beneath those rugged elms, that yew-tree's shade,
   Where heaves the turf in many a mouldering heap,
Each in his narrow cell for ever laid,
   The rude forefathers of the hamlet sleep.

The breezy call of incense-breathing morn,
   The swallow twittering from the straw-built shed,
The cock's shrill clarion, or the echoing horn,
   No more shall rouse them from their lowly bed.

For them no more the blazing hearth shall burn,
   Or busy housewife ply her evening care:
No children run to lisp their sire's return,
   Or climb his knee the envied kiss to share.

Oft did the harvest to their sickle yield,
   Their furrow oft the stubborn glebe has broke:
How jocund did they drive their team afield!
   How bowed the woods beneath their sturdy stroke!

Let not ambition mock their useful toil,
   Their homely joys, and destiny obscure;
Nor grandeur hear with a disdainful smile
   The short and simple annals of the poor.

The boast of heraldry, the pomp of power,
   And all that beauty, all that wealth e'er gave,
Awaits alike the inevitable hour.
   The paths of glory lead but to the grave.

Nor you, ye proud, impute to these the fault,
   If memory o'er their tomb no trophies raise,
Where through the long-drawn aisle and fretted vault
   The pealing anthem swells the note of praise.

Can storied urn or animated bust
   Back to its mansion call the fleeting breath?
Can honour's voice provoke the silent dust,
   Or flattery soothe the dull cold ear of death?

Perhaps in this neglected spot is laid
   Some heart once pregnant with celestial fire;
Hands, that the rod of empire might have swayed,
   Or waked to extasy the living lyre.

But knowledge to their eyes her ample page
   Rich with the spoils of time did ne'er unroll;
Chill penury repressed their noble rage,
   And froze the genial current of the soul.

Full many a gem of purest ray serene,
   The dark unfathomed caves of ocean bear,
Full many a flower is born to blush unseen,
   And waste its sweetness on the desert air.

Some village-Hampden, that with dauntless breast
   The little tyrant of his fields withstood,
Some mute inglorious Milton here may rest,
   Some Cromwell guiltless of his country's blood.

The applause of listening senates to command,
   The threats of pain and ruin to despise,
To scatter plenty o'er a smiling land,
   And read their history in a nation's eyes,

Their lot forbad: nor circumsribed alone
   Their growing virtues, but their crimes confined;
Forbad to wade through slaughter to a throne,
   And shut the gates of mercy on mankind,

The struggling pangs of conscious truth to hide,
   To quench the blushes of ingenuous shame,
Or heap the shrine of luxury and pride
   With incense kindled at the Muse's flame.

Far from the madding crowd's ignoble strife,
  Their sober wishes never learned to stray;
Along the cool sequestered vale of life
  They kept the noiseless tenor of their way.

Yet even these bones from insult to protect
  Some frail memoral still erected nigh,
With uncouth rhymes and shapeless sculpture decked,
  Implores the passing tribute of a sigh.

Their name, their years, spelt by the unlettered Muse,
  The place of fame and elegy supply:
And many a holy text around she strews,
  That teach the rustic moralist to die.

For who, to dumb forgetfulness a prey,
  This pleasing anxious being e'er resigned,
Left the warm precincts of the cheerful day,
  Nor cast one longing lingering look behind?

On some fond breast the parting soul relies,
  Some pious drops the closing eye requires;
E'en from the tomb the voice of nature cries,
  E'en in our ashes live their wonted fires.

For thee, who mindful of the unhonoured dead,
  Dost in these lines their artless tale relate;
If chance, by lonely contemplation led,
  Some kindred spirit shall inquire thy fate—

Haply some hoary-headed swain may say,
  'Oft have we seen him at the peep of dawn
Brushing with hasty steps the dews away
  To meet the sun upon the upland lawn.

'There at the foot of yonder nodding beech,
  That wreathes its old fantastic roots so high,
His listless length at noontide would he stretch,
  And pore upon the brook that babbles by.

'Hard by yon wood, now smiling as in scorn,
  Muttering his wayward fancies he would rove,
Now drooping, woeful-wan, like one forlorn,
  Or crazed with care, or crossed in hopeless love.

'One morn I missed him on the customed hill,
  Along the heath, and near his favourite tree;
Another came; nor yet beside the rill,
  Nor up the lawn, nor at the wood was he:

'The next, with dirges due in sad array
   Slow through the church-way path we saw him borne.
Approach and read (for though can'st read) the lay,
   Graved on the stone beneath yon aged thorn.'

(There scattered oft, the earliest of the year,
   By hands unseen, are showers of violets found:
The redbreast loves to bill and warble there,
   And little footsteps lightly print the ground.)

The Epitaph

Here rests his head upon the lap of Earth
   A Youth, to Fortune and to Fame unknown.
Fair Science frowned not on his humble birth,
   And Melancholy marked him for her own.

Large was his bounty, and his soul sincere,
   Heaven did a recompense as largely send:
He gave to Misery all he had, a tear,
   He gained from Heaven ('twas all he wished) a friend.

No farther seek his merits to disclose,
   Or draw his frailties from their dread abode,
(There they alike in trembling hope repose,)
   The bosom of his Father and his God.

On a Favourite Cat, Drowned
in a Tub of Gold Fishes

'Twas on a lofty vase's side,
Where China's gayest art had dyed
   The azure flowers that blow;
Demurest of the tabby kind,
The pensive Selima reclined,
   Gazed on the lake below.

Her conscious tail her joy declared;
The fair round face, the snowy beard,
   The velvet of her paws,
Her coat, that with the tortoise vies,
Her ears of jet, and emerald eyes,
   She saw; and purred applause.

Still had she gazed; but 'midst the tide
Two angel forms were seen to glide,
   The genii of the stream:
Their scaly armour's Tyrian hue
Through richest purple to the view
   Betrayed a golden gleam.

The hapless nymph with wonder saw:
A whisker first and then a claw,
   With many an ardent wish,
She stretched in vain to reach the prize.
What female heart can gold despise?
   What cat's averse to fish?

Presumptuous maid! with looks intent
Again she stretched, again she bent,
   Nor knew the gulf between—
Malignant Fate sat by, and smiled—
The slippery verge her feet beguiled,
   She tumbled headlong in.

Eight times emerging from the flood
She mewed to every watery god,
   Some speedy aid to send.
No dolphin came, no nereid stirred:
Nor cruel Tom, nor Susan heard.
   A favourite has no friend!

From hence, ye beauties undeceived,
Know, one false step is ne'er retrieved,
   And be with caution bold.
Not all that tempts your wandering eyes
And heedless hearts, is lawful prize;
   Nor all that glisters, gold.

Oliver Goldsmith

From The Deserted Village

Beside yon straggling fence that skirts the way,
With blossomed furze unprofitably gay,
There, in his noisy mansion, skilled to rule,
The village master taught his little school;

A man severe he was, and stern to view,
I knew him well, and every truant knew;
Well had the boding tremblers learned to trace
The day's disasters in his morning face;
Full well they laughed with counterfeited glee
At all his jokes, for many a joke had he;
Full well the busy whisper, circling round,
Conveyed the dismal tidings when he frowned;
Yet he was kind, or, if severe in aught,
The love he bore to learning was in fault;
The village all declared how much he knew;
'Twas certain he could write and cipher too;
Lands he could measure, terms and tides presage,
And e'en the story ran that he could gauge;
In arguing too the parson owned his skill,
For e'en though vanquished, he could argue still;
While words of learned length and thundering sound
Amazed the gazing rustics ranged around,
And still they gazed, and still the wonder grew,
That one small head could carry all he knew.

From The Vicar of Wakefield

[Song]

When lovely woman stoops to folly
And finds too late that men betray,
What charm can soothe her melancholy,
What art can wash her guilt away?

The only art her guilt to cover,
To hide her shame from every eye,
To give repentance to her lover,
And wring his bosom – is to die.

William Cowper

'God moves in a mysterious way'

God moves in a mysterious way,
    His wonders to perform;
He plants his footsteps in the sea,
    And rides upon the storm.

Deep in unfathomable mines
    Of never failing skill,
He treasures up his bright designs,
    And works his sovereign will.

Ye faithful saints fresh courage take;
    The clouds ye so much dread
Are big with mercy, and shall break
    In blessings on your head.

Judge not the Lord by feeble sense,
    But trust him for his grace;
Behind a frowning providence,
    He hides a smiling face.

His purposes will ripen fast,
    Unfolding every hour;
The bud may have a bitter taste,
    But sweet will be the flower.

Blind unbelief is sure to err,
    And scan his work in vain;
God is his own interpreter,
    And he will make it plain.

From The Task

England, with all thy faults, I love thee still:
My country! and, while yet a nook is left
Where English minds and manners may be found,
Shall be constrained to love thee. Though thy clime
Be fickle, and thy year most part deformed
With dripping rains, or withered by a frost,
I would not yet exchange thy sullen skies,

And fields without a flower, for warmer France
With all her vines; nor for Ausonia's groves
Of golden fruitage, and her myrtle bowers.
To shake thy senate, and from heights sublime
Of patriot eloquence to flash down fire
Upon thy foes, was never meant my task:
But I can feel thy fortunes, and partake
Thy joys and sorrows, with as true a heart
As any thunderer there. And I can feel
Thy follies, too; and with a just disdain
Frown at effeminates, whose very looks
Reflect dishonour on the land I love.
How, in the name of soldiership and sense,
Should England prosper, when such things, as smooth
And tender as a girl, all essenced o'er
With odours, and as profligate as sweet;
Who sell their laurel for a myrtle wreath,
And love when they should fight; when such as these
Presume to lay their hand upon the ark
Of her magnificent and awful cause?
Time was when it was praise and boast enough
In every clime, and travel where we might,
That we were born her children. Praise enough
To fill the ambition of a private man,
That Chatham's language was his mother tongue,
And Wolfe's great name compatriot with his own.
Farewell those honours, and farewell with them
The hope of such hereafter! They have fallen
Each in his field of glory; one in arms,
And one in council – Wolfe upon the lap
Of smiling victory that moment won,
And Chatham heart-sick of his country's shame!
They made us many soldiers. Chatham, still
Consulting England's happiness at home,
Secured it by an unforgiving frown,
If any wronged her. Wolfe, where'er he fought,
Put so much of his heart into his act,
That his example had a magnet's force,
And all were swift to follow whom all loved.
Those suns are set. Oh, rise some other such!
Or all that we have left is empty talk
Of old achievements, and despair of new.

'I am monarch of all I survey'

*Supposed to be written by Alexander Selkirk, during his
solitary abode in the island of Juan Fernandez*

I am monarch of all I survey;
My right there is none to dispute;
From the centre al! round to the sea
I am lord of the fowl and the brute.
O Solitude! where are the charms
That sages have been in thy face?
Better dwell in the midst of alarms,
Than reign in this horrible place.

I am out of humanity's reach,
I must finish my journey alone,
Never hear the sweet music of speech;
I start at the sound of my own.
The beasts that roam over the plain
My form with indifference see;
They are so unacquainted with man,
Their tameness is shocking to me.

Society, friendship, and love
Divinely bestowed upon man,
O, had I the wings of a dove
How soon would I taste you again!
My sorrows I then might assuage
In the ways of religion and truth,
Might learn from the wisdom of age,
And be cheered by the sallies of youth.

Ye winds that have made me your sport,
Convey to this desolate shore
Some cordial endearing report
Of a land I shall visit no more:
My friends, do they now and then send
A wish or a thought after me?
O tell me I yet have a friend,
Though a friend I am never to see.

How fleet is a glance of the mind!
Compared with the speed of its flight,
The tempest itself lags behind,
And the swift-winged arrows of light.

When I think of my own native land
In a moment I seem to be there;
But alas! recollection at hand
Soon hurries me back to despair.

But the sea-fowl is gone to her nest,
The beast is laid down in his lair;
Even here is a reason of rest,
And I to my cabin repair.
There's mercy in every place,
And mercy, encouraging thought!
Gives even affliction a grace
And reconciles man to his lot.

Isaac Bickerstaffe

From Love in a Village

There was a jolly miller once,
    Lived on the river Dee;
He danced and sang from morn till night,
    No lark so blithe as he.
And this the burden of his song,
    For ever used to be:
I care for nobody, not I,
    If nobody cares for me.

Richard Brinsley Sheridan

From School for Scandal

[Song]

Here's to the maiden of bashful fifteen;
    Here's to the widow of fifty;
Here's to the flaunting extravagant queen,
    And here's to the housewife that's thrifty.
        Let the toast pass.
        Drink to the lass,
I'll warrant she'll prove an excuse for the glass.

Here's to the charmer whose dimples we prize;
　　Now to the maid who has none, sir:
Here's to the girl with a pair of blue eyes,
　　And here's to the nymph with but one, sir.
　　　　Let the toast pass, etc.

Here's to the maid with a bosom of snow;
　　Now to her that's as brown as a berry:
Here's to the wife with a face full of woe,
　　And now to the damsel that's merry.

For let them be clumsy, or let them be slim,
　　Young or ancient, I care not a feather;
So fill a pint bumper quite up to the brim,
　　And let us e'en toast them together.

William Blake

From Songs of Innocence

The Lamb

　　Little Lamb, who made thee?
　　Dost thou know who made thee?
Gave thee life, and bid thee feed
By the stream and o'er the mead;
Gave thee clothing of delight,
Softest clothing, woolly, bright;
Gave thee such a tender voice,
Making all the vales rejoice?
　　Little Lamb, who made thee?
　　Dost thou know who made thee?

　　Little Lamb, I'll tell thee,
　　Little Lamb, I'll tell thee:
He is called by thy name,
For he calls himself a Lamb.
He is meek, and he is mild;
He became a little child.
I a child, and thou a lamb,
We are called by his name.
　　Little Lamb, God bless thee!
　　Little Lamb, God bless thee!

From Songs of Experience

The Tiger

Tiger! Tiger! burning bright
In the forests of the night,
What immortal hand or eye
Could frame thy fearful symmetry?

In what distant deeps or skies
Burnt the fire of thine eyes?
On what wings dare he aspire?
What the hand dare seize the fire?

And what shoulder, and what art,
Could twist the sinews of thy heart?
And when thy heart began to beat,
What dread hand? and what dread feet?

What the hammer? what the chain?
In what furnace was thy brain?
What was anvil? what dread grasp
Dare its deadly terrors clasp?

When the stars threw down their spears,
And watered heaven with their tears,
Did he smile his work to see?
Did he who made the Lamb make thee?

Tiger! Tiger! burning bright
In the forests of the night,
What immortal hand or eye,
Dare frame thy fearful symmetry?

The Sick Rose

O Rose, thou art sick!
The invisible worm
That flies in the night,
In the howling storm,

Has found out thy bed
Of crimson joy,
And his dark secret love
Does thy life destroy.

Infant Sorrow

My mother groaned, my father wept,
Into the dangerous world I leapt;
Helpless, naked, piping loud,
Like a fiend hid in a cloud.

Struggling in my father's hands,
Striving against my swaddling bands,
Bound and weary, I thought best
To sulk upon my mother's breast.

The Chimney Sweeper

A little black thing among the snow,
Crying "weep! 'weep!' in notes of woe!
'Where are thy father and mother, say?'
'They are both gone up to the church to pray.

'Because I was happy upon the heath,
And smiled among the winter's snow,
They clothed me in the clothes of death,
And taught me to sing the notes of woe.

'And because I am happy and dance and sing,
They think they have done me no injury,
And are gone to praise God and his priest and king,
Who make up a heaven of our misery.'

From Auguries of Innocence

To see a world in a grain of sand
And heaven in a wild flower,
Hold infinity in the palm of your hand
And eternity in an hour.
A robin red breast in a cage
Puts all Heaven in a rage.
A dove house filled with doves and pigeons
Shudders Hell through all its regions.
A dog starved at his master's gate
Predicts the ruin of the state.
A horse misused upon the road
Calls to Heaven for human blood.

Each outcry of the hunted hare
A fibre from the brain does tear.
A skylark wounded in the wing,
A cherubim does cease to sing.
The game cock clipped and armed for fight
Does the rising sun affright.
Every wolf's and lion's howl
Raises from Hell a human soul.
The wild deer, wandering here and there,
Keeps the human soul from care.
The lamb misused breeds public strife
And yet forgives the butcher's knife.
The bat that flits at close of eve
Has left the brain that won't believe.
The owl that calls upon the night
Speaks the unbeliever's fright.
He who shall hurt the little wren
Shall never be beloved by men.
He who the ox to wrath has moved
Shall never be by woman loved.
The wanton boy that kills the fly
Shall feel the spider's enmity.
He who torments the chafer's sprite
Weaves a bower in endless night.
The caterpillar on the leaf
Repeats to thee thy mother's grief.
Kill not the moth nor butterfly,
For the last judgment draweth nigh.
He who shall train the horse to war
Shall never pass the polar bar.
The beggar's dog and widow's cat,
Feed them and thou wilt grow fat.
The gnat that sings his summer's song
Poison gets from slander's tongue.
The poison of the snake and newt
Is the sweat of envy's foot.
The poison of the honey bee
Is the artist's jealousy.
The prince's robes and beggar's rags
Are toadstools on the miser's bags.
A truth that's told with bad intent
Beats all the lies you can invent.
It is right it should be so;

Man was made for joy and woe;
And when this we rightly know
Through the world we safely go.

From Milton

And did those feet in ancient time
Walk upon England's mountains green?
And was the holy lamb of God
On England's pleasant pastures seen?

And did the countenance divine
Shine forth upon our clouded hills?
And was Jerusalem builded here
Among those dark satanic mills?

Bring me my bow of burning gold:
Bring me my arrows of desire:
Bring me my spear: O clouds unfold!
Bring me my chariot of fire.

I will not cease from mental fight,
Nor shall my sword sleep in my hand
Till we have built Jersusalem
In England's green and pleasant land.

Robert Burns

Auld Lang Syne

Should auld acquaintance be forgot,
  And never brought to min'?
Should auld acquaintance be forgot,
  And auld lang syne?

Surely ye'll be your pint-stowp,
  And surely I'll be mine;
And we'll take a cup o' kindness yet
  For auld lang syne!

We twa hae rin about the braes,
    And pu'd the gowans fine;
But we've wandered monie a weary fit
    Sin' auld lang syne.

We twa hae paidl't i' the burn,
    Frae mornin' sun till dine;
But seas between us braid hae roared
    Sin auld lang syne.

And there's a hand, my trusty fiere,
    And gie's a hand o' thine;
And we'll tak a right guid-willie waught
    For auld lang syne.

For auld lang syne, my dear,
    For auld lang syne,
We'll tak a cup o' kindness yet
    For auld lang syne.

Song

My luve is like a red, red rose,
    That's newly sprung in June:
My luve is like the melodie,
    That's sweetly played in tune.

As fair art thou, my bonnie lass,
    So deep in luve am I;
And I will luve thee still, my dear,
    Till a' the seas gang dry.

Till a' the seas gang dry, my dear,
    And the rocks melt wi' the sun;
And I will luve thee still, my dear,
    While the sands o' life shall run.

And fare-thee-well, my only luve!
    And fare-thee-well, a while!
And I will come again, my luve,
    Tho' it were ten thousaand mile!

To a Mouse

On Turning Her up in Her Nest with the Plough, November 1785

Wee, sleeket, cowrin, tim'rous beastie,
O, what a panic's in thy breastie!
Thou need na start awa sae hasty,
　　　　　　　Wi' bickerin brattle!
I wad be laith to rin an' chase thee,
　　　　　　　Wi' murderin pattle!

I'm truly sorry man's dominion,
Has broken nature's social union,
An' justifies that ill opinion,
　　　　　　　Which makes thee startle
At me, thy poor, earth-born companion,
　　　　　　　An' fellow-mortal!

I doubt na, whyles, but thou may thieve;
What then? poor beastie, thou maun live!
A daimen icker in a thrave
　　　　　　　'S a sma' request;
I'll get a blessin wi' the lave,
　　　　　　　An' never miss 't!

Thy wee bit housie, too, in ruin!
It's silly wa's the win's are strewin
An' naething, now, to big a new ane,
　　　　　　　O' foggage green!
An' bleak December's winds ensuin,
　　　　　　　Baith snell an' keen!

Thou saw the fields laid bare an' waste,
An' weary winter comin fast,
An' cozie here, beneath the blast,
　　　　　　　Thou thought to dwell—
Till crash! the cruel coulter past
　　　　　　　Out thro' thy cell.

That wee bit heap o' leaves an' stibble,
Has cost thee mony a weary nibble!
Now thou's turn'd out, for a' thy trouble,
　　　　　　　But house or hald,
To thole the winter's sleety dribble,
　　　　　　　An' cranreuch could!

But mousie, thou art no thy lane,
In proving foresight maybe vain;
The best-laid schemes o' mice an' men
        Gang aft agley,
An' lea'e us nought but grief an' pain,
        For promis'd joy!

Still thou art blest, compar'd wi' me!
The present only toucheth thee:
But och! I backward cast my e'e,
        On prospects drear!
An' forward, tho' I canna see,
        I guess an' fear!

'Scots, wha hae wi' Wallace bled'

Scots, wha hae wi' Wallace bled
Scots, wham Bruce has aften led,
Welcome to your gory bed,
    Or to victory!

Now's the day, and now's the hour;
See the front o' battle lour,
See approach proud Edward's power—
    Chains and slavery!

Wha will be a traitor knave?
Wha can fill a coward's grave?
Wha sae base as be a slave?—
    Let him turn, and flee!

Wha for Scotland's king and law
Freedom's sword will strongly draw,
Freeman stand or freeman fa',
    Let him follow me!

By oppression's woes and pains,
By your sons in servile chains,
We will drain our dearest veins,
    But they shall be free!

Lay the proud usurpers low!
Tyrants fall in every foe!
Liberty's in every blow!
    Let us do, or die!

'Ae fond kiss, and then we sever'

Ae fond kiss, and then we sever;
Ae fareweel, and then for ever!
Deep in the heart-wrung tears I'll pledge thee,
Warring sighs and groans I'll wage thee!
Who shall say that Fortune grieves him
While the star of hope she leaves him?
Me, nae cheerfu' twinkle lights me,
Dark despair around benights me.

I'll ne'er blame my partial fancy;
Naething could resist my Nancy;
But to see her was to love her,
Love but her, and love for ever.
Had we never loved sae kindly,
Had we never loved sae blindly,
Never met – or never parted,
We had ne'er been broken-hearted.

Fare thee weel, thou first and fairest!
Fare thee weel, thou best and dearest!
Thine be ilka joy and treasure,
Peace, enjoyment, love, and pleasure!
Ae fond kiss, and then we sever!
Ae fareweel, alas, for ever!
Deep in heart-wrung tears I'll pledge thee,
Warring sighs and groans I'll wage thee!

William Wordsworth

'My heart leaps up when I behold'

My heart leaps up when I behold
   A rainbow in the sky;
So was it when my life began;
So is it now I am a man;
So be it when I shall grow old,
   Or let me die!
The child is father of the man
And I could wish my days to be
Bound each to each by natural piety.

To the Cuckoo

O blithe new-comer! I have heard,
I hear thee and rejoice.
O Cuckoo! shall I call thee bird,
Or but a wandering voice;

While I am lying on the grass
Thy twofold shout I hear;
From hill to hill it seems to pass
At once far off, and near.

Though babbling only to the vale,
Of sunshine and of flowers,
Thou bringest unto me a tale
Of visionary hours.

Thrice welcome, darling of the Spring!
Even yet thou art to me
No bird, but an invisible thing,
A voice, a mystery;

The same whom in my schoolboy days
I listened to; that cry
Which made me look a thousand ways
In bush, and tree, and sky.

To seek thee did I often rove
Through woods and on the green;
And thou wert still a hope, a love;
Still longed for, never seen.

And I can listen to thee yet;
Can lie upon the plain
And listen, till I do beget
That golden time again.

O blessed bird! the earth we pace
Again appears to be
An unsubstantial, faery place;
That is fit home for thee!

'She dwelt among the untrodden ways'

She dwelt among the untrodden ways
   Beside the springs of Dove,
A maid whom there were none to praise
   And very few to love:

A violet by a mossy stone
   Half hidden from the eye!
—Fair as a star, when only one
   Is shining in the sky.

She lived unknown, and few could know
   When Lucy ceased to be;
But she is in her grave, and, oh,
   The difference to me!

'A slumber did my spirit seal'

A slumber did my spirit seal;
   I had no human fears:
She seemed a thing that could not feel
   The touch of earthly years.

No motion has she now, no force;
   She neither hears nor sees;
Rolled round in earth's diurnal course,
   With rocks, and stones, and trees.

'I wandered lonely as a cloud'

I wandered lonely as a cloud
That floats on high o'er vales and hills,
When all at once I saw a crowd,
A host, of golden daffodils;
Beside the lake, beneath the trees,
Fluttering and dancing in the breeze.

Continuous as the stars that shine
And twinkle on the milky way,
They stretched in never-ending line
Along the margin of a bay:
Ten thousand saw I at a glance,
Tossing their heads in sprightly dance.

The waves beside them danced; but they
Out-did the sparkling waves in glee:
A poet could not but be gay,
In such a jocund company:
I gazed – and gazed – but little thought
What wealth the show to me had brought:

For oft, when on my couch I lie
In vacant or in pensive mood,
They flash upon that inward eye
Which is the bliss of solitude;
And then my heart with pleasure fills
And dances with the daffodils.

Lines Composed a Few Miles above Tintern Abbey, on revisiting the banks of the Wye during a tour, July 13, 1798

Five years have past; five summers, with the length
Of five long winters! and again I hear
These waters, rolling from their mountain-springs
With a soft inland murmur. – Once again
Do I behold these steep and lofty cliffs,
That on a wild secluded scene impress

Thoughts of more deep seclusion; and connect
The landscape with the quiet of the sky.
The day is come when I again repose
Here, under this dark sycamore, and view
These plots of cottage-ground, these orchard-tufts,
Which at this season, with their unripe fruits,
Are clad in one green hue, and lose themselves
'Mid groves and copses. Once again I see
These hedge-rows, little lines
Of sportive wood run wild: these pastoral farms,
Green to the very door; and wreaths of smoke
Sent up, in silence, from among the trees!
With some uncertain notice, as might seem
Of vagrant dwellers in the houseless woods,
Or of some Hermit's cave, where by his fire
The Hermit sits alone.
                              These beauteous forms,
Through a long absence, have not been to me
As is a landscape to a blind man's eye:
But oft, in lonely rooms, and 'mid the din
Of towns and cities, I have owed to them,
In hours of weariness, sensations sweet,
Felt in the blood, and felt along the heart;
And passing even into my purer mind,
With tranquil restoration:- feelings too
Of unremembered pleasure: such, perhaps,
As have no slight or trivial influence
On that best portion of a good man's life,
His little, nameless, unremembered, acts
Of kindness and of love. Nor less, I trust,
To them I may have owned another gift,
Of aspect more sublime; that blessed mood,
In which the burthen of the mystery,
In which the heavy and the weary weight
Of all this unintelligible world,
Is lightened:- that serene and blessed mood,
In which the affections gently lead us on—
Until, the breath of this corporeal frame
And even the motion of our human blood
Almost suspended, we are laid asleep
In body, and become a living soul:
While with an eye made quiet by the power

Of harmony, and the deep power of joy,
We see into the life of things.
                    If this
Be but a vain belief, yet, oh! how oft—
In darkness and amid the many shapes
Of joyless daylight; when the fretful stir
Unprofitable, and the fever of the world,
Have hung upon the beatings of my heart—
How oft, in spirit, have I turned to thee,
O sylvan Wye! thou wanderer through the woods,
How often has my spirit turned to thee!

And now, with gleams of half-extinguished thought
With many recognitions dim and faint,
And somewhat of a sad perplexity,
The picture of the mind revives again:
While here I stand, not only with the sense
Of present pleasure, but with pleasing thoughts
That in this moment there is life and food
For future years. And so I dare to hope,
Though changed, no doubt, from what I was when first
I came among these hills; when like a roe
I bounded o'er the mountains, by the sides
Of the deep rivers, and the lonely streams,
Wherever nature led: more like a man
Flying from something that he dreads than one
Who sought the thing he loved. For nature then
(The coarser pleasures of my boyish days,
And their glad animal movements all gone by)
To me was all in all. – I cannot paint
What then I was. The sounding cataract
Haunted me like a passion: the tall rock,
The mountain, and the deep and gloomy wood,
Their colours and their forms, were then to me
An appetite; a feeling and a love,
That had no need of a remoter charm,
By thought supplied, nor any interest
Unborrowed from the eye. – That time is past,
And all its aching joys are now no more,
And all its dizzy raptures. Not for this
Faint I, nor mourn nor murmur; other gifts
Have followed; for such loss, I would believe,
Abundant recompense. For I have learned

To look on nature, not as in the hour
Of thoughtless youth; but hearing oftentimes
The still, sad music of humanity,
Nor harsh nor grating, though of ample power
To chasten and subdue. And I have felt
A presence that disturbs me with the joy
Of elevated thoughts; a sense sublime
Of something far more deeply interfused,
Whose dwelling is the light of setting suns,
And the round ocean and the living air,
And the blue sky, and in the mind of man:
A motion and a spirit, that impels
All thinking things, all objects of all thought,
And rolls through all things. Therefore am I still
A lover of the meadows and the woods,
And mountains; and of all that we behold
From this green earth; of all the mighty world
Of eye, and ear – both what they half create,
And what perceive; well pleased to recognise
In nature and the language of the sense
The anchor of my purest thoughts, the nurse,
The guide, the guardian of my heart, and soul
Of all my moral being.
                              Nor perchance.
If I were not thus taught, should I the more
Suffer my genial spirits to decay:
For thou art with me here upon the banks
Of this fair river; thou my dearest friend,
My dear, dear friend; and in thy voice I catch
The language of my former heart, and read
My former pleasures in the shooting lights
Of thy wild eyes. Oh! yet a little while
May I behold in thee what I was once,
My dear, dear sister! and this prayer I make,
Knowing that nature never did betray
The heart that loved her! 'tis her privilege,
Through all the years of this our life, to lead
From joy to joy: for she can so inform
The mind that is within us, so impress
With quietness and beauty, and so feed
With lofty thoughts, that neither evil tongues,
Rash judgments, nor the sneers of selfish men,
Nor greetings where no kindness is, nor all

The dreary intercourse of daily life,
Shall e'er prevail against us, or disturb
Our cheerful faith, that all which we behold
Is full of blessings. Therefore let the moon
Shine on thee in thy solitary walk;
And let the misty mountain-winds be free
To blow against thee: and, in after years,
When these wild ecstasies shall be matured
Into a sober pleasure; when thy mind
Shall be a mansion for all lovely forms.
Thy memory be as a dwelling-place
For all sweet sounds and harmonies; oh! then,
If solitude, or fear, or pain, or grief,
Should be thy portion, with what healing thoughts
Of tender joy wilt thou remember me,
And these my exhortations! Nor, perchance—
If I should be where I no more can hear
Thy voice, nor catch from thy wild eyes these gleams
Of past existence – wilt thou then forget
That on the banks of this delightful stream
We stood together; and that I, so long
A worshipper of nature, hither came
Unwearied in that service: rather say
With warmer love – oh! with far deeper zeal
Of holier love. Nor wilt thou then forget
That after many wanderings, many years
Of absence, these steep woods and lofty cliffs,
And this green pastoral landscape, were to me
More dear, both for themselves and for thy sake!

'The world is too much with us; late and soon'

The world is too much with us; late and soon,
Getting and spending, we lay waste our powers:
Little we see in nature that is ours;
We have given our hearts away, a sordid boon!
This sea that bares her bosom to the moon;
The winds that will be howling at all hours,
And are up-gathered now like sleeping flowers;
For this, for everything, we are out of tune;
It moves us not. – Great God! I'd rather be

A pagan suckled in a creed outworn;
So might I, standing on this pleasant lea,
Have glimpses that would make me less forlorn;
Have sight of Proteus rising from the sea;
Or hear old Triton blow his wreathed horn.

The Solitary Reaper

Behold her, single in the field,
Yon solitary Highland Lass!
Reaping and singing by herself;
Stop here, or gently pass!
Alone she cuts and binds the grain,
And sings a melancholy strain;
O listen! for the vale profound
Is overflowing with the sound.

No nightingale did ever chaunt
More welcome notes to weary bands
Of travellers in some shady haunt,
Among Arabian sands;
A voice so thrilling ne'er was heard
In spring-time from the cuckoo-bird,
Breaking the silence of the seas
Among the farthest Hebrides.

Will no one tell me what she sings?
Perhaps the plaintive numbers flow
For old, unhappy, far-off things,
And battles long ago;
Or is it some more humble lay,
Familiar matter of to-day?
Some natural sorrow, loss, or pain,
That has been, and may be again?

Whate'er the theme, the maiden sang
As if her song could have no ending;
I saw her singing at her work,
And o'er the sickle bending;—
I listened, motionless and still;
And, as I mounted up the hill,
The music in my heart I bore
Long after it was heard no more.

Composed upon Westminster Bridge

Earth has not anything to show more fair:
Dull would he be of soul who could pass by
A sight so touching in its majesty:
This city now doth, like a garment, wear
The beauty of the morning; silent, bare,
Ships, towers, domes, theatres, and temples lie
Open unto the fields, and to the sky;
All bright and glittering in the smokeless air.
Never did sun more beautifully steep
In his first splendour, valley, rock, or hill;
Ne'er saw I, never felt, a calm so deep!
The river glideth at his own sweet will;
Dear God! the very houses seem asleep;
And all that mighty heart is lying still!

London: 1802

Milton! thou shouldst be living at this hour:
England hath need of thee: she is a fen
Of stagnant waters: altar, sword, and pen,
Fireside, the heroic wealth of hall and bower,
Have forefeited their ancient English dower
Of inward happiness. We are selfish men;
Oh! raise us up, return to us again;
And give us manners, virtue, freedom, power.
Thy soul was like a star, and dwelt apart;
Thou hadst a voice whose sound was like the sea:
Pure as the naked heavens, majestic, free,
So didst thou travel on life's common way,
In cheerful godliness; and yet thy heart
The lowliest duties on herself did lay.

Walter Scott

From The Lay of the Last Minstrel

Breathes there the man, with soul so dead,
Who never to himself hath said,
   This is my own, my native land!
Whose heart hath ne'er within him burned,
As home his footsteps he hath turned,
   From wandering on a foreign strand!
If such there breathe, go, mark him well;
For him no minstrel raptures swell;
High though his titles, proud his name,
Boundless his wealth as wish can claim;
Despite those titles, power, and pelf,
The wretch, concentred all in self,
Living, shall forfeit fair renown,
And, doubly dying, shall go down
To the vile dust, from whence he sprung,
Unwept, unhonoured, and unsung.

Lochinvar

O, young Lochinvar is come out of the west,
Through all the wide Border his steed was the best;
And save his good broad-sword he weapons had none,
He rode all unarmed, and he rode all alone.
So faithful in love, and so dauntless in war,
There never was knight like the young Lochinvar.

He stayed not for brake, and he stopped not for stone;
He swam the Eske river where ford there was none;
But, ere he alighted at Netherby gate,
The bridge had consented, the gallant came late:
For a laggard in love, and a dastard in war,
Was to wed the fair Ellen of brave Lochinvar.

So boldly he entered the Netherby Hall,
Among bride's-men, and kinsmen, and brothers, and all:
Then spoke the bride's father, his hand on his sword,
(For the poor craven bridegroom said never a word,)
'O come ye in peace here, or come ye in war,
Or to dance at our bridal, young Lord Lochinvar?'

'I long wooed your daughter, my suit you denied—
Love swells like the Solway, but ebbs like its tide—
And now am I come, with this lost love of mine,
To lead but one measure, drink one cup of wine.
There are maidens in Scotland more lovely by far,
That would gladly be bride to the young Lochinvar.'

The bride kissed the goblet; the knight took it up,
He quaffed off the wine, and he threw down the cup.
She looked down to blush, and she looked up to sigh,
With a smile on her lips, and a tear in her eye.
He took her soft hand, ere her mother could bar—
'Now tread we a measure!' said young Lochinvar.

So stately his form, and so lovely her face,
That never a hall such a galliard did grace;
While her mother did fret, and her father did fume,
And the bridegroom stood dangling his bonnet and plume;
And the bride-maidens whispered, ''Twere better by far
To have matched our fair cousin with young Lochinvar.'

One touch to her hand, and one word in her ear,
When they reached the hall-door, and the charger stood near;
So light to the croupe the fair lady he swung,
So light to the saddle before her he sprung!
'She is won! we are gone, over bank, bush, and scaur;
They'll have fleet steeds that follow,' quoth young Lochinvar.

There was mounting 'mong Graemes of the Netherby clan;
Forsters, Fenwicks, and Musgraves, they rode and they ran:
There was racing, and chasing, on Cannobie Lee,
But the lost bride of Netherby ne'er did they see.
So daring in love, and so dauntless in war,
Have ye e'er heard of gallant like young Lochinvar?

Samuel Taylor Coleridge

Kubla Khan

In Xanadu did Kubla Khan
    A stately pleasure-dome decree:
Where Alph, the sacred river, ran
Through caverns measureless to man
    Down to a sunless sea.

So twice five miles of fertile ground
With walls and towers wer girdled round:
And there were gardens bright with sinuous rills,
Where blossomed many an incense-bearing tree,
And here were forests ancient as the hills,
Enfolding sunny spots of greenery.

But oh! that deep romantic chasm which slanted
Down the green hill athwart a cedarn cover!
A savage place! as holy and enchanted
As e'er beneath a waning moon was haunted
By woman wailing for her demon-lover!
And from his chasm, with ceaseless turmoil seething,
As if this earth in fast thick pants were breathing,
A mighty fountain momently was forced,
Amid whose swift half-intermitted burst
Huge fragments vaulted like rebounding hail,
Or chaffy grain beneath the thresher's flail:
And 'mid these dancing rocks at once and ever
It flung up momently the sacred river.
Five miles meandering with a mazy motion
Through wood and dale the sacred river ran,
Then reached the caverns measureless to man,
And sank in tumult to a lifeless ocean:
And 'mid this tumult Kubla heard from far
Ancestral voices prophesying war!

    The shadow of the dome of pleasure
    Floated midway on the waves;
    Where was heard the mingled measure
    From the fountain and the caves.
It was a miracle of rare device,
A sunny pleasure-dome with caves of ice!

    A damsel with a dulcimer
    In a vision once I saw:
    It was an Abyssinian maid,
    And on her dulcimer she played,
    Singing of Mount Albora.
    Could I revive within me
    Her sympathy and song,
    To such a deep delight 'twould win me,
That with music loud and long,
I would build that dome in air,

That sunny dome! those caves of ice!
And all who heard should see them there,
And all should cry, Beware! Beware!
His flashing eyes, his floating hair!
Weave a circle round him thrice,
And close your eyes with holy dread,
For he on honey-dew hath fed,
And drunk the milk of Paradise.

Robert Southey

The Inchcape Rock

No stir in the air, no stir in the sea,
The ship was as still as she could be;
Her sails from heaven received no motion,
Her keel was steady in the ocean.

Without either sign or sound of their shock,
The waves flowed over the Inchcape Rock;
So little they rose, so little they fell,
They did not move the Inchcape bell.

The Abbot of Aberbrothok
Had placed that bell on the Inchcape Rock;
On a buoy in the storm it floated and swung,
And over the waves its warning rung.

When the rock was hid by the surge's swell,
The mariners heard the warning bell:
And then they knew the perilous rock,
And blessed the Abbot of Aberbrothok.

The sun in heaven was shining gay,
All things were joyful on that day;
The sea-birds screamed as they wheeled around,
And there was joyance in their sound.

The buoy of the Inchcape bell was seen,
A darker speck on the ocean green;
Sir Ralph the Rover walked his deck,
And he fixed his eye on the darker speck.

He felt the cheering power of spring,
It made him whistle, it made him sing;
His heart was mirthful to excess—
But the Rover's mirth was wickedness.

His eye was on the Inchcape float:
Quoth he, 'My men, put out the boat,
And row me to the Inchcape Rock
And I'll plague the Abbot of Aberbrothok.'

The boat is lowered, the boatmen row,
And to the Inchcape Rock they go;
Sir Ralph bent over from the boat,
And he cut the bell from the Inchcape float.

Down sunk the bell with a gurgling sound—
The bubbles rose and burst around;
Quoth Sir Ralph, 'The next who comes to the Rock
Won't bless the Abbot of Aberbrothok.'

Sir Ralph the Rover sailed away;
He scoured the seas for many a day;
And, now grown rich with plundered store,
He steers his course for Scotland's shore.

So thick a haze o'erspreads the sky
They cannot see the sun on high;
The wind hath blown a gale all day,
At evening it hath died away.

On the deck the Rover takes his stand,
So dark it is they see no land.
Quoth Sir Ralph, 'It will be lighter soon,
For there is the dawn of the rising moon.'

'Canst hear', said one, 'the breakers roar?
For methinks we should be near the shore.
Now where we are we cannot tell,
But I wish I could hear the Inchcape bell.'

They hear no sound – the swell is strong;
Though the wind hath fallen they drift along
Till the vessel strikes with a shivering shock—
'Oh! heavens! it is the Inchcape Rock!'

Sir Ralph the Rover tore his hair,
And curst himself in his despair:
The waves rush in on every side,
The ship is sinking beneath the tide.

But even in his dying fear,
One dreadful sound could the Rover hear—
A sound as if, with the Inchcape bell,
The Devil below was ringing his knell.

The Old Man's Comforts

and how he gained them

You are old, Father William, the young man cried,
    The few locks which are left you are grey;
You are hale, Father William, a hearty old man,
    Now tell me the reason, I pray.

In the days of my youth, Father William replied,
    I remembered that youth would fly fast,
And abused not my health and my vigour at first,
    That I never might need them at last.

You are old, Father William, the young man cried,
    And pleasures with youth pass away;
And yet you lament not the days that are gone,
    Now tell me the reason, I pray.

In the days of my youth, Father William replied,
    I remembered that youth could not last;
I thought of the future, whatever I did,
    That I never might grieve for the past.

You are old, Father William, the young man cried,
    And life must be hastening away;
You are cheerful, and love to converse upon death,
    Now tell me the reason, I pray.

I am cheerful, young man, Father William replied,
    Let the cause thy attention engage;
In the days of my youth I remembered my God!
    And He hath not forgotten my age.

Thomas Campbell

'Ye mariners of England'

Ye mariners of England
  That guard our native seas!
Whose flag has braved a thousand years
  The battle and the breeze!
Your glorious standard launch again
  To match another foe;
And sweep through the deep,
  While the stormy winds do blow!
While the battle rages loud and long
  And the stormy winds do blow.

The spirits of your fathers
  Shall start from every wave—
For the deck it was their field of fame,
  And ocean was their grave:
Where Blake and mighty Nelson fell
  Your manly hearts shall glow,
As ye sweep through the deep,
  While the stormy winds do blow!
While the battle rages loud and long
  And the stormy winds do blow.

Britannia needs no bulwarks,
  No towers along the steep;
Her march is o'er the mountain-waves,
  Her home is on the deep.
With thunders from her native oak
  She quells the floods below,
As they roar on the shore,
  When the stormy winds do blow!
When the battle rages loud and long,
  And the stormy winds do blow.

The meteor flag of England
  Shall yet terrific burn;
Till danger's troubled night depart
  And the star of peace return.

Then, then, ye ocean-warriors!
  Our song and feast shall flow
To the fame of your name,
  When the storm has ceased to blow!
When the fiery fight is heard no more,
  And the storm has ceased to blow.

Walter Savage Landor

'I strove with none, for none was worth my strife'

I strove with none, for none was worth my strife:
  Nature I loved, and next to nature, art:
I warmed both hands before the fire of life;
  It sinks; and I am ready to depart.

Thomas Moore

'Oft in the stilly night'

Oft in the stilly night,
  Ere slumber's chain has bound me,
Fond memory brings the light
  Of other days around me.
    The smiles, the tears,
    Of boyhood's years,
The words of love then spoken,
    The eyes that shone,
    Now dimmed and gone,
The cheerful hearts now broken!
Thus in the stilly night,
    Ere slumber's chain has bound me,
Sad memory brings the light
  Of other days around me.

When I remember all
  The friends, so linked together,
I've seen around me fall,
  Like leaves in wintry weather;
    I feel like one,

Who treads alone
Some banquet-hall, deserted,
   Whose lights are fled,
   Whose garlands dead,
And all, but he, departed!
Thus in the stilly night,
   Ere slumber's chain has bound me,
Sad memory brings the light
   Of other days around me.

Francis Scott Key

The Star-Spangled Banner

O say, can you see, by the dawn's early light,
   What so proudly we hailed at the twilight's last
      gleaming—
   Whose broad stripes and bright stars, through the clouds of
      the fight,
   O'er the ramparts we watched were so gallantly
      streaming!
And the rocket's red glare, the bombs bursting in air,
Gave proof through the night that our flag was still there;
O! say, does that star-spangled banner yet wave
O'er the land of the free, and the home of the brave?

On that shore dimly seen through the mists of the deep,
   Where the foe's haughty host in dread silence reposes,
What is that which the breeze, o'er the towering steep,
   As it fitfully blows, now conceals, now discloses?
Now it catches the gleam of the morning's first beam,
In full glory reflected now shines on the stream;
'Tis the star-spangled banner; O long may it wave
O'er the land of the free, and the home of the brave!

And where is that band who so vauntingly swore
   That the havoc of war and the battle's confusion
A home and a country should leave us no more?
   Their blood has washed out their foul footsteps'
      pollution.
No refuge could save the hireling and slave
From the terror of flight, or the gloom of the grave;

And the star-spangled banner in triumph doth wave
O'er the land of the free, and the home of the brave.

O! thus be it ever, when freemen shall stand
  Between their loved homes and the war's desolation!
Blessed with victory and peace, may the heav'n-rescued
    land
  Praise the power that hath made and preserved us a
    nation.
Then conquer we must, when our cause it is just,
And this be our motto – '*In God is our trust*':
And the star-spangled banner in triumph shall wave
O'er the land of the free, and the home of the brave.

Leigh Hunt

Abou Ben Adhem

Abou Ben Adhem (may his tribe increase!)
Awoke one night from a deep dream of peace,
And saw, within the moonlight in his room,
Making it rich, and like a lily in bloom,
An angel writing in a book of gold:
Exceeding peace had made Ben Adhem bold,
And to the presence in the room he said,
'What writest thou?' The vision raised its head,
And with a look made of all sweet accord,
Answered, 'The names of those who love the Lord.'
And is mine one?' said Abou. 'Nay, not so,'
Replied the angel. Abou spoke more low,
But cheerly still; and said, 'I pray thee, then,
Write me as one that loves his fellow men.'
The angel wrote, and vanished. The next night
It came again with a great wakening light,
And showed the names whom love of God has blest,
And lo! ben Adhem's name led all the rest.

Thomas Love Peacock

The War Song of Dinas Vawr

The mountain sheep are sweeter,
But the valley sheep are fatter;
We therefore deemed it meeter
To carry off the latter.
We made an expedition;
We met a host and quelled it;
We forced a strong position,
And killed the men who held it.

On Dyfed's richest valley,
Where herds of kine were browsing,
We made a mighty sally,
To furnish our carousing.
Fierce warriors rushed to meet us;
We met them, and o'erthrew them:
They struggled hard to beat us;
But we conquered them, and slew them.

As we drove our prize at leisure,
The king marched forth to catch us:
His rage surpassed all measure,
But his people could not match us.
He fled to his hall-pillars;
And, ere our force we led off,
Some sacked his house and cellars,
While others cut his head off.

We there, in strife bewildering,
Spilt blood enough to swim in:
We orphaned many children,
And widowed many women.
The eagles and the ravens
We glutted with our foemen;
The heroes and the cravens,
The spearmen and the bowmen.

We brought away from battle,
And much their land bemoaned them,
Two thousand head of cattle,
And the head of him who owned them:

Ednyfed, King of Dyfed,
His head was borne before us;
His wine and beasts supplied our feasts,
And his overthrow, our chorus.

George Gordon, Lord Byron

'When we two parted'

When we two parted
    In silence and tears,
Half broken-hearted
    To sever for years,
Pale grew thy cheek and cold,
    Colder thy kiss;
Truly that hour foretold
    Sorrow to this.

The dew of the morning
    Sunk chill on my brow—
It felt like the warning
    Of what I feel now.
Thy vows are all broken,
    And light is thy fame;
I hear thy name spoken,
    And share in its shame.

They name thee before me,
    A knell to mine ear;
A shudder comes o'er me—
    Why wert thou so dear?
They know not I knew thee,
    Who knew thee too well:
Long, long shall I rue thee,
    Too deeply to tell.

In secret we met—
    In silence I grieve,
That thy heart could forget,
    Thy spirit deceive.
If I should meet thee
    After long years,
How should I greet thee?
    With silence and tears.

From Childe Harold's Pilgrimage

[The Eve of Waterloo]

There was a sound of revelry by night,
And Belgium's capital had gathered then
Her beauty and her chivalry, and bright
The lamps shone o'er fair women and brave men;
A thousand hearts beat happily; and when
Music arose with its voluptuous swell,
Soft eyes looked love to eyes which spake again,
And all went merry as a marriage-bell;
But hush! hark! a deep sound strikes like a rising knell!

Did ye not hear it? No, 'twas but the wind,
Or the car rattling o'er the stony street;
On with the dance! let joy be unconfined;
No sleep till morn, when youth and pleasure meet
To chase the glowing hours with flying feet—
But hark! that heavy sound breaks in once more,
As if the clouds its echo would repeat;
And nearer, clearer, deadlier than before!
Arm! Arm! it is – it is – the cannon's opening roar!

Within a windowed niche of that high hall
Sate Brunswick's fated chieftain; he did hear
That sound the first amidst the festival,
And caught its tone with death's prophetic ear;
And when they smiled because he deemed it near,
His heart more truly knew that peal too well
Which stretched his father on a bloody bier,
And roused the vengeance blood alone could quell:
He rushed into the field, and, foremost fighting, fell.

Ah! then and there was hurrying to and fro.
And gathering tears, and tremblings of distress,
And cheeks all pale, which but an hour ago
Blushed at the praise of their own loveliness;
And there were sudden partings, such as press
The life from out young hearts, and choking sighs
Which ne'er might be repeated; who could guess
If ever more should meet those mutual eyes
Since upon night so sweet such awful morn could rise?

And there was mounting in hot haste: the steed,
The mustering squadron, and the clattering car,
Went pouring forward with impetuous speed,
And swiftly forming in the ranks of war;
And the deep thunder peal on peal afar;
And near, the beat of the alarming drum
Roused up the soldier ere the morning star;
While thronged the citizens with terror dumb,
Or whispering, with white lips – 'The foe! They come!
　　they come!'

And wild and high the 'Cameron's gathering' rose!
The war-note of Lochiel, which Albyn's hills
Have heard, and heard, too, have her Saxon foes:
How in the moon of night that pibroch thrills,
Savage and shrill! But with the breath which fills
Their mountain-pipe, so fill the mountaineers
With the fierce native daring which instils
The stirring memory of a thousand years,
And Evan's, Donald's fame rings in each clansman's ears!

And Ardennes waves above them her green leaves,
Dewy with nature's tear-drops as they pass,
Grieving, if aught inanimate e'er grieves,
Over the unreturning brave – alas!
Ere evening to be trodden like the grass
Which now beneath them, but above shall grow
In its next verdure, when this fiery mass
Of living valour, rolling on the foe
And burning with high hope, shall moulder cold and low.

Last noon beheld them full of lusty life,
Last eve in beauty's circle proudly gay,
The midnight brought the signal-sound of strife,
The morn the marshalling in arms – the day
Battle's magnificently-stern array!
The thunder-clouds close o'er it, which when rent
The earth is covered thick with other clay,
Which her own clay shall cover, heaped and pent,
Rider and horse – friend, foe – in one red burial blent!

She Walks in Beauty

She walks in beauty, like the night
   Of cloudless climes and starry skies;
And all that's best of dark and bright
   Meet in her aspect and her eyes:
Thus mellowed to that tender light
   Which heaven to gaudy day denies.

One shade the more, one ray the less,
   Had half impaired the nameless grace
Which waves in every raven tress,
   Or softly lightens o'er her face,
Where thoughts serenely sweet express
   How pure, how dear their dwelling-place.

And on that cheek, and o'er that brow,
   So soft, so calm, yet eloquent,
The smiles that win, the tints that glow,
   But tell of days in goodness spent,
A mind at peace with all below,
   A heart whose love is innocent!

The Destruction of Sennacherib

The Assyrian came down like the wolf on the fold,
And his cohorts were gleaming in purple and gold;
And the sheen of their spears was like stars on the sea,
When the blue wave rolls nightly on deep Galilee.

Like the leaves of the forest when summer is green,
That host with their banners at sunset were seen:
Like the leaves of the forest when autumn hath blown,
That host on the morrow lay withered and strown.

For the Angel of Death spread his wings on the blast,
And breathed on the face of the foe as he passed:
And the eyes of the sleepers waxed deadly and chill,
And their hearts but once heaved, and for ever grew still!

And there lay the steed with his nostril all wide,
But through it there rolled not the breath of his pride:
And the foam of his gasping lay white on the turf,
And cold as the spray of the rock-beating surf.

And there lay the rider, distorted and pale,
With the dew on his brow and the rust on his mail;
And the tents wcrc all silent, the banners alone,
The lances unlifted, the trumpet unblown.

And the widows of Ashur are loud in their wail,
And the idols are broke in the temple of Baal;
And the might of the Gentile, unsmote by the sword,
Hath melted like snow in the glance of the Lord!

'So, we'll go no more a roving'

So, we'll go no more a roving
    So late into the night,
Thought the heart be still as loving,
    And the moon be still as bright.

For the sword outwears its sheath,
    And the soul wears out the breast,
And the heart must pause to breathe,
    And love itself have rest.

Though the night was made for loving,
    And the day returns too soon,
Yet we'll go no more a roving
    By the light of the moon.

Charles Wolfe

The Burial of Sir John Moore after Corunna

Not a drum was heard, not a funeral note,
    As his corse to the rampart we hurried;
Not a soldier discharged his farewell shot
    O'er the grave where our hero we buried.

We buried him darkly at dead of night,
    The sods with our bayonets turning,
By the struggling moonbeam's misty light
    And the lantern dimly burning.

No useless coffin enclosed his breast,
   Not in sheet or in shroud we wound him;
But he lay like a warrior taking his rest
   With his martial cloak around him.

Few and short were the players we said,
   And we spoke not a word of sorrow;
But we steadfastly gazed on the face that was dead,
   And we bitterly thought of the morrow.

We thought, as we hollowed his narrow bed
   And smoothed down his lonely pillow,
That the foe and the stranger would tread o'er his head,
   And we far away on the billow!

Lightly they'll talk of the spirit that's gone,
   And o'er his cold ashes upbraid him—
But little he'll reck, if they let him sleep on
   In the grave where a Briton has laid him.

But half of our heavy task was done
   When the clock struck the hour for retiring;
And we heard the distant and random gun
   That the foe was sullenly firing.

Slowly and sadly we laid him down,
   From the field of his fame fresh and gory;
We carved not a line, and we raised not a stone,
   But we left him alone with his glory.

John Howard Payne

Home, Sweet Home

'Mid pleasures and palaces though we may roam,
Be it ever so humble, there's no place like home;
A charm from the sky seems to hallow us there,
Which, seek through the world, is ne'er met with elsewhere.
   Home, home, sweet, sweet home!
There's no place like home! There's no place like home!

An exile from home, splendour dazzles in vain;
Oh, give me my lowly thatched cottage again!
The birds singing gaily, that came at my call—
Give me them – and the peace of mind, dearer than all!
   Home, home, etc.

I gaze on the moon as I trace the drear wild,
And feel that my mother now thinks of her child,
As she looks on that moon from our own cottage door
Through the woodbine, whose fragrance shall cheer me no more.

How sweet 'tis to sit 'neath a fond father's smile,
And the cares of a mother to soothe and beguile!
Let others delight 'mid new pleasure to roam,
But give me, oh, give me, the pleasures of home.

To thee I'll return, overburdened with care;
The heart's dearest solace will smile on me there;
No more from that cottage again will I roam;
Be it ever so humble, there's no place like home.

Percy Bysshe Shelley

Ozymandias

I met a traveller from an antique land
Who said: 'Two vast and trunkless legs of stone
Stand in the desert . . . Near them, on the sand,
Half sunk, a shattered visage lies, whose frown,
And wrinkled lip, a sneer of cold command,
Tell that its sculptor well those passions read
Which yet survive, stamped on these lifeless things,
The hand that mocked them, and the heart that fed:
And on the pedestal these words appear:
"My name is Ozymandias, king of kings:
Look on my works, ye mighty, and despair!"
Nothing beside remains. Round the decay
Of that colossal wreck, boundless and bare
The lone and level sands stretch far away.'

From To a Skylark

Hail to thee, blithe Spirit!
Bird thou never wert,
That from Heaven, or near it,
Pourest thy full heart
In profuse strains of unpremeditated art.

Higher still and higher
  From the earth thou springest
Like a cloud of fire;
  The blue deep thou wingest,
And singing still dost soar, and soaring ever singest.

In the golden lightning
  Of the sunken sun,
O'er which clouds are brightening,
  Thou dost float and run;
Like an unbodied joy whose race is just begun.

'Music, when soft voices die'

Music, when soft voices die,
Vibrates in the memory—
Odours, when sweet violets sicken,
Live within the sense they quicken.

Rose leaves, when the rose is dead,
Are heaped for the beloved's bed;
And so thy thoughts, when thou art gone,
Love itself shall slumber on.

'One word is too often profaned'

One word is too often profaned
  For me to profane it,
One feeling too falsely disdained
  For thee to disdain it;
One hope is too like despair
  For prudence to smother,
And pity from thee more dear
  Than that from another.

I can give not what men call love,
    But wilt thou accept not
The worship the heart lifts above
    And the Heavens reject not—
The desire of the moth for the star,
    Of the night for the morrow,
The devotion to something afar
    From the sphere of our sorrow?

Felicia D. Hemans

Casabianca

The boy stood on the burning deck,
    Whence all but he had fled;
The flame that lit the battle's wreck
    Shone round him o'er the dead.

Yet beautiful and bright he stood,
    As born to rule the storm;
A creature of heroic blood,
    A proud though childlike form.

The flames rolled on; he would not go
    Without his father's word;
That father, faint in death below,
    His voice no longer heard.

He called aloud, 'Say, Father, say,
    If yet my task be done!'
He knew not that the chieftain lay
    Unconscious of his son.

'Speak, Father!' once again he cried,
    'If I may yet be gone!'
And but the booming shots replied,
    And fast the flames rolled on.

Upon his brow he felt their breath,
    And in his waving hair,
And looked from that lone post of death
    In still yet brave despair;

And shouted but once more aloud,
  'My father! must I stay?'
While o'er him fast, through sail and shroud,
  The wreathing fires made way.

They wrapped the ship in splendour wild,
  They caught the flag on high,
And streamed above the gallant child,
  Like banners in the sky.

There came a burst of thunder sound;
  The boy – Oh! where was he?
Ask of the winds, that far around
  With fragments strewed the sea—

With mast and helm and pennon fair,
  That well had borne their part—
But the noblest thing that perished there
  Was that young, faithful heart.

John Keats

On First Looking into Chapman's Homer

Much have I travelled in the realms of gold,
  And many goodly states and kingdoms seen;
  Round many western islands have I been
Which bards in fealty to Apollo hold.
Oft of one wide expanse had I been told
  That deep-browed Homer ruled as his demesne;
  Yet did I never breathe its pure serene
Till I heard Chapman speak out loud and bold:
Then felt I like some watcher of the skies
  When a new planet swims into his ken;
Or like stout Cortez when with eagle eyes
  He stared at the Pacific – and all his men
Looked at each other with a wild surmise—
  Silent, upon a peak in Darien.

From Endymion

A thing of beauty is a joy for ever:
Its loveliness increases; it will never
Pass into nothingness; but still will keep
A bower quiet for us, and a sleep
Full of sweet dreams, and health, and quiet breathing.
Therefore, on every morrow, are we wreathing
A flowery band to bind us to the earth,
Spite of despondence, of the inhuman dearth
Of noble natures, of the gloomy days,
Of all the unhealthy and o'er-darkened ways
Made for our searching: yes, in spite of all,
Some shape of beauty moves away the pall
From our dark spirits. Such the sun, the moon,
Trees old and young, sprouting a shady boon
For simple sheep; and such are daffodils
With the green world they live in; and clear rills
That for themselves a cooling covert make
'Gainst the hot season; the mid-forest brake,
Rich with a sprinkling of fair musk-rose blooms:
And such too is the grandeur of the dooms
We have imagined for the mighty dead;
All lovely tales that we have heard or read:
An endless fountain of immortal drink
Pouring unto us from the heaven's brink.

La Belle Dame Sans Merci

O what can ail thee, knight-at-arms,
    Alone and palely loitering?
The sedge is withered from the lake,
    And no birds sing.

O what can ail thee, knight-at-arms!
    So haggard and so woe-begone?
The squirrel's granary is full,
    And the harvest's done.

I see a lily on thy brow
    With anguish moist and fever dew,
And on thy cheek a fading rose
    Fast withereth too.

I met a lady in the meads,
  Full beautiful – a faery's child,
Her hair was long, her foot was light,
  And her eyes were wild.

I made a garland for her head,
  And bracelets too, and fragrant zone;
She looked at me as she did love,
  And made sweet moan.

I set her on my pacing steed,
  And nothing else saw all day long,
For sidelong would she bend, and sing
  A faery's song.

She found me roots of relish sweet,
  And honey wild, and manna dew,
And sure in language strange she said—
  'I love thee true.'

She took me to her elfin grot,
  And there she wept, and sighed full sore.
And there I shut her wild, wild eyes
  With kisses four.

And there she lulled me asleep,
  And there I dreamed – Ah! woe betide!
The latest dream I ever dreamed
  On the cold hill side.

I saw pale kings and princes too,
  Pale warriors, death-pale were they all;
They cried – 'La Belle Dame sans Merci
  Hath thee in thrall!'

I saw their starved lips in the gloam,
  With horrid warning gaped wide,
And I awoke and found me here,
  On the cold hill side.

And this is why I sojourn here,
  Alone and palely loitering,
Though the sedge is withered from the lake,
  And no birds sing.

To Sleep

O soft embalmer of the still midnight,
    Shutting with careful fingers and benign,
Our gloom-pleased eyes, embowered from the light,
    Enshaded in forgetfulness divine:
O soothest Sleep! If so it please thee, close
    In midst of this thine hymn my willing eyes,
Or wait the 'Amen', ere thy poppy throws
    Around my bed its lulling charities.
Then save me, or the passed day will shine
Upon my pillow, breeding many woes—
    Save me from curious conscience, that still lords
Its strength for darkness, burrowing like a mole;
    Turn the key deftly in the oiled wards,
And seal the hushed casket of my soul.

Ode to a Nightingale

My heart aches, and a drowsy numbness pains
    My sense, as though of hemlock I had drunk,
Or emptied some dull opiate to the drains
    One minute past, and Lethe-wards had sunk:
'Tis not through envy of thy happy lot,
    But being too happy in thine happiness—
        that though, light-winged Dryad of the trees,
            In some melodious plot
Of beechen green, and shadows numberless,
Singest of summer in full-throated ease.

O, for a draught of vintage! that hath been
    Cooled a long age in the deep-delved earth,
Tasting of Flora and the country green,
    Dance, and Provençal song, and sunburnt mirth!
O for a beaker full of the warm South,
    Full of the true, the blushful Hippocrene,
        With beaded bubbles winking at the brim,
            And purple-stained mouth;
    That I might drink, and leave the world unseen,
    And with thee fade away into the forest dim:

Fade far away, dissolve, and quite forget
  What thou among the leaves hast never known,
The weariness, the fever, and the fret
  Here, where men sit and hear each other groan;
Where palsy shakes a few, sad, last gray hairs,
  Where youth grows pale, and spectre-thin, and dies;
    Where but to think is to be full of sorrow
      And leaden-eyed despairs,
Where beauty cannot keep her lustrous eyes,
  Or new love pine at them beyond to-morrow.

Away! away! for I will fly to thee,
  Not charioted by Bacchus and his pards,
But on the viewless wings of poesy,
  Though the dull brain perplexes and retards:
Already with thee! tender is the night,
  And haply the Queen-Moon is on her throne,
    Clustered around by all her starry fays;
      But here there is no light,
Save what from heaven is with the breezes blown
  Through verdurous glooms and winding mossy ways.

I cannot see what flowers are at my feet,
  Nor what soft incense hangs upon the boughs,
But, in embalmed darkness, guess each sweet
  Wherewith the seasonable month endows
The grass, the thicket, and the fruit-tree wild:
  White hawthorn, and the pastoral eglantine;
    Fast fading violets covered up in leaves;
      And mid-May's eldest child,
The coming musk-rose, full of dewy wine,
  The murmurous haunt of flies on summer eves.

Darkling I listen; and, for many a time
  I have been half in love with easeful death,
Called him soft names in many a mused rhyme,
  To take into the air my quiet breath;
Now more than ever seems it rich to die,
  To cease upon the midnight with no pain,
    While thou art pouring forth thy soul abroad
      In such an ecstasy!
Still wouldst thou sing, and I have ears in vain—
  To thy high requiem become a sod.

Thou wast not born for death, immortal bird!
  No hungry generations tread thee down;
The voice I hear this passing night was heard
  In ancient days by emperor and clown:
Perhaps the self-same song that found a path
  Through the sad heart of Ruth, when, sick for home,
    She stood in tears amid the alien corn;
            The same that oft-times hath
  Charmed magic casements, opening on the foam
  Of perilous seas, in faery lands forlorn.

Forlorn! the very word is like a bell
  To toll me back from thee to my sole self!
Adieu! the fancy cannot cheat so well
  As she is famed to do, deceiving elf.
Adieu! adieu! thy plaintive anthem fades
  Past the near meadows, over the still stream,
    Up the hill-side; and now 'tis buried deep
            In the next valley-glades:
  Was it a vision, or a waking dream?
    Fled is that music: Do I wake or sleep?

Ode on a Grecian Urn

Thou still unravished bride of quietness,
  Thou foster-child of silence and slow time,
Sylvan historian, who canst thus express
  A flowery tale more sweetly than our rhyme:
What leaf-fringed legend haunts about thy shape
  Of deities or mortals, or of both,
    In Tempe or the dales of Arcady?
  What men or gods are these? What maidens loth?
What mad pursuit? What struggle to escape?
  What pipes and timbrels? What wild ecstasy?

Heard melodies are sweet, but those unheard
  Are sweeter; therefore, ye soft pipes, play on;
Not to the sensual ear, but, more endeared,
  Pipe to the spirit ditties of no tone:
Fair youth, beneath the trees, thou canst not leave
  Thy song, nor ever can those trees be bare;
    Bold lover, never never canst thou kiss,

Though winning near the goal – yet, do not grieve;
 She cannot fade, though thou hast not thy bliss,
  For ever wilt thou love, and she be fair!

Ah, happy, happy boughs! that cannot shed
 Your leaves, nor ever bid the Spring adieu:
And, happy melodist, unwearied,
 For ever piping songs for ever new;
More happy love! more happy, happy love!
 For ever warm, and still to be enjoyed,
  For ever panting, and for ever young;
All breathing human passion far above,
 That leaves a heart high-sorrowful and cloyed,
  A burning forehead, and a parching tongue.

Who are these coming to the sacrifice?
 To what green altar, O mysterious priest,
Lead'st thou that heifer lowing at the skies,
 And all her silken flanks with garlands drest?
What little town by river or sea shore,
 Or mountain-built with peaceful citadel,
  Is emptied of this folk, this pious morn?
And, little town, thy streets for evermore
 Will silent be; and not a soul to tell
  Why thou are desolate, can e'er return.

O attic shape! Fair attitude! with brede
 Of marble men and maidens overwrought,
With forest branches and the trodden weed;
 Thou, silent form, dost tease us out of thought
As doth eternity: Cold pastoral!
 When old age shall this generation waste,
  Thou shalt remain, in midst of other woe
Than ours, a friend to man, to whom thou say'st,
 'Beauty is truth, truth beauty' – that is all
  Ye know on earth, and all ye need to know.

To Autumn

 Season of mists and mellow fruitfulness,
  Close bosom-friend of the maturing sun;
 Conspiring with him how to load and bless

With fruit the vines that round the thatch-eaves run;
To bend with apples the mossed cottage-trees,
    And fill all fruit with ripeness to the core;
        To swell the gourd, and plump the hazel shells
    With a sweet kernel; to set budding more,
And still more, later flowers for the bees,
Until they think warm days will never cease,
        For summer has o'er brimmed their clammy cells.

Who hath not seen thee oft amid thy store?
    Sometimes whoever seeks abroad may find
Thee sitting careless on a granary floor,
    Thy hair soft-lifted by the winnowing wind;
Or on a half-reaped furrow sound asleep,
    Drowsed with the fume of poppies, while thy hook
        Spares the next swath and all its twined flowers:
And sometimes like a gleaner thou dost keep
Steady thy laden head across a brook;
Or by a cider-press, with patient look,
        Thou watchest the last oozings hours by hours.

Where are the songs of spring? Ay, where are they?
    Think not of them, thou hast thy music too—
While barred clouds bloom the soft-dying day,
    And touch the stubble-plains with rosy hue;
Then in a wailful choir the small gnats mourn
    Among the river sallows, borne aloft
        Or sinking as the light wind lives or dies;
    And full-grown lambs loud bleat from hilly bourn;
Hedge-crickets sing; and now with treble soft
The red-breast whistles from a garden-croft;
        And gathering swallows twitter in the skies.

Thomas Hood

The Song of the Shirt

With fingers weary and worn,
    With eyelids heavy and red,
A woman sat, in unwomanly rags,
    Plying her needle and thread—

Stitch! stitch! stitch!
In poverty, hunger and dirt,
    And still with a voice of dolorous pitch
She sang the 'Song of the Shirt'!

    'Work! work! work!
While the cock is crowing aloof!
    And work – work – work,
Till the stars shine through the roof!
It's O! to be a slave
    Along with the barbarous Turk,
Where women has never a soul to save,
    If this is Christian work!

 . 'Work – work – work
Till the brain begins to swim;
    Work – work – work
Till the eyes are heavy and dim!
Seam, and gusset, and band,
    Band, and gusset, and seam,
Till over the buttons I fall asleep,
    And sew them on in a dream!

'O! men, with sisters dear!
    O! men! with mothers and wives!
It is not linen you're wearing out,
    But human creatures' lives!
        Stitch – stitch – stitch,
    In poverty, hunger, and dirt,
Sewing at once, with a double thread,
    A shroud as well as a shirt.

'But why do I talk of death?
    That phantom of grisly bone,
I hardly fear his terrible shape,
    It seems so like my own—
    It seems so like my own,
    Because of the fasts I keep,
Oh! God! that bread should be so dear,
    And flesh and blood so cheap!

    'Work – work – work!
My labour never flags;
And what are its wages? A bed of straw,
    A crust of bread – and rags.
That shattered roof – and this naked floor—

A table – a broken chair—
And a wall so blank, my shadow I thank
   For sometimes falling there!

  'Work – work – work!
From weary chime to chime,
  Work – work – work—
As prisoners work for crime!
   Band, and gusset, and seam,
   Seam, and gusset, and band,
Till the heart is sick, and the brain benumbed,
   As well as the weary hand.

  'Work – work – work,
In the dull December light,
  And work – work – work,
When the weather is warm and bright—
   While underneath the eaves
   The brooding swallows cling
As if to show me their sunny backs
   And twit me with the Spring.

  'Oh! but to breathe the breath
Of the cowslip and primrose sweet—
  With the sky above my head,
And the grass beneath my feet,
   For only one short hour
   To feel as I used to feel,
Before I knew the woes of want
   And the walk that costs a meal!

  'Oh but for one short hour!
  A respite however brief!
No blessed leisure for love or hope,
  But only time for grief!
   A little weeping would ease my heart,
   But in their briny bed
My tears must stop, for every drop
   Hinders needle and thread!'

With fingers weary and worn,
  With eyelids heavy and red,
A woman sat in unwomanly rags,
  Plying her needle and thread—
  - Stitch! stitch! stitch!
   In poverty, hunger, and dirt,

And still with a voice of dolorous pitch,
Would that its tone could reach the rich!
She sang this 'Song of the Shirt'!

'I remember, I remember'

I remember, I remember,
 The house where I was born,
The little window where the sun
 Came peeping in at morn:
He never came a wink too soon,
 Nor brought too long a day;
But now, I often wish the night
 Had borne my breath away.

I remember, I remember,
 The roses, red and white;
The violets, and the lily-cups,
 Those flowers made of light!
The lilacs where the robin built,
 And where my brother set
The laburnum on his birthday—
 The tree is living yet!

I remember, I remember,
 Where I was used to swing;
And thought the air must rush as fresh
 To swallows on the wing;
My spirit flew in feathers then,
 That is so heavy now,
And summer pools could hardly cool
 The fever on my brow!

I remember, I remember,
 The fir trees dark and high;
I used to think their slender tops
 Were close against the sky:
It was a childish ignorance,
 But now 'tis little joy
To know I'm farther off from Heaven
 Than when I was a boy.

Thomas Babington, Lord Macaulay

From Horatius

Lars Porsena of Clusium
　By the Nine Gods he swore
That the great house of Tarquin
　Should suffer wrong no more.
By the Nine Gods he swore it,
　And named a trysting day,
And bade his messengers ride forth,
East and west and south and north,
　To summon his array.

East and west and south and north
　The messengers ride fast,
And tower and town and cottage
　Have heard the trumpet's blast.
Shame on the false Etruscan
　Who lingers in his home,
When Porsena of Clusium
　Is on the march for Rome.

The horsemen and the footmen
　Are pouring in amain,
From many a stately market-place;
　From many a fruitful plain;
From many a lonely hamlet,
　Which, hid by beech and pine,
Like an eagle's nest, hangs on the crest
　Of purple Apennine.

. . .

There be thirty chosen prophets,
　The wisest of the land,
Who always by Lars Porsena
　Both morn and evening stand:
Evening and morn the Thirty
　Have turned the verses o'er,
Traced from the right on linen white
　By mighty seers of yore.

And with one voice the Thirty
   Have their glad answer given:
'Go forth, go forth, Lars Porsena;
   Go forth, beloved of Heaven;
Go, and return in glory
   To Clusium's royal dome;
And hang round Nurscia's altars
   The golden shields of Rome.'

And now hath every city
   Sent up her tale of men;
The foot are fourscore thousand,
   The horse are thousands ten.
Before the gates of Sutrium
   Is met the great array.
A proud man was Lars Porsena
   Upon the trysting day.

. . .

Fast by the royal standard,
   O'erlooking all the war,
Lars Porsena of Clusium
   Sat in his ivory car.
By the right wheel rode Mamilius,
   Prince of the Latian name;
And by the left false Sextus,
   That wrought the deed of shame.

But when the face of Sextus
   Was seen among the foes,
A yell that rent the firmament
   From all the town arose.
On the house-tops was no woman
   But spat towards him and hissed.
No child but screamed out curses,
   And shook its little fist.

But the Consul's brow was sad,
   And the Consul's speech was low,
And darkly looked he at the wall,
   And darkly at the foe.
'Their van will be upon us
   Before the bridge goes down;
And if they once may win the bridge,
   What hope to save the town?'

Then out spake brave Horatius,
    The Captain of the Gate:
'To every man upon this earth
    Death cometh soon or late.
And how can man die better
    Than facing fearful odds,
For the ashes of his fathers,
    And the temples of his Gods,

'And for the tender mother
    Who dandled him to rest,
And for the wife who nurses
    His baby at her breast,
And for the holy maidens
    Who feed the eternal flame,
To save them from false Sextus
    That wrought the deed of shame?

'Hew down the bridge, Sir Consul,
    With all the speed ye may;
I, with two more to help me,
    Will hold the foe in play.
In yon strait path a thousand
    May well be stopped by three.
Now who will stand on either hand,
    And keep the bridge with me?'

Then out spake Spurius Lartius;
    A Ramnian proud was he:
'Lo, I will stand at thy right hand,
    And keep the bridge with thee.'
And out spake strong Herminius;
    Of Titian blood was he:
'I will abide on thy left side,
    And keep the bridge with thee.'

'Horatius,' quoth the Consul,
    'As thou sayest, so let it be.'
And straight against that great array
    Forth went the dauntless Three.
For Romans in Rome's quarrel
    Spared neither land nor gold,
Nor son nor wife, nor limb nor life,
    In the brave days of old.

From The Armada

Night sank upon the dusky beach, and on the purple sea,
Such night in England ne'er had been, nor e'er again shall be.
From Eddystone to Berwick bounds, from Lynn to Milford Bay,
That time of slumber was as bright and busy as the day;
For swift to east and swift to west the ghastly war-flame spread,
High on Saint Michael's Mount it shone: it shone on Beachy Head.
Far on the deep the Spaniard saw, along each southern shire,
Cape beyond cape, in endless range, those twinkling points of fire.
The fisher left his skiff to rock on Tamar's glittering waves:
The rugged miners poured to war from Mendip's sunless caves:
O'er Longleat's towers, o'er Cranbourne's oaks, the fiery herald
      flew;
He roused the shepherds of Stonehenge, the rangers of Beaulieu.
Right sharp and quick the bells all night rang out from Bristol
      town,
And ere the day three hundred horse had met on Clifton down;
The sentinel on Whitehall gate looked forth into the night,
And saw o'erhanging Richmond Hill the streak of blood-red light.
Then bugle's note and cannon's roar the deathlike silence broke,
And with one start, and with one cry, the royal city woke.
At once on all her stately gates arose the answering fires;
At once the wild alarum clashed from all her reeling spires;
From all the batteries of the Tower pealed loud the voice of fear;
And all the thousand masts of Thames sent back a louder cheer:
And from the furthest wards was heard the rush of hurrying feet,
And the broad streams of pikes and flags rushed down each
      roaring street;
And broader still became the blaze, and louder still the din,
As fast from every village round the horse came spurring in:
And eastward straight from wild Blackheath the warlike errand
      went,
And roused in many an ancient hall the gallant squires of Kent.
Southward from Surrey's pleasant hills flew those bright couriers
      forth;
High on bleak Hampstead's swarthy moor they started for the
      north;
And on, and on, without a pause, untired they bounded still;
All night from tower to tower they sprang; they sprang from hill to
      hill:
Till the proud peak unfurled the flag o'er Darwin's rocky dales,
Till like volcanoes flared to heaven the stormy hills of Wales,

Till twelve fair counties saw the blaze on Malvern's lonely height,
Till streamed in crimson on the wind the Wrekin's crest of light,
Till broad and fierce the star came forth on Ely's stately fane,
And tower and hamlet rose in arms o'er all the boundless plain;
Till Belvoir's lordly terraces the sign to Lincoln sent,
And Lincoln sped the message on o'er the wide vale of Trent;
Till Skiddaw saw the fire that burned on Gaunt's embattled pile,
And the red glare on Skiddaw roused the burghers of Carlisle.

Ralph Waldo Emerson

Hymn

Sung at the Completion of the Concord Monument 19 April 1836

By the rude bridge that arched the flood,
    Their flag to April's breeze unfurled,
Here once the embattled farmers stood,
    And fired the shot heard round the world.

The foe long since in silence slept;
    Alike the conqueror silent sleeps;
And time the ruined bridge was swept
    Down the dark stream which seaward creeps.

On this green bank, by this soft stream,
    We set to-day a votive stone;
That memory may their deed redeem,
    When, like our sires, our sons are gone.

Spirit, that made those heroes dare
    To die, or leave their children free,
Bid time and nature gently spare
    The shaft we raise to them and thee.

Robert Stephen Hawker

The Song of the Western Men

A good sword and a trusty hand!
   A merry heart and true!
King James's men shall understand
   What Cornish lads can do.

And have they fixed the where and when?
   And shall Trelawny die?
Here's twenty thousand Cornish men
   Will see the reason why!

Out spake their captain brave and bold,
   A merry wight was he:
'If London Tower were Michael's hold
   We'd set Trelawny free!

'We'll cross the Tamar, land to land—
   The Severn is no stay—
All side by side, and hand to hand,
   And who shall bid us nay?

'And when we come to London Wall,
   A pleasant sight to view,
Come forth! Come forth, ye cowards all!
   To better men than you.

'Trelawny he's in keep and hold,
   Trelawny he may die;
But here's twenty thousand Cornish bold
   Will see the reason why!'

Elizabeth Barrett Browning

Grief

I tell you, hopeless grief is passionless;
   That only men incredulous of despair,
   Half-taught in anguish, through the midnight air
Beat upward to God's throne in loud access
Of shrieking and reproach. Full desertness

In souls as countries lieth silent – bare
Under the blenching, vertical eye-glare
Of the absolute Heavens. Deep-hearted man, express
Grief for thy dead in silence like to death—
    Most like a monumental statue set
In everlasting watch and moveless woe
Till itself crumble to the dust beneath.
    Touch it; the marble eyelids are not wet:
If it could weep, it could arise and go.

A Musical Instrument

What was he doing, the great god Pan,
    Down in the reeds by the river?
Spreading ruin and scattering ban,
Splashing and paddling with hoofs of a goat,
And breaking the golden lilies afloat
    With the dragon-fly on the river.

He tore out a reed, the great god Pan,
    From the deep cool bed of the river:
The limpid water turbidly ran,
And the broken lilies a-dying lay,
And the dragon-fly had fled away,
    Ere he brought it out of the river.

High on the shore sat the great god Pan,
    While turbidly flowed the river;
And hacked and hewed as a great god can,
With his hard bleak steel at the patient reed,
Till there was not a sign of a leaf indeed
    To prove it fresh from the river.

He cut it short, did the great god Pan
    (How tall it stood in the river!),
Then drew the pith, like the heart of a man,
Steadily from the outside ring,
And notched the poor dry empty thing
    In holes, as he sat by the river.

'This is the way,' laughed the great god Pan
  (Laughed while he sat by the river),
'The only way, since gods began
To make sweet music, they could succeed.'
Then, dropping his mouth to a hole in the reed,
  He blew in power by the river.

Sweet, sweet, sweet, O Pan!
  Piercing sweet by the river!
Blinding sweet, O great god Pan!
The sun on the hill forgot to die,
And the lilies revived, and the dragon-fly
  Came back to dream on the river.

Yet half a beast is the great god Pan,
  To laugh as he sits by the river,
Making a poet out of a man:
The true gods sigh for the cost and pain—
For the reed which grows nevermore again
  As a reed with the reeds in the river.

'How do I love thee? Let me count the ways'

How do I love thee? Let me count the ways.
I love thee to the depth and breadth and height
My soul can reach, when feeling out of sight
For the ends of being and ideal grace.
I love thee to the level of every day's
Most quiet need, by sun and candlelight.
I love thee freely, as men strive for right;
I love thee purely, as they turn from praise.
I love thee with the passion put to use
In my old griefs, and with my childhood's faith.
I love thee with a love I seemed to lose
With my lost saints – I love thee with the breath,
Smiles, tears, of all my life! – and, if God choose,
I shall but love thee better after death.

Henry Wadsworth Longfellow

The Village Blacksmith

Under a spreading chestnut-tree
  The village smithy stands;
The smith, a mighty man is he,
  With large and sinewy hands;
And the muscles of his brawny arms
  Are strong as iron bands.

His hair is crisp, and black, and long,
  His face is like the tan;
His brow is wet with honest sweat,
  He earns whate'er he can,
And looks the whole world in the face,
  For he owes not any man.

Week in, week out, from morn till night,
  You can hear his bellows blow;
You can hear him swing his heavy sledge,
  With measured beat and slow,
Like a sexton ringing the village bell,
  When the evening sun is low.

And children coming home from school
  Look in at the open door;
They love to see the flaming forge,
  And hear the bellows roar,
And catch the burning sparks that fly
  Like chaff from a threshing-floor.

He goes on Sunday to the church,
  And sits among his boys;
He hears the parson pray and preach,
  He hears his daughter's voice,
Singing in the village choir,
  And it makes his heart rejoice.

It sounds to him like her mother's voice,
  Singing in Paradise!
He needs must think of her once more,
  How in the grave she lies;
And with his hard, rough hand he wipes
  A tear out of his eyes.

Toiling – rejoicing – sorrowing,
  Onward through life he goes;
Each morning sees some task begin,
  Each evening sees it close;
Something attempted, something done,
  Has earned a night's repose.

Thanks, thanks to thee, my worthy friend,
  For the lesson thou hast taught!
Thus at the flaming forge of life
  Our fortunes must be wrought;
Thus on its sounding anvil shaped
  Each burning deed and thought.

Paul Revere's Ride

Listen, my children, and you shall hear
Of the midnight ride of Paul Revere,
On the eighteenth of April, in Seventy-five;
Hardly a man is now alive
Who remembers that famous day and year.

He said to his friend, 'If the British march
By land or sea from the town tonight,
Hang by lantern aloft in the belfry arch
Of the North Church tower as a signal light—
One, if by land, and two, if by sea;
And I on the opposite shore will be,
Ready to ride and spread the alarm
Through every Middlesex village and farm,
For the country folk to be up and to arm.'

Then he said, 'Good night!' and with muffled oar
Silently rowed to the Charlestown shore,
Just as the moon rose over the bay,
Where swinging wide at her moorings lay
The Somerset, British man-of-war;
A phantom ship, with each mast and spar
Across the moon like a prison bar,
And a huge black hulk, that was magnified
By its own reflection in the tide.

Meanwhile, his friend, through alley and street,
Wanders and watches with eager ears,
Till in the silence around him he hears
The muster of men at the barrack door,
The sound of arms, and the tramp of feet,
And the measured tread of the grenadiers,
Marching down to their boats on the shore.

Then he climbed the tower of the Old North Church,
By the wooden stairs, with stealthy tread,
To the belfry-chamber overhead,
And startled the pigeons from their perch
On the sombre rafters, that round him made
Masses and moving shapes of shade—
By the trembling ladder, steep and tall,
To the highest window in the wall,
Where he paused to listen and look down
A moment on the roofs of the town,
And the moonlight flowing over all.

Beneath, in the churchyard, lay the dead,
In their night-encampment on the hill,
Wrapped in silence so deep and still
That he could hear, like a sentinel's tread,
The watchful night-wind, as it went
Creeping along from tent to tent,
And seeming to whisper, 'All is well!'
A moment only he feels the spell
Of the place and the hour, and the secret dread
Of the lonely belfry and the dead;
For suddenly all his thoughts are bent
On a shadowy something far away,
Where the river widens to meet the bay—
A line of black that bends and floats
On the rising tide, like a bridge of boats.

Meanwhile, impatient to mount and ride,
Booted and spurred, with a heavy stride
On the opposite shore walked Paul Revere.
Now he patted his horse's side,
Now gazed at the landscape far and near,
Then, impetuous, stamped the earth,
And turned and tightened his saddle-girth;
But mostly he watched with eager search

The belfry-tower of the Old North Church,
As it rose above the graves on the hill,
Lonely and spectral and sombre and still.
And lo! as he looks, on the belfry's height
A glimmer, and then a gleam of light!
He springs to the saddle, the bridle he turns,
But lingers and gazes, till full on his sight
A second lamp in the belfry burns!

A hurry of hoofs in a village street,
A shape in the moonlight, a bulk in the dark,
And beneath, from the pebbles, in passing, a spark
Struck out by a steed flying fearless and fleet;
That was all! And yet, through the gloom and the light
The fate of a nation was riding that night;
And the spark struck out by that steed in his flight,
Kindled the land into flame with its heat.

He has left the village and mounted the steep,
And beneath him, tranquil and broad and deep,
Is the Mystic, meeting the ocean tides;
And under the alders, that skirt its edge,
Now soft on the sand, now loud on the ledge,
Is heard the tramp of his steed as he rides.

It was twelve by the village clock
When he crossed the bridge into Medford town.
He heard the crowing of the cock,
And the barking of the farmer's dog,
And felt the damp of the river fog,
That rises after the sun goes down.

It was one by the village clock,
When he galloped into Lexington.
He saw the gilded weathercock
Swim in the moonlight as he passed,
And the meeting-house windows, blank and bare,
Gaze at him with a spectral glare,
As if they already stood aghast
At the bloody work they would look upon.

It was two by the village clock,
When he came to the bridge in Concord town.
He heard the bleating of the flock,
And the twitter of birds among the trees,
And felt the breath of the morning breeze

Blowing over the meadows brown.
And one was safe and asleep in his bed
Who at the bridge would be first to fall,
Who that day would be lying dead,
Pierced by a British musket-ball.

You know the rest. In the books you have read,
How the British Regulars fired and fled—
How the farmers gave them ball for ball,
From behind each fence and farmyard wall,
Chasing the redcoats down the lane,
Then crossing the fields to emerge again
Under the trees at the turn of the road,
And only pausing to fire and load.
So through the night rode Paul Revere;
And so through the night went his cry of alarm
To every Middlesex village and farm—
A cry of defiance, and not of fear,
A voice in the darkness, a knock at the door,
And a word that shall echo for evermore!

For, borne on the night-wind of the past,
Through all our history, to the last,
In the hour of darkness and peril and need,
The people will waken and listen to hear
The hurrying hoofbeats of that steed,
And the midnight message of Paul Revere.

The Wreck of the 'Hesperus'

It was the schooner *Hesperus*,
    That sailed the wintry sea;
And the skipper had taken his little daughter,
    To bear him company.

Blue were her eyes as the fairy flax,
    Her cheeks like the dawn of day,
And her bosom white as the hawthorn buds
    That ope in the month of May.

The skipper he stood beside the helm,
    His pipe was in his mouth,
And watched how the veering flaw did blow
    The smoke now West, now South.

Then up and spake an old Sailor,
   Had sailed the Spanish Main,
'I pray thee, put into yonder port,
   For I fear a hurricane.

'Last night, the moon had a golden ring,
   And to-night no moon we see!'
The skipper, he blew a whiff from his pipe,
   And a scornful laugh laughed he.

Colder and louder blew the wind,
   A gale from the North-east;
The snow fell hissing in the brine,
   And the billows frothed like yeast.

Down came the storm, and smote amain
   The vessel in its strength;
She shuddered and paused, like a frighted steed,
   Then leaped her cable's length.

'Come hither! come hither! my little daughter,
   And do not tremble so!
For I can weather the roughest gale
   That ever wind did blow.'

He wrapped her warm in his seaman's coat
   Against the stinging blast;
He cut a rope from a broken spar,
   And bound her to the mast.

'O father! I hear the church-bells ring,
   O say, what may it be?
''Tis a fog-bell on a rock-bound coast!'—
   And he steered for the open sea.

'O father! I hear the sound of guns,
   O say, what may it be?'
'Some ship in distress that cannot live
   In such an angry sea!'

'O father! I see a gleaming light,
   O say, what may it be?'
But the father answered never a word—
   A frozen corpse was he.

Lashed to the helm, all stiff and stark,
   With his face turned to the skies,
The lantern gleamed through the gleaming snow
   On his fixed and glassy eyes.

Then the maiden clasped her hands and prayed
    That saved she might be;
And she thought of Christ, who stilled the waves
    On the Lake of Galilee.

And fast through the midnight, dark and drear,
    Through the whistling sleet and snow,
Like a sheeted ghost, the vessel swept
    Towards the reef of Norman's Woe.

And ever the fitful gusts between
    A sound came from the land;
It was the sound of the trampling surf
    On the rocks and the hard sea-sand.

The breakers were right beneath her bows,
    She drifted a dreary wreck,
And a whooping billow swept the crew
    Like icicles from her deck.

She struck where the white and fleecy waves
    Looked soft as carded wool,
But the cruel rocks they gored her sides
    Like the horns of an angry bull.

Her rattling shrouds, all sheathed in ice,
    With the masts went by the board;
Like a vessel of glass she stove and sank,
    Ho! ho! the breakers roared.

At daybreak on the bleak sea-beach
    A fisherman stood aghast,
To see the form of a maiden fair
    Lashed close to a drifting mast.

The salt sea was frozen on her breast,
    The salt tears in her eyes;
And he saw her hair like the brown sea-weed
    On the billows fall and rise.

Such was the wrest of the *Hesperus*,
    In the midnight and the snow!
Christ save us from a death like this,
    On the reef of Norman's Woe!

From The Song of Hiawatha

By the shores of Gitchee Gumee,
By the shining Big-Sea-Water,
Stood the wigwam of Nokomis,
Daughter of the Moon, Nokomis.
Dark behind it rose the forest,
Rose the black and gloomy pine-trees,
Rose the firs with cones upon them;
Bright before it beat the water,
Beat the clear and sunny water,
Beat the shining Big-Sea-Water.
    There the wrinkled old Nokomis
Nursed the little Hiawatha,
Rocked him in his linden cradle,
Bedded soft in moss and rushes,
Safely bound with reindeer sinews;
Stilled his fretful wail by saying,
'Hush! the Naked Bear will hear thee!'
Lulled him into slumber, singing,
'Ewa-yea! my little owlet!
Who is this, that lights the wigwam?
With his great eyes lights the wigwam?
Ewa-yea! my little owlet!'
    Many things Nokomis taught him
Of the stars that shine in heaven;
Showed him Ishkoodah, the comet,
Ishkoodah, with fiery tresses;
Showed the Death-Dance of the spirits,
Warriors with their plumes and war-clubs,
Flaring far away to northward
In the frosty nights of Winter;
Showed the broad white road in heaven,
Pathway of the ghosts, the shadows,
Running straight across the heavens,
Crowded with the ghosts, the shadows.
    At the door on summer evenings
Sat the little Hiawatha;
Heard the whispering of the pine-trees,
Heard the lapping of the water,
Sounds of music, words of wonder;
'Minne-wawa!' said the pine-trees,
'Mudway-aushka!' said the water.

Saw the fire-fly, Wah-wah-taysee,
Flitting through the dusk of evening,
With the twinkle of its candle
Lighting up the brakes and bushes,
And he sang the song of children,
Sang the song Nokomis taught him:
'Wah-wah-taysee, little fire-fly,
Little, flitting, white-fire insect,
Little, dancing, white-fire creature,
Light me with your little candle,
Ere upon my bed I lay me,
Ere in sleep I close my eye-lids!'

Saw the moon rise from the water,
Rippling, rounding from the water,
Saw the flecks and shadows on it,
Whispered, 'What is that, Nokomis?'
And the good Nokomis answered:
'Once a warrior, very angry,
Seized his grandmother, and threw her
Up into the sky at midnight;
Right against the moon he threw her;
'Tis her body that you see there.'

. . .

Then the little Hiawatha
Learned of every bird its language,
Learned their names and all their secrets,
How they built their nests in summer,
Where they hid themselves in winter,
Talked with them whene'er he met them,
Called them 'Hiawatha's Chickens'.

Of all beasts he learned the language,
Learned their names and all their secrets,
How the beavers built their lodges,
Where the squirrels hid their acorns,
How the reindeer ran so swiftly,
Why the rabbit was so timid,
Talked with them whene'er he met them,
Called them 'Hiawatha's Brothers'.

Excelsior

The shades of night were falling fast,
As through an Alpine village passed
A youth, who bore, 'mid snow and ice,
A banner with the strange device,
      Excelsior!

His brow was sad; his eye beneath
Flashed like a falchion from its sheath;
And like a silver clarion rung
The accents of that unknown tongue,
      Excelsior!

In happy homes he saw the light
Of household fires gleam warm and bright,
Above, the spectral glaciers shone,
And from his lips escaped a groan,
      Excelsior!

'Try not the pass,' the old man said:
'Dark lowers the tempest overhead;
The roaring torrent is deep and wide.'
And loud that clarion voice replied,
      Excelsior!

'Oh, stay,' the maiden said, 'and rest
Thy weary head upon this breast!'
A tear stood in his bright blue eye,
But still he answered with a sigh,
      Excelsior!

'Beware the pine-tree's withered branch!
Beware the awful avalanche!'
This was the peasant's last good-night:
A voice replied, far up the height:
      Excelsior!

At break of day, as heavenward
The pious monks of Saint Bernard
Uttered the oft-repeated prayer,
A voice cried through the startled air,
      Excelsior!

A traveller, by the faithful hound,
Half-buried in the snow was found,
Still grasping in his hands of ice
That banner with the strange device,
    Excelsior!

There in the twilight cold and gray,
Lifeless, but beautiful, he lay,
And from the sky, serene and far,
A voice fell, like a falling star:
    Excelsior!

A Psalm of Life

What the Heart of the Young Man Said to the Psalmist

Tell me not, in mournful numbers,
    Life is but an empty dream!
For the soul is dead that slumbers,
    And things are not what they seem.

Life is real! Life is earnest!
    And the grave is not its goal;
Dust thou art, to dust returnest,
    Was not spoken of the soul.

Not enjoyment, and not sorrow,
    Is our destined end or way;
But to act, that each to-morrow
    Finds us farther than to-day.

Art is long, and time is fleeting,
    And our hearts, though stout and brave,
Still, like muffled drums, are beating
    Funeral marches to the grave.

In the world's broad field of battle,
    In the bivouac of life,
Be not like dumb, driven cattle!
    Be a hero in the strife!

Trust no future, howe'er pleasant!
    Let the dead past bury its dead!
Act — act in the living present!
    Heart within, and God o'erhead!

Lives of great men all remind us
 We can make our lives sublime,
And, departing, leave behind us
 Footprints on the sands of time;

Footprints, that perhaps another,
 Sailing o'er life's solemn main,
A forlorn and shipwrecked brother,
 Seeing, shall take heart again.

Let us, then, be up and doing,
 With a heart for any fate;
Still achieving, still pursuing,
 Learn to labour and to wait.

Samuel Francis Smith

America

My country, 'tis of thee,
Sweet land of liberty,
 Of thee I sing;
Land where my fathers died,
Land of the pilgrims' pride,
From every mountain-side
 Let freedom ring.

My native country, thee,
Land of the noble free,
 Thy name I love;
I love thy rocks and rills,
Thy woods and templed hills;
My heart with rapture thrills
 Like that above.

Let music swell the breeze,
And ring from all the trees
 Sweet freedom's song;
Let mortal tongues awake,
Let all that breathe partake,
Let rocks their silence break—
 The sound prolong.

Our fathers' God, to Thee,
Author of liberty,
    To Thee we sing;
Long may our land be bright
With freedom's holy light;
Protect us by Thy might,
    Great God, our King.

Edgar Allan Poe

The Raven

Once upon a midnight dreary, while I pondered, weak and weary,
Over many a quaint and curious volume of forgotten lore,
While I nodded, nearly napping, suddenly there came a tapping
As of someone gently rapping, rapping at my chamber door.
' 'Tis some visitor,' I muttered, 'tapping at my chamber door—
    Only this and nothing more.'

Ah, distinctly I remember it was in the bleak December,
And each separate dying ember wrought its ghost upon the floor.
Eagerly I wished the morrow – vainly had I sought to borrow
From my books surcease of sorrow, sorrow for the lost Lenore—
For the rare and radiant maiden whom the angels name Lenore—
    Nameless here for evermore.

And the silken, sad, uncertain rustling of each purple curtain
Thrilled me – filled me with fantastic terrors never felt before;
So that now to still the beating of my heart, I stood repeating,
'Tis some visitor entreating entrance at my chamber door—
Some late visitor entreating entrance at my chamber door—
    This it is and nothing more.

Presently my soul grew stronger, hesitating then no longer,
'Sir,' I said, 'or madam, truly your forgiveness I implore;
But the fact is I was napping, and so gently you came rapping,
And so faintly you came tapping, tapping at my chamber door,
That I scarce was sure I heard you', here I opened wide the door—
    Darkness there and nothing more.

Deep into that darkness peering, long I stood there wondering,
    fearing,
Doubting, dreaming dreams no mortal ever dared to dream before;
But the silence was unbroken, and the darkness gave no token,
And the only word there spoken was the whispered word 'Lenore!'
This I whispered, and an echo murmured back the word
    'Lenore'—
    Merely this, and nothing more.

Back into the chamber turning, all my soul within me burning,
Soon again I heard a tapping somewhat louder than before.
'Surely,' said I, 'surely that is something at my window lattice;
Let me see then what thereat is, and this mystery explore—
Let my heart be still a moment and this mystery explore—
    'Tis the wind, and nothing more!'

Open here I flung a shutter, when with many a flirt and flutter
In there stepped a stately raven of the saintly days of yore;
Not the least obeisance made he; not an instant stopped or stayed
    he;
But with mien of lord or lady, perhced above my chamber door—
Perched upon a bust of Pallas, just above my chamber door—
    Perched and sat, and nothing more.

Then this ebony bird beguiling my sad fancy into smiling,
By the grave and stern decorum of the countenance it wore,
'Though thy crest be shorn and shaven, thou,' I said, 'art sure no
    craven,
Ghastly, grim and ancient raven wandering from the nightly shore,
Tell me what thy lordly name is on the night's Plutonian shore':
    Quoth the raven, 'Nevermore!'

Much I marvelled this ungainly fowl to hear discourse so plainly,
Though its answer little meaning – little relevancy bore;
For we cannot help agreeing that no living human being
Ever yet was blest with seeing bird above his chamber door,
Bird or beast upon the sculptured bust above his chamber door,
    With such a name as 'Nevermore'.

But the raven, sitting lonely on the placid bust, spoke only
That one word, as if his soul in that one word he did outpour;
Nothing further then he uttered – not a feather then he fluttered—
Till I scarcely more than muttered, 'Other friends have flown
    before—
On the morrow he will leave me, as my hopes have flown before.'
    Then the bird said 'Nevermore'.

Startled at the stillness broken by reply so aptly spoken,
'Doubtless,' said I, 'what it utters is its only stock and store,
Caught from some unhappy master whom unmerciful disaster
Followed fast and followed faster, till his songs one burden bore—
Till the dirges of his hope that melancholy burden bore
   Of 'Never – nevermore'.

But the raven still beguiling all my sad soul into smiling,
Straight I wheeled a cushioned seat in front of bird, and bust, and
    door;
Then, upon the velvet sinking, I betook myself to linking
Fancy unto fancy, thinking what this ominous bird of yore—
What this grim, ungainly, ghastly, gaunt and ominous bird of yore
   Meant in croaking 'Nevermore'.

This I sat engaged in guessing, but no syllable expressing
To the fowl whose fiery eyes now burnt into my bosom's core;
This and more I sat divining, with my head at ease reclining
On the cushions velvet lining that the lamp-light gloated o'er,
But whose velvet violet lining, with the lamp-light gloating o'er,
   She shall press, ah, nevermore!

Then, methought, the air grew denser, perfumed from an unseen
    censer
Swung by seraphim whose foot-falls tinkled on the tufted floor.
'Wretch,' I cried, 'thy God hath lent thee – by these angels he hath
    sent thee
Respite – respite and nepenthe from thy memories of Lenore!
Quaff, oh quaff this kind nepenthe, and forget this lost Lenore!'
   Quoth the raven, 'Nevermore.'

'Prophet!' said I, 'thing of evil! – prophet still, if bird or devil!
Whether tempter sent, or whether tempest tossed thee here ashore,
Desolate yet all undaunted, on this desert land enchanted—
On this home by horror haunted – tell me truly, I implore—
Is there – is there balm in Gilead? tell me – tell me, I implore!
   Quoth the raven, 'Nevermore.'

'Prophet!' said I, 'thing of evil – prophet still, if bird or devil!
By that heaven that bends above us, by that God we both adore—
Tell this soul, with sorrow laden, if within the distant Aidenn
It shall clasp a sainted maiden whom the angels name Lenore—
Clasp a rare and radiant maiden whom the angels name Lenore.'
   Quoth the raven 'Nevermore'.

'Be that word our sign of parting, bird or fiend!' I shrieked
    upstarting—
'Get thee back into the tempest and the night's Plutonian shore!
Leave no black plume as a token of the lie thy soul hath spoken!
Leave my loneliness unbroken, quit the bust above my door!
Take thy beak from out my heart and take thy form from off my
    door!'
   Quoth the raven 'Nevermore'.

And the raven never flitting, still is sitting, still is sitting,
On the pallid bust of Pallas just above my chamber door;
And his eyes have all the seeming of a demon's that is dreaming,
And the lamp-light o'er him streaming throws his shadow on the
    floor;
And my soul from out that shadow that is floating on the floor
Shall be lifted – nevermore.

Annabel Lee

It was many and many a year ago,
    In a kingdom by the sea,
That a maiden there lived whom you may know
    By the name of Annabel Lee;
And this maiden she lived with no other thought
    Than to love and be loved by me.

She was a child, and *I* was a child,
    In this kingdom by the sea;
But we loved with a love that was more than love—
    I and my Annabel Lee;
With a love that the winged seraphs of Heaven
    Coveted her and me.

And this was the reason that, long ago,
    In this kingdom by the sea,
A wind blew out of a cloud by night,
    Chilling my Annabel Lee;

So that her highborn kinsmen came
    And bore her away from me,
To shut her up in a sepulchre
    In this kingdom by the sea.

The angels, not half so happy in Heaven,
    Went envying her and me—
Yes! that was the reason (as all men know,
    In this kingdom by the sea)
That the wind came out of the cloud chilling
    And killing my Annabel Lee.

But our love it was stronger by far than the love
    Of those who were older than we—
    Of many far wiser than we—
And neither the angels in Heaven above,
    Nor the demons down under the sea,
Can ever dissever my soul from the soul
    Of the beautiful Annabel Lee!

For the moon never beams, without bringing me dreams
    Of the beautiful Annabel Lee;
And the stars never rise, but I feel the bright eyes
    Of the beautiful Annabel Lee;
And so, all the night-tide, I lie down by the side
Of my darling – my darling – my life and my bride,
    In the sepulchre there by the sea,
    In her tomb by the sounding sea.

Edward Fitzgerald

From The Rubaíyát of Omar Khayyám of Naishapur

Awake! for Morning in the Bowl of Night
Has flung the Stone that puts the Stars to Flight:
    And Lo! the Hunter of the East has caught
The Sultán's Turret in a Noose of Light.

Dreaming when Dawn's Left Hand was in the Sky
I heard a Voice within the Tavern cry:
    'Awake, my Little ones, and fill the Cup
Before Life's Liquor in its Cup be dry.'

And, as the Cock crew, those who stood before
The Tavern shouted: 'Open then the Door!
    You know how little while we have to stay,
And, once departed, may return no more.'

. . .

But come with old Khayyám, and leave the Lot
Of Kaikobád and Kaikhosrú forgot:
  Let Rustum lay about him as he will,
Or Hátim Tai cry Supper – heed them not.

With me along some Strip of Herbage strown
That just divides the desert from the sown,
  Where name of Slave and Sultán scarce is known,
And pity Sultán Máhmúd on his Throne.

Here with a Loaf of Bread beneath the Bough,
A Flask of Wine, a Book of Verse – and Thou
  Beside me singing in the Wilderness—
And Wilderness is Paradise enow.

'How sweet is mortal Sovranty!' – think some:
Others: 'How blest the Paradise to come!'
  Ah, take the Cash in hand and wave the Rest;
Oh, the brave Music of a *distant* Drum!

Look to the Rose that blows about us – 'Lo,
Laughing,' she says, 'into the World I blow:
  At once the silken Tassel of my Purse
Tear, and its Treasure on the Garden throw.'

The Worldly Hope men set their Hearts upon
Turns Ashes – or it prospers; and anon,
  Like Snow upon the Desert's dusty Face,
Lighting a little House or two – is gone.

And those who husbanded the Golden Grain,
And those who flung it to the Winds like Rain,
  Alike to no such aureate Earth are turned
As, buried once, Men want dug up again.

Think, in this battered Caravanserai
Whose Doorways are alternate Night and Day,
  How Sultán after Sultán with his Pomp
Abode his Hour or two, and went his way.

They say the Lion and the Lizard keep
The Courts where Jamshýd gloried and drank deep:
  And Bahrám, that great Hunter – the Wild Ass
Stamps o'er his Head, and he lies fast asleep.

Alfred, Lord Tennyson

The Lady of Shalott

I

On either side the river lie
Long fields of barley and of rye,
That clothe the wold and meet the sky;
And through the field the road runs by
　　To many-towered Camelot;
And up and down the people go,
Gazing where the lilies blow
Round an island there below,
　　The island of Shalott.

Willows whiten, aspens quiver,
Little breezes dusk and shiver
Through the wave that runs for ever
By the island in the river
　　Flowing down to Camelot.
Four grey walls, and four grey towers,
Overlook a space of flowers,
And the silent isle embowers
　　The Lady of Shalott.

By the margin, willow-veiled,
Slide the heavy barges trailed
By slow horses; and unhailed
The shallop flitteth silken-sailed
　　Skimming down to Camelot:
But who hath seen her wave her hand?
Or at the casement seen her stand?
Or is she known in all the land,
　　The Lady of Shalott?

Only reapers, reaping early
In among the bearded barley,
Hear a song that echoes cheerly
From the river winding clearly,
　　Down to towered Camelot:
And by the moon the reaper weary,
Piling sheaves in uplands airy,
Listening, whispers ' 'Tis the fairy
　　Lady of Shalott.'

II

There she weaves by night and day
A magic web with colours gay.
She has heard a whisper say,
A curse is on her if she stay
     To look down to Camelot.
She knows not what the curse may be,
And so she weaveth steadily,
And little other care hath she,
     The Lady of Shalott.

And moving through a mirror clear
That hangs before her all the year,
Shadows of the world appear.
There she sees the highway near
     Winding down to Camelot:
There the river eddy whirls,
And there the surly village-churls,
And the red cloaks of market-girls,
     Pass onward from Shalott.

Sometimes a troop of damsels glad,
An abbot on an ambling pad,
Sometimes a curly shepherd-lad,
Or long-haired page in crimson clad,
     Goes by to towered Camelot;
And sometimes through the mirror blue
The knights come riding two and two:
She hath no loyal knight and true,
     The Lady of Shalott.

But in her web she still delights
To weave the mirror's magic sights,
For often through the silent nights
A funeral, with plumes and lights
     And music, went to Camelot:
Or when the moon was overhead,
Came two young lovers lately wed;
'I am half sick of shadows,' said
     The Lady of Shalott.

III

A bow-shot from her bower-eaves,
He rode between the barley-sheaves,
The sun came dazzling through the leaves,
And flamed upon the brazen greaves
      Of bold Sir Lancelot.
A red-cross knight for ever kneeled
To a lady in his shield,
That sparkled on the yellow field,
      Beside remote Shalott.

The gemmy bridle glittered free,
Like to some branch of stars we see
Hung in the golden Galaxy.
The bridle bells rang merrily
      As he rode down to Camelot:
And from his blazoned baldric slung
A mighty silver bugle hung,
And as he rode his armour rung,
      Beside remote Shalott.

All in the blue unclouded weather
Thick-jewelled shone the saddle-leather,
The helmet and the helmet-feather
Burned like one burning flame together,
      As he rode down to Camelot.
As often through the purple night,
Below the starry clusters bright,
Some bearded meteor, trailing light,
      Moves over still Shalott.

His broad clear brow in sunlight glowed;
On burnished hooves his war-horse trode;
From underneath his helmet flowed
His coal-black curls as on he rode,
      As he rode down to Camelot.
From the bank and from the river
He flashed into the crystal mirror,
'Tirra lirra,' by the river
      Sang Sir Lancelot.

She left the web, she left the loom,
She made three paces through the room,
She saw the water-lily bloom,
She saw the helmet and the plume,

She looked down to Camelot.
Out flew the web and floated wide;
The mirror cracked from side to side;
'The curse is come upon me,' cried
        The Lady of Shalott.

IV

In the stormy east-wind straining,
The pale yellow woods were waning,
The broad stream in his banks complaining,
Heavily the low sky raining
        Over towered Camelot;
Down she came and found a boat
Beneath a willow left afloat,
And round about the prow she wrote
        The Lady of Shalott.

And down the river's dim expanse—
Like some bold seer in a trance,
Seeing all his own mischance—
With a glassy countenance
        Did she look to Camelot.
And at the closing of the day
She loosed the chain, and down she lay;
The broad stream bore her far away,
        The Lady of Shalott.

Lying, robed in snowy white
That loosely flew to left and right—
The leaves upon her falling light—
Through the noises of the night
        She floated down to Camelot:
And as the boat-head wound along
The willowy hills and fields among,
They heard her singing her last song,
        The Lady of Shalott.

Heard a carol, mournful, holy,
Chanted loudly, chanted lowly,
Till her blood was frozen slowly,
And her eyes were darkened wholly,
        Turned to towered Camelot.
For ere she reached upon the tide
The first house by the water-side,
Singing in her song she died,
        The Lady of Shalott.

Under tower and balcony,
By garden-wall and gallery,
A gleaming shape she floated by,
Dead-pale between the houses high,
    Silent into Camelot.
Out upon the wharfs they came,
Knight and burgher, lord and dame,
And round the prow they read her name,
    The Lady of Shalott.

Who is this? and what is here?
And in the lighted palace near
Died the sound of royal cheer;
And they crossed themselves for fear,
    All the knights at Camelot:
But Lancelot mused a little space;
He said, 'She has a lovely face;
God in His mercy lend her grace,
    The Lady of Shalott.'

From The May Queen

You must wake and call me early, call me early, mother dear;
To-morrow'll be the happiest time of all the glad New-year;
Of all the glad New-year, mother, the maddest merriest day;
For I'm to be Queen o' the May, mother, I'm to be Queen o' the
    May.

There's many a black black eye, they say, but none so bright as
    mine;
There's Margaret and Mary, there's Kate and Caroline:
But none so fair as little Alice in all the land they say,
So I'm to be Queen o' the May, mother, I'm to be Queen o' the
    May.

I sleep so sound all night, mother, that I shall never wake,
If you do not call me loud when the day begins to break:
But I must gather knots of flowers, and buds and garlands gay,
For I'm to be Queen o' the May, mother, I'm to be Queen o' the
    May.

The Lotos-Eaters

'Courage!' he said, and pointed toward the land,
'This mounting wave will roll us shoreward soon.'
In the afternoon they came unto a land
In which it seemed always afternoon.
All round the coast the languid air did swoon,
Breathing like one that hath a weary dream.
Full-faced above the valley stood the moon;
And like a downward smoke, the slender stream
Along the cliff to fall and pause and fall did seem.

A land of streams! Some, like a downward smoke,
Slow-dropping veils of thinnest lawn, did go;
And some through wavering lights and shadows broke,
Rolling a slumbrous sheet of foam below.
They saw the gleaming river seaward flow
From the inner land: far off, three mountain-tops,
Three silent pinnacles of aged snow,
Stood sunset-flushed: and, dewed with showery drops,
Up-clomb the shadowy pine above the woven copse.

The charmed sunset lingered low adown
In the red West: through mountain clefts the dale
Was seen far inland, and the yellow down
Bordered with palm, and many a winding vale
And meadow, set with slender galingale;
A land where all things always seemed the same!
And round about the keel with faces pale,
Dark faces pale against that rosy flame,
The mild-eyed melancholy Lotos-eaters came.

Branches they bore of that enchanted stem,
Laden with flower and fruit, whereof they gave
To each, but whoso did receive of them,
And taste, to him the gushing of the wave
Far far away did seem to mourn and rave
On alien shores; and if his fellow spake,
His voice was thin, as voices from the grave;
And deep-asleep he seemed, yet all awake,
And music in his ears his beating heart did make.

They sat them down upon the yellow sand,
Between the sun and moon upon the shore;
And sweet it was to dream of Fatherland,

Of child, and wife, and slave; but evermore
Most weary seemed the sea, weary the oar,
Weary the wandering fields of barren foam.
The some one said, 'We will return no more;'
And all at once they sang, 'Our island home
Is far beyond the wave; we will no longer roam.'

'Break, break, break'

Break, break, break
    On thy cold grey stones, O Sea!
And I would that my tongue could utter
    The thoughts that arise in me.

O well for the fisherman's boy,
    That he shouts with his sister at play!
O well for the sailor lad,
    That he sings in his boat on the bay!

And the stately ships go on
    To their haven under the hill;
But O for the touch of a vanished hand,
    And the sound of a voice that is still!

Break, break, break
    At the foot of thy crags, O Sea!
But the tender grace of a day that is dead
    Will never come back to me.

From The Princess

[1]

The splendour falls on castle walls
    And snowy summits old in story:
The long light shakes across the lakes,
    And the wild cataract leaps in glory.
Blow, bugle, blow, set the wild echoes flying,
Blow, bugle; answer, echoes, dying, dying, dying.

O hark, O hear! how thin and clear,
    And thinner, clearer, farther going!
O sweet and far from cliff and scar
    The horns of Elfland faintly blowing!
Blow, let us hear the purple glens replying:
Blow, bugle; answer, echoes, dying, dying, dying.

O love, they die in yon rich sky,
    They faint on hill or field or river:
Our echoes roll from soul to soul,
    And grow for ever and for ever.
Blow, bugle, blow, set the wild echoes flying,
And answer, echoes, answer, dying, dying, dying.

[2]

Tears, idle tears, I know not what they mean,
Tears from the depth of some divine despair
Rise in the heart, and gather to the eyes,
In looking on the happy Autumn-fields,
And thinking of the days that are no more.

Fresh as the first beam glittering on a sail,
That brings our friends up from the underworld,
Sad as the last which reddens over one
That sinks with all we love below the verge;
So sad, so fresh, the days that are no more.

Ah, sad and strange as in dark summer dawns
The earliest pipe of half-awakened birds
To dying ears, when unto dying eyes
The casement slowly grows a glimmering square;
So sad, so strange, the days that are no more.

Dear as remembered kisses after death,
And sweet as those by hopeless fancy feigned
On lips that are for others; deep as love,
Deep at first love, and wild with all regret;
O Death in Life, the days that are no more.

From In Memoriam

[1]

I envy not in any moods
    The captive void of noble rage,
    The linnet born within the cage,
That never knew the summer woods:

I envy not the beast that takes
    His licence in the field of time,
    Unfettered by the sense of crime,
To whom a conscience never wakes;

Nor, what may count itself as blest,
    The heart that never plighted troth
    But stagnates in the weeds of cloth;
Nor any want-begotten rest.

I hold it true, whate'er befall;
    I feel it, when I sorrow most;
    'Tis better to have loved and lost
Than never to have loved at all.

[2]

Ring out, wild bells, to the wild sky,
    The flying cloud, the frosty light:
    The year is dying in the night;
Ring out, wild bells, and let him die.

Ring out the old, ring in the new,
    Ring, happy bells, across the snow:
    The year is going, let him go;
Ring out the false, ring in the true,

Ring out the grief that saps the mind,
    For those that here we see no more;
    Ring out the feud of rich and poor,
Ring in redress to all mankind.

Ring out a slowly dying cause,
    And ancient forms of party strife;
    Ring in the nobler modes of life,
With sweeter manners, purer laws.

Ring out the want, the care, the sin,
  The faithless coldness of the times;
  Ring out, ring out my mournful rhymes,
But ring the fuller minstrel in.

Ring out false pride in place and blood,
  The civic slander and the spite;
  Ring in the love of truth and right,
Ring in the common love of good.

Ring out old shapes of foul disease;
  Ring out the narrowing lust of gold;
  Ring out the thousand wars of old,
Ring in the thousand years of peace.

Ring in the valiant man and free,
  The larger heart, the kindlier hand;
  Ring out the darkness of the land,
Ring in the Christ that is to be.

The Charge of the Light Brigade

Half a league, half a league,
  Half a league onward,
All in the valley of Death
  Rode the six hundred.
'Forward, the Light Brigade!
Charge for the guns!' he said:
Into the valley of Death
  Rode the six hundred.

'Forward, the Light Brigade!'
Was there a man dismayed?
Not though the soldier knew
  Someone had blundered:
Their's not to make reply,
Their's not to reason why,
Their's but to do and die,
Into the valley of Death
  Rode the six hundred.

Cannon to right of them,
Cannon to left of them,
Cannon in front of them
    Volleyed and thundered;
Stormed at with shot and shell,
Boldly they rode and well,
Into the jaws of Death,
Into the mouth of Hell
    Rode the six hundred.

Flashed all their sabres bare,
Flashed as they turned in air,
Sabring the gunners there,
Charging an army, while
    All the world wondered:
Plunged in the battery-smoke
Right through the line they broke;
Cossack and Russian
Reeled from the sabre-stroke
    Shattered and sundered.
Then they rode back, but not,
    Not the six hundred.

Cannon to right of them,
Cannon to left of them,
Cannon behind them
    Volleyed and thundered;
Stormed at with shot and shell,
While horse and hero fell,
They that had fought so well
Came through the jaws of Death
Back from the mouth of Hell,
All that was left of them,
    Left of six hundred.

When can their glory fade?
O the wild charge they made!
    All the world wondered.
Honour the charge they made!
Honour the Light Brigade,
    Noble six hundred!

From Maud

Come into the garden, Maud,
   For the black bat, night, has flown,
Come into the garden, Maud,
   I am here at the gate alone;
And the woodbine spices are wafted abroad,
   And the musk of the rose is blown.

For a breeze of morning moves,
   And the planet of Love is on high,
Beginning to faint in the light that she loves
   On a bed of daffodil sky,
To faint in the light of the sun she loves,
   To faint in his light, and to die.

All night have the roses heard
   The flute, violin, bassoon;
All night has the casement jessamine stirred
   To the dancers dancing in tune;
Till a silence fell with the waking bird,
   And a hush with the setting moon.

I said to the lily, 'There is but one
   With whom she has heart to be gay.
When will the dancers leave her alone?
   She is weary of dance and play.'
Now half to the setting moon are gone,
   And half to the rising day;
Low on the sand and loud on the stone
   The last wheel echoes away.

I said to the rose, 'The brief night goes
   In babble and revel and wine.
O young lord-lover, what sighs are those
   For one that will never be thine?
But mine, but mine,' so I sware to the rose,
   'For ever and ever, mine.'

And the soul of the rose went into my blood,
   As the music clashed in the hall;
And long by the garden lake I stood,
   For I heard your rivulet fall
From the lake to the meadow and on to the wood,
   Our wood, that is dearer than all;

From the meadow your walks have left so sweet
    That whenever a March-wind sighs
He sets the jewel-point of your feet
    In violets blue as your eyes,
To the woody hollows in which we meet
    And the valleys of Paradise.

The slender acacia would not shake
    One long milk-bloom on the tree;
The white lake-blossom fell into the lake,
    As the pimpernel dozed on the lea;
But the rose was awake all night for your sake,
    Knowing your promise to me;
The lilies and roses were all awake,
    They sighed for the dawn and thee.

Queen rose of the rosebud garden of girls,
    Come hither, the dances are done,
In gloss of satin and glimmer of pearls,
    Queen lily and rose in one;
Shine out, little head, sunning over with curls.
    To the flowers, and be their sun.

There has fallen a splendid tear
    From the passion-flower at the gate.
She is coming, my life, my fate;
The red rose cries, 'She is near, she is near;'
    And the white rose weeps, 'She is late;'
The larkspur listens, 'I hear, I hear;'
    And the lily whispers, 'I wait'.

She is coming, my own, my sweet;
    Were it ever so airy a tread,
My heart would hear her and beat,
    Were it earth in an earthy bed;
My dust would hear her and beat,
    Had I lain for a century dead;
Would start and tremble under her feet,
    And blossom in purple and red.

From The Brook

I come from haunts of coot and hern,
   I make a sudden sally
And sparkle out among the fern,
   To bicker down a valley.

By thirty hills I hurry down,
   Or slip between the ridges,
By twenty thorps, a little town,
   And half a hundred bridges.

Till last by Philip's farm I flow
   To join the brimming river,
For men may come and men may go,
   But I go on for ever.

I chatter over stony ways,
   In little sharps and trebles,
I bubble into eddying bays,
   I babble on the pebbles.

With many a curve my banks I fret
   By many a field and fallow,
And many a fairy foreland set
   With willow-weed and mallow.

I chatter, chatter, as I flow
   To join the brimming river,
For men may come and men may go,
   But I go on for ever.

I wind about, and in and out,
   With here a blossom sailing,
And here and there a lusty trout,
   And here and there a grayling.

And here and there a foamy flake
   Upon me, as I travel
With many a silvery waterbreak
   Above the golden gravel,

And draw them all along, and flow
   To join the brimming river,
For men may come and men may go,
   But I go on for ever.

I steal by lawns and grassy plots,
   I slide by hazel covers;
I move the sweet forget-me-nots
   That grow for happy lovers.

I slip, I slide, I gloom, I glance,
   Among my skimming swallows;
I make the netted sunbeam dance
   Against my sandy shallows.

I murmur under moon and stars
   In brambly wildernesses;
I linger by my shingly bars;
   I loiter round my cresses;

And out again I curve and flow
   To join the brimming river,
For men may come and men may go,
   But I go on for ever.

The Revenge

A Ballad of the Fleet

At Flores in the Azores Sir Richard Grenville lay,
And a pinnace, like a fluttered bird, came flying from far away:
'Spanish ships of war at sea! we have sighted fifty-three!'
Then sware Lord Thomas Howard: ' 'Fore God I am no coward;
But I cannot meet them here, for my ships are out of gear,
And the half my men are sick. I must fly, but follow quick.
We are six ships of the line; can we fight with fifty-three?'

Then spake Sir Richard Grenville: 'I know you are no coward;
You fly them for a moment to fight with them again.
But I've ninety men and more that are lying sick ashore.
I should count myself the coward if I left them, my Lord Howard,
To these Inquisition dogs and the devildoms of Spain.'

So Lord Howard passed away with five ships of war that day,
Till he melted like a cloud in the silent summer heaven;
But Sir Richard bore in hand all his sick men from the land
Very carefully and slow,
Men of Bideford in Devon,
And we laid them on the ballast down below;

For we brought them all aboard,
And they blest him in their pain, that they were not left to Spain,
To the thumbscrew and the stake, for the glory of the Lord.

He had only a hundred seamen to work the ship and to fight,
And he sailed away from Flores till the Spaniard came in sight,
With his huge sea-castles heaving upon the weather bow.
'Shall we fight or shall we fly?
Good Sir Richard, tell us now,
For to fight is but to die!
There'll be little of us left by the time this sun be set.'
And Sir Richard said again: 'We be all good English men.
Let us bang these dogs of Seville, the children of the devil,
For I never turned my back upon Don or devil yet.'

Sir Richard spoke and he laughed, and we roared a hurrah, and so
The little Revenge ran on sheer into the heart of the foe,
With her hundred fighters on deck, and her ninety sick below;
For half of their fleet to the right and half to the left were seen,
And the little Revenge ran on through the long sea-lane between.

Thousands of their soldiers looked down from their decks and
     laughed,
Thousands of their seamen made mock at the mad little craft
Running on and on, till delayed
By their mountain-like San Philip that, of fifteen hundred tons,
And up-shadowing high above us with her yawning tiers of guns,
Took the breath from our sails, and we stayed.

And while now the great San Philip hung above us like a cloud
Whence the thunderbolt will fall
Long and loud,
Four galleons drew away
From the Spanish fleet that day,
And two upon the larboard and two upon the starboard lay,
And the battle-thunder broke from them all.
But anon the great San Philip, she bethought herself and went
Having that within her womb that had left her ill content;
And the rest they came aboard us, and they fought us hand to
     hand,
For a dozen times they came with their pikes and musqueteers,
And a dozen times we shook 'em off as a dog that shakes his ears
When he leaps from the water to the land.

And the sun went down, and the stars came out far over the
     summer sea,

But never a moment ceased the fight of the one and the fifty-three.
Ship after ship, the whole night long, their high-built galleons
     came,
Ship after ship, the whole night long, with her battle-thunder and
     flame;
Ship after ship, the whole night long, drew back with her dead and
     her shame.
For some were sunk and many were shattered, and so could fight
     us no more—
God of battles, was ever a battle like this in the world before?

For he said 'Fight on! Fight on!'
Though his vessel was all but a wreck;
And it chanced that, when half of the short summer night was
     gone,
With a grisly wound to be dressed he had left the deck,
But a bullet struck him that was dressing it suddenly dead,
And himself he was wounded again in the side and the head,
And he said 'Fight on! Fight on!'

And the night went down, and the sun smiled out far over the
     summer sea,
And the Spanish fleet with broken sides lay round us all in a ring;
But they dared not touch us again, for they feared that we still
     could sting,
So they watched what the end would be.
And we had not fought them in vain,
But in perilous plight were we,
Seeing forty of our poor hundred were slain,
And half of the rest of us maimed for life
In the crash of the cannonades and the desperate strife;
And the sick men down in the hold were most of them stark and
     cold,
And the pikes were all broken or bent, and the powder was all of it
     spent;
And the masts and the rigging were lying over the side;
But Sir Richard cried in his English pride,
'We have fought such a fight for a day and a night
As may never be fought again!
We have won great glory, my men!
And a day less or more
At sea or ashore,
We die – does it matter when?
Sink me the ship, Master Gunner – sink her, split her in twain!
Fall into the hands of God, not into the hands of Spain!'

And the gunner said 'Ay, ay,' but the seamen made reply:
'We have children, we have wives,
And the Lord hath spared our lives.
We will make the Spaniard promise, if we yield, to let us go;
We shall live to fight again and to strike another blow.'
And the lion there lay dying, and they yielded to the foe.

And the stately Spanish men to their flagship bore him then,
Where they laid him by the mast, old Sir Richard caught at last,
And they praised him to his face with their courtly foreign grace;
But he rose upon their decks, and he cried:
'I have fought for Queen and Faith like a valiant man and true;
I have only done my duty as a man is bound to do:
With a joyful spirit I Sir Richard Grenville die!'
And he fell upon their decks, and he died.

And they stared at the dead that had been so valiant and true,
And had holden the power and glory of Spain so cheap
That he dared her with one little ship and his English few;
Was he devil or man? He was devil for aught they knew,
But they sank his body with honour down into the deep,
And they manned the Revenge with a swarthier alien crew,
And away she sailed with her loss and longed for her own;
When a wind from the lands they had ruined awoke from sleep,
And the water began to heave and the weather to moan,
And or ever that evening ended a great gale blew,
And a wave like the wave that is raised by an earthquake grew,
Till it smote on their hulls and their sails and their masts and their
    flags,
And the whole sea plunged and fell on the shot-shattered navy of
    Spain,
And the little Revenge herself went down by the island crags
To be lost evermore in the main.

Oliver Wendell Holmes

Old Ironsides

[*Written with reference to the proposed breaking up
of the U.S. frigate* Constitution]

Ay, tear her tattered ensign down!
    Long has it waved on high,
And many an eye has danced to see
    That banner in the sky;
Beneath it rung the battle-shout,
    And burst the cannon's roar:
The meteor of the ocean air
    Shall sweep the clouds no more!

Her deck, once red with heroes' blood,
    Where knelt the vanquished foe,
When winds were hurrying o'er the flood
    And waves were white below,
No more shall feel the victor's tread,
    Or know the conquered knee:
The harpies of the shore shall pluck
    The eagle of the sea!

O better that her shattered hulk
    Should sink beneath the wave!
Her thunders shook the mighty deep,
    And there should be her grave:
Nail to the mast her holy flag,
    Set every threadbare sail,
And give her to the god of storms,
    The lightning and the gale!

Robert Browning

From Pippa Passes

[Song]

The year's at the spring,
And the day's at the morn;
Morning's at seven;
The hill-side's dew-pearled;
The lark's on the wing;
The snail's on the thorn;
God's in his heaven—
All's right with the world!

How They Brought the Good News
from Ghent to Aix

I sprang to the stirrup, and Joris, and he;
I galloped, Dirck galloped, we galloped all three;
'God speed!' cried the watch, as the gate-bolts undrew;
'Speed!' echoed the wall to us galloping through;
Behind shut the postern, the lights sank to rest,
And into the midnight we galloped abreast.

Not a word to each other; we kept the great pace,
Neck by neck, stride by stride, never changing our place.
I turned in my saddle and made its girths tight,
Then shortened each stirrup, and set the pique right,
Rebuckled the cheek-strap, chained slacker the bit,
Nor galloped less steadily Roland a whit.

'Twas moonset at starting; but while we drew near
Lokeren, the cocks crew and twilight dawned clear;
At Boom, a great yellow star came out to see;
At Düffeld, 'twas morning as plain as could be;
And from Mecheln church-steeple we heard the half-chime,
So, Joris broke silence with, 'Yet there is time!'

At Aershot, up leaped of a sudden the sun,
And against him the cattle stood black every one,
To stare through the mist at us galloping past,
And I saw my stout galloper Roland at last,
With resolute shoulders, each butting away
The haze, as some bluff river headland its spray:

And his low head and crest, just one sharp ear bent back
For my voice, and the other pricked out on his track;
And one eye's black intelligence – ever that glance
O'er its white edge at me, his own master, askance!
And the thick heavy spume-flakes which aye and anon
His fierce lips shook upwards in galloping on.

By Hasselt, Dirck groaned; and cried Joris, 'Stay spur!
Your Roos galloped bravely, the fault's not in her,
We'll remember at Aix' – for one heard the quick wheeze
Of her chest, saw the stretched neck and staggering knees,
And sunk tail, and horrible heave of the flank,
As down on her haunches she shuddered and sank.

So, we were left galloping, Joris and I,
Past Looz and past Tongres, no cloud in the sky;
The broad sun above laughed a pitiless laugh,
'Neath our feet broke the brittle bright stubble like chaff;
Till over by Dalhem a dome-spire sprang white,
And 'Gallop', gasped Joris, 'for Aix is in sight!'

'How they'll greet us!' – and all in a moment his roan
Rolled neck and croup over, lay dead as a stone;
And there was my Roland to bear the whole weight
Of the news which alone could save Aix from her fate,
With his nostrils like pits full of blood to the brim,
And with circles of red for his eye-socket's rim.

Then I cast loose my buffcoat, each holster let fall,
Shook off both my jack-boots, let go belt and all,
Stood up in the stirrup, leaned, patted his ear,
Called my Roland his pet-name, my horse without peer;
Clapped my hands, laughed and sang, any noise, bad or good,
Till at length into Aix Roland galloped and stood.

And all I remember is – friends flocking round
As I sat with his head 'twixt my knees on the ground;
And no voice but was praising this Roland of mine,
As I poured down his throat our last measure of wine,
Which (the burgesses voted by common consent)
Was no more than his due who brought good news from Ghent.

The Lost Leader

Just for a handful of silver he left us,
    Just for a riband to stick in his coat—
Found the one gift of which fortune bereft us,
    Lost all the others she lets us devote;
They, with the gold to give, doled him out silver,
    So much was theirs who so little allowed:
How all our copper had gone for his service!
    Rags – were they purple, his heart had been proud!
We that had loved him so, followed him, honoured him,
    Lived in his mild and magnificent eye,
Learned his great language, caught his clear accents,
    Made him our pattern to live and to die!
Shakespeare was of us, Milton was for us,
    Burns, Shelley, were with us – they watch from their graves!
He alone breaks from the van and the freemen
    —He alone sinks to the rear and the slaves!

We shall march prospering – not through his presence;
    Songs may inspirit us – not from his lyre;
Deeds will be done – while he boasts his quiescence,
    Still bidding crouch whom the rest bade aspire:
Blot out his name, then, record one lost soul more,
    One task more declined, one more footpath untrod,
One more devils'-triumph and sorrow for angels,
    One wrong more to man, one more insult to God!
Life's night begins: let him never come back to us!
    There would be doubt, hesitation and pain,
Forced praise on our part – the glimmer of twilight,
    Never glad confident morning again!
Best fight on well, for we taught him – strike gallantly,
    Menace our heart ere we master his own;
Then let him receive the new knowledge and wait us,
    Pardoned in heaven, the first by the throne!

Home-thoughts, from Abroad

O to be in England
Now that April's there,
And whoever wakes in England
Sees, some morning, unaware,

That the lowest boughs and the brushwood sheaf
Round the elm-tree bole are in tiny leaf,
While the chaffinch sings on the orchard bough
In England – now!

And after April, when May follows,
And the whitethroat builds, and all the swallows!
Hark, where my blossomed pear-tree in the hedge
Leans to the field and scatters on the clover
Blossoms and dewdrops – at the bent spray's edge—
That's the wise thrush; he sings each song twice over,
Lest you should think he never could recapture
The first fine careless rapture!
And though the fields look rough with hoary dew,
All will be gay when noontide wakes anew
The buttercups, the little children's dower
—Far brighter than this gaudy melon-flower!

Home-thoughts, from the Sea

Nobly, nobly Cape Saint Vincent to the North-west died away;
Sunset ran, one glorious blood-red reeking into Cadiz Bay;
Bluish 'mid the burning water, full in face Trafalgar lay;
In the dimmest North-east distance dawned Gibraltar grand and
    gray;
'Here and here did England help me: how can I help England?' –
    say,
Whoso turns as I, this evening, turn to God to praise and pray,
While Jove's planet rises yonder, silent over Africa.

Meeting at Night

The grey sea and the long black land;
And the yellow half-moon large and low;
And the startled little waves that leap
In fiery ringlets from their sleep,
As I gain the cove with pushing prow,
And quench its speed i' the slushy sand.

Then a mile of warm sea-scented beach;
Three fields to cross till a farm appears;
A tap at the pane, the quick sharp scratch
And blue spurt of a lighted match,
And a voice less loud, through its joys and fears,
Then the two hearts beating each to each!

Parting at Morning

Round the cape of a sudden came the sea,
And the sun looked over the mountain's rim:
And straight was a path of gold for him,
And the need of a world of men for me.

Edward Lear

The Owl and the Pussy-Cat

The Owl and the Pussy-cat went to sea
   In a beautiful pea-green boat:
They took some honey, and plenty of money
   Wrapped up in a five-pound note.
The Owl looked up to the stars above,
   And sang to a small guitar,
'O lovely Pussy, O Pussy, my love,
   What a beautiful Pussy you are!'

Pussy said to the Owl, 'You elegant fowl,
   How charmingly sweet you sing!
Oh! let us be married; too long we have tarried:
   But what shall we do for a ring?'
They sailed away, for a year and a day,
   To the land where the Bong-tree grows;
And there in a wood a Piggy-wig stood,
   With a ring at the end of his nose.

'Dear Pig, are you willing to sell for one shilling
   Your ring?' Said the Piggy, 'I will.'
So they took it away, and were married next day
   By the turkey who lives on the hill.

They dined on mince and slices of quince,
    Which they ate with a runcible spoon;
And hand in hand, on the edge of the sand,
    They danced by the light of the moon.

The Jumblies

They went to sea in a Sieve, they did,
    In a Sieve they went to sea:
In spite of all their friends could say,
On a winter's morn, on a stormy day,
    In a Sieve they went to sea!
And when the Sieve turned round and round,
And everyone cried, 'You'll all be drowned!'
They called aloud, 'Our Sieve ain't big,
But we don't care a button! We don't care a fig!
    In a Sieve we'll go to sea!'
        Far and few, far and few,
            Are the lands where the Jumblies live;
            Their heads are green, and their hands are blue,
            And they went to sea in a Sieve.

They sailed away in a Sieve, they did,
    In a Sieve they sailed so fast,
With only a beautiful pea-green veil
Tied with a riband by way of a sail,
    To a small tobacco-pipe mast;
And everyone said, who saw them go,
'O won't they be soon upset, you know!
For the sky is dark, and the voyage is long,
And happen what may, it's extremely wrong
    In a Sieve to sail so fast!'
        Far and few, far and few, etc.

The water it soon came in, it did,
    The water it soon came in;
So to keep them dry, they wrapped their feet
In a pinky paper all folded neat,
    And they fastened it down with a pin.
And they passed the night in a crockery-jar,
And each of them said, 'How wise we are!
Though the sky be dark, and the voyage be long,
Yet we never can think we were rash or wrong,
    While round in our Sieve we spin!'

And all night long they sailed away;
  And when the sun went down,
They whistled and warbled a moony song
To the echoing sound of a coppery gong,
  In the shade of the mountains brown.
'O Timballoo! How happy we are,
When we live in a sieve and a crockery-jar,
And all night long in the moonlight pale,
We sail away with a pea-green sail,
  In the shade of the mountains brown!'

They sailed to the Western Sea, they did,
  To a land all covered with trees,
And they bought an Owl, and a useful Cart,
And a pound of Rice, and a Cranberry Tart,
  And a hive of silvery Bees.
And they bought a Pig, and some green Jackdaws,
And a lovely Monkey with lollipop paws,
And forty bottles of Ring-Bo-Ree,
  And no end of Stilton Cheese.

And in twenty years they all came back,
  In twenty years or more,
And everyone said, 'How tall they've grown!
For they've been to the Lakes, and the Torrible Zone,
  And the hills of the Chankly Bore;
And they drank their health, and gave them a feast
Of dumplings made of beautiful yeast;
And everyone said, 'If we only live,
We too will go to sea in a Sieve,
  To the hills of the Chankly Bore!'

Emily Brontë

'No coward soul is mine'

No coward soul is mine
No trembler in the world's storm-troubled sphere.
I see Heaven's glories shine,
And faith shines equal, arming me from fear.

O God within my breast,
Almighty ever-present Deity!
Life, that in me hast rest
As I, undying Life, have power in Thee.

Vain are the thousand creeds
That move men's hearts; unutterably vain;
Worthless as withered weeds
Or idlest froth amid the boundless main,

To waken doubt in one
Holding so fast by Thy infinity
So surely anchored on
The steadfast rock of immortality.

With wide-embracing love
The spirit animates eternal years
Pervades and broods above,
Changes, sustains, dissolves, creates and rears.

Though earth and moon were gone,
And suns and universes ceased to be
And Thou wert left alone
Every existence would exist in Thee.

There is not room for death
Nor atom that his might could render void
Thou – Thou art Being and Breath
And what Thou art may never be destroyed.

Charles Kingsley

The Sands of Dee

'O Mary, go and call the cattle home,
    And call the cattle home,
    And call the cattle home
Across the sands of Dee';
The western wind was wild and dank with foam,
    And all alone went she.

The western tide crept up along the sand,
    And o'er and o'er the sand,
    And round and round the sand,

As far as eye could see.
The rolling mist came down and hid the land:
And never home came she.

'Oh! is it weed, or fish, or floating hair—
    A tress of golden hair,
    A drowned maiden's hair
Above the nets at sea?
Was never salmon yet that shone so fair
    Among the stakes on Dee.'

They rowed her in across the rolling foam,
    The cruel crawling foam,
    The cruel hungry foam,
To her grave beside the sea:
But still the boatmen hear her call the cattle home
    Across the sands of Dee.

The Last Buccaneer

Oh, England is a pleasant place for them that's rich and high,
But England is a cruel place for such poor folks as I;
And such a port for mariners I ne'er shall see again,
As the pleasant Isle of Avès, beside the Spanish Main.

They were forty craft in Avès that were both swift and stout,
All furnished well with small arms and cannons round about;
And a thousand men in Avès made laws so fair and free
To choose their valiant captains and obey them loyally.

Thence we sailed against the Spaniard with his hoards of plate and
    gold,
Which he wrung with cruel tortures from Indian folk of old;
Likewise the merchant captains, with hearts as hard as stone,
Who flog men and keel-haul them, and starve them to the bone.

Oh, the palms grew high in Avès, and fruits that shone like gold,
And the colibris and parrots they were gorgeous to behold;
And the negro maids to Avès from bondage fast did flee,
To welcome gallant sailors, a-sweeping in from sea.

Oh, sweet it was in Avès to hear the landward breeze,
A-swing with good tobacco in a net between the trees,
With a negro lass to fan you, while you listened to the roar
Of the breakers on the reef outside, that never touched the shore.

But Scripture saith, an ending to all fine things must be;
So the King's ships sailed on Avès, and quite put down were we.
All day we fought like bulldogs, but they burst the booms at night,
And I fled in a piragua, sore wounded, from the fight.

Nine days I floated starving, and a negro lass beside,
Till for all I tried to cheer her, the poor young thing she died;
But as I lay a-gasping, a Bristol sail came by,
And brought me home to England here, to beg until I die.

And now I'm old and going – I'm sure I can't tell where;
One comfort is, this world's so hard, I can't be worse off there;
If I might but be a sea-dove, I'd fly across the main,
To the pleasant Isle of Avès, to look at it once again.

Arthur Hugh Clough

'Say not the struggle nought availeth'

Say not the struggle nought availeth,
　　The labour and the wounds are vain,
The enemy faints not, nor faileth,
　　And as things have been, things remain.

If hopes were dupes, fears may be liars;
　　It may be, in yon smoke concealed,
Your comrades chase e'en now the fliers,
　　And, but for you, possess the field.

For while the tired waves, vainly breaking,
　　Seem here no painful inch to gain,
Far back through creeks and inlets making
　　Comes, silent, flooding in, the main,

And not by eastern windows only,
　　When daylight comes, comes in the light,
In front the sun climbs slow, how slowly,
　　But westward, look, the land is bright.

Walt Whitman

O Captain! My Captain!

O Captain! my Captain! our fearful trip is done,
The ship has weathered every rack, the prize we sought is won,
The port is near, the bells I hear, the people all exulting,
While follow eyes the steady keel, the vessel grim
    and daring;
      But O heart! heart! heart!
        O the bleeding drops of red!
          Where on the deck my Captain lies,
           Fallen cold and dead.

O Captain! my Captain! rise up and hear the bells;
Rise up – for you the flag is flung – for you the bugle trills,
For you bouquets and ribboned wreaths – for you the
    shores a-crowding,
For you they call, the swaying mass, their eager faces
    turning;
      Here, Captain! dear father!
        This arm beneath your head!
          It is some dream that on the deck
           You've fallen cold and dead.

My Captain does not answer, his lips are pale and still,
My father does not feel my arm, he has no pulse nor will;
The ship is anchored safe and sound, its voyage closed and done,
From fearful trip the victor ship comes in with object won;
      Exult, O shores! and sing, O bells!
      But I, with mournful tread,
        Walk the deck my Captain lies,
          Fallen cold and dead.

From Song of Myself

Houses and rooms are full of perfumes, the shelves are crowded
    with perfumes,
I breathe the fragrance myself and know it and like it,
The distillation would intoxicate me also, but I shall not let it.

The atmosphere is not a perfume, it has no taste of the distillation,
    it is odourless,
It is for my mouth forever, I am in love with it.
I will go to the bank by the wood and become undisguised and
    naked,
I am mad for it to be in contact with me.

The smoke of my own breath
Echoes, ripples, buzzed whispers, love-root, silk-thread, crotch and
    vine,
My respiration and inspiration, the beating of my heart, the
    passing of blood and air through my lungs.
The sniff of green leaves and dry leaves, and of the shore and dark-
    coloured sea-rocks, and of hay in the barn,
The sound of the belched words of my voice loosed to the eddies
    of the wind,
A few light kisses, a few embraces, a reaching around of arms,
The play of shine and shade on the trees as the supple boughs wag,
The delight alone or in the rush of the streets, or along the fields
    and hill-sides,
The feeling of health, the full-noon trill, the song of me rising from
    bed and meeting the sun.

Have you reckoned a thousand acres much? have you reckoned the
    earth much?
Have you practised so long to learn to read?
Have you felt so proud to get at the meaning of poems?

Stop this day and night with me and you shall possess the origin of
    all poems,
You shall possess the good of the earth and sun (there are millions
    of suns left)
You shall no longer take things at second or third hand, nor look
    through the eyes of the dead, nor feed on the spectres in
    books,
You shall not look through my eyes either, nor take things from
    me,
You shall listen to all sides and filter them from your self.

Julia Ward Howe

Battle-Hymn of the Republic

Mine eyes have seen the glory of the coming of the Lord:
He is trampling out the vintage where the grapes of wrath are
    stored;
He hath loosed the fateful lightning of His terrible swift sword:
    His truth is marching on.

I have seen Him in the watch-fires of a hundred circling camps;
They have builded Him an altar in the evening dews and damps;
I can read His righteous sentence by the dim and flaring lamps:
    His day is marching on.

I have read a fiery gospel, writ in burnished rows of steel:
'As ye deal with my contemners, so with you my grace shall deal;
Let the hero, born of woman, crush the serpent with his heel,
    Since God is marching on.'

I have read a fiery gospel, writ in burnished rows of steel:
'As ye deal with my contemners, so with you my grace shall deal;
Let the hero, born of woman, crush the serpent with his heel,
    Since God is marching on.'

He has sounded forth the trumpet that shall never call retreat;
He is sifting out the hearts of men before His judgement-seat:
O, be swift, my soul, to answer Him! be jubilant, my feet!
    Our God is marching on.

In the beauty of the lilies. Christ was born across the sea,
With a glory in His bosom that transfigures you and me;
As He died to make men holy, let us die to make men free,
    While God is marching on.

He is coming like the glory of the morning on the wave,
He is wisdom to the mighty, He is succour to the brave,
So the world shall be His footstool, and the soul of wrong His
    slave,
    Our God is marching on!

Matthew Arnold

From Sohrab and Rustum

So, on the bloody sand, Sohrab lay dead;
And the great Rustum drew his horseman's cloak
Down o'er his face, and sat by his dead son.
As those black granite pillars, once high-reared
By Jemshid in Persepolis, to bear
His house, now 'mid their broken flights of steps
Lie prone, enormous, down the mountain side—
So in the sand lay Rustum by his son.
    And night came down over the solemn waste,
And the two gazing hosts, and that sole pair,
And darkened all; and a cold fog, with night,
Crept from the Oxus. Soon a hum arose,
As of a great assembly loosed, and fires
Began to twinkle through the fog; for now
Both armies moved to camp, and took their meal;
The Persians took it on the open sands
Southward, the Tartars by the river marge;
And Rustum and his son were left alone.
    But the majestic river floated on,
Out of the mist and hum of that low land,
Into the frosty starlight, and there moved,
Rejoicing, through the hushed Chorasmian waste,
Under the solitary moon; he flowed
Right for the polar star, past Orgunjè,
Brimming, and bright, and large; then sands begin
To hem his watery march, and dam his streams,
And split his currents; that for many a league
The shorn and parcelled Oxus strains along
Through beds of sand and matted rushy isles—
Oxus, forgetting the bright speed he had
In his high mountain cradle in Pamere,
A foiled circuitous wanderer – till at last
The longed-for dash of waves is heard, and wide
His luminous home of waters opens, bright
And tranquil, from whose floor the new-bathed stars
Emerge, and shine upon the Aral Sea.

Dover Beach

The sea is calm to-night.
The tide is full, the moon lies fair
Upon the straits; on the French coast the light
Gleams and is gone; the cliffs of England stand,
Glimmering and vast, out in the tranquil bay.
Come to the window, sweet is the night-air!
Only, from the long line of spray
Where the sea meets the moon-blanched land,
Listen! you hear the grating roar
Of pebbles which the waves draw back, and fling,
At their return, up the high strand,
Begin, and cease, and then again begin,
With tremulous cadence slow, and bring
The eternal note of sadness in.

Sophocles long ago
Heard it on the Aegaean, and it brought
Into his mind the turbid ebb and flow
Of human misery; we
Find also in the sound a thought,
Hearing it by this distant northern sea.

The Sea of Faith
Was once, too, at the full, and round earth's shore
Lay like the folds of a bright girdle furled.
But now I only hear
Its melancholy, long, withdrawing roar,
Retreating, to the breath
Of the night-wind, down the vast edges drear
And naked shingles of the world.

Ah, love, let us be true
To one another! for the world, which seems
To lie before us like a land of dreams,
So various, so beautiful, so new,
Hath really neither joy, nor love, nor light,
Nor certitude, nor peace, nor help for pain;
And we are here as on a darkling plain
Swept with confused alarms of struggle and flight,
Where ignorant armies clash by night.

Requiescat

Strew on her roses, roses,
    And never a spray of yew!
In quiet she reposes;
    Ah, would that I did too!

Her mirth the world required;
    She bathed it in smiles of glee.
But her heart was tired, tired,
    And now they let her be.

Her life was turning, turning,
In mazes of heat and sound.
But for peace her soul was yearning,
    And now peace laps her round.

Her cabined, ample spirit,
    It fluttered and failed for breath.
To-night it doth inherit
    The vasty hall of death.

William Johnson Cory

Heraclitus

They told me, Heraclitus, they told me you were dead,
They brought me bitter news to hear and bitter tears to shed.
I wept as I remembered how often you and I
Had tired the sun with talking and sent him down the sky.

And now that thou art lying, my dear old Carian guest,
A handful of grey ashes, long, long ago at rest,
Still are thy pleasant voices, thy nightingales, awake;
For death, he taketh all away, but them he cannot take.

William Allingham

Four Ducks on a Pond

Four ducks on a pond,
A grass-bank beyond,
A blue sky of spring,
White clouds on the wing;
What a little thing
To remember for years—
To remember with tears.

Adelaide Anne Procter

A Lost Chord

Seated one day at the organ,
I was weary and ill at ease,
And my fingers wandered idly
Over the noisy keys.

I know not what I was playing,
Or what I was dreaming then;
But I struck one chord of music,
Like the sound of a great Amen.

It flooded the crimson twilight
Like the close of an angel's psalm,
And it lay on my fevered spirit
With a touch of infinite calm.

It quieted pain and sorrow,
Like love overcoming strife;
It seemed the harmonious echo
From our discordant life.

It linked all perplexed meanings
Into one perfect peace.
And trembled away into silence,
As if it were loath to cease.

I have sought, but I seek it vainly,
That one lost chord divine,
That came from the soul of the organ
And entered into mine.

It may be that death's bright angel
Will speak in that chord again—
It may be that only in Heaven
I shall hear that grand Amen.

Dante Gabriel Rossetti

From The Blessed Damozel

The blessed damozel leaned out
  From the gold bar of Heaven;
Her eyes were deeper than the depth
  Of waters stilled at even;
She had three lilies in her hand,
  And the stars in her hair were seven.

Her robe, ungirt from clasp to hem,
  No wrought flowers did adorn,
But a white rose of Mary's gift,
  For service meetly worn;
Her hair that lay along her back
  Was yellow like ripe corn.

Her seemed she scarce had been a day
  One of God's choristers;
The wonder was not yet quite gone
  From that still look of hers;
Albeit, to them she left, her day
  Had counted as ten years.

(To one, it is ten years of years.
  ... Yet now, and in this place,
Surely she leaned o'er me – her hair
  Fell all about my face. ...
Nothing: the autumn-fall of leaves.
  The whole year sets apace.)

It was the rampart of God's house
    That she was standing on;
By God built over the sheer depth
    The which is space begun;
So high, that looking downward thence
She scarce could see the sun.

It lies in Heaven, across the flood
    Of ether, as a bridge.
Beneath, the tides of day and night
    With flame and darkness ridge
The void, as low as where this earth
    Spins like a fretful midge.

Around her, lovers, newly met
    'Mid deathless love's acclaims,
Spoke evermore among themselves
    Their heart-remembered names;
And the souls mounting up to God
    Went by her like thin flames.

And still she bowed herself and stooped
    Out of the circling charm;
Until her bosom must have made
    The bar she leaned on warm,
And the lilies lay as if asleep
    Along her bended arm.

Sudden Light

I have been here before,
    But when or how I cannot tell:
I know the grass beyond the door,
    The sweet keen smell,
The sighing sound, the lights around the shore.

You have been mine before—
    How long ago I may not know:
But just when at that swallow's soar
    Your neck turned so,
Some veil did fall – I knew it all of yore.

Has this been thus before?
    And shall not thus time's eddying flight
Still with our lives our love restore
    In death's despite,
And day and night yield one delight once more?

Emily Dickinson

'Because I could not stop for death'

Because I could not stop for death,
He kindly stopped for me;
The carriage held but just ourselves
And immortality.

We slowly drove, he knew no haste,
And I had put away
My labour, and my leisure too,
For his civility.

We passed the school, where children strove
At recess, in the ring;
We passed the fields of gazing grain,
We passed the setting sun.

Or rather, he passed us;
The dews grew quivering and chill,
For only gossamer my gown,
My tippet only tulle.

We paused before a house that seemed
A swelling of the ground;
The roof was scarcely visible,
The cornice in the ground.

Since then 'tis centuries, and yet
Feels shorter than the day
I first surmised the horses' heads
Were toward eternity.

'Success is counted sweetest'

Success is counted sweetest
By those who ne'er succeed.
To comprehend a nectar
Requires sorest need.

Not one of all the purple host
Who took the flag today
Can tell the definition
So clear of victory

As he defeated – dying—
On whose forbidden ear
The distant strains of triumph
Burst agonized and clear!

'My life closed twice before its close'

My life closed twice before its close;
    It yet remains to see
If immortality unveil
    A third event to me

So huge, so hopeless to conceive,
    As these that twice befell.
Parting is all we know of heaven,
    And all we need of hell.

Christina Rossetti

From Goblin Market

Morning and evening
Maids heard the goblins cry:
'Come buy our orchard fruits,
Come buy, come buy:
Apples and quinces,
Lemons and oranges,
Plump unpecked cherries,
Melons and raspberries,
Bloom-down-cheeked peaches,
Swart-headed mulberries,

Wild free-born cranberries,
Crab-apples, dewberries,
Pine-apples, blackberries,
Apricots, strawberries;
All ripe together
In summer weather,
Morns that pass by,
Fair eves that fly;
Come buy, come buy:
Our grapes fresh from the vine,
Pomegranates full and fine,
Dates and sharp bullaces,
Rare pears and greengages,
Damons and bilberries,
Taste them and try:
Currants and gooseberries,
Bright-fire-like barberries,
Figs to fill your mouth,
Citrons from the South,
Sweet to tongue and sound to eye;
Come buy, come buy.'

Remember

Remember me when I am gone away,
   Gone far away into the silent land;
    When you can no more hold me by the hand,
Nor I half turn to go yet turning stay.
Remember me when no more day by day
   You tell me of our future that you planned:
   Only remember me; you understand
It will be late to counsel then or pray.
Yet if you should forget me for a while
   And afterwards remember, do not grieve:
   For if the darkness and corruption leave
    A vestige of the thoughts that once I had,
Better by far you should forget and smile
   Than that you should remember and be sad.

A Birthday

My heart is like a singing bird
 Whose nest is in a watered shoot:
My heart is like an apple-tree
 Whose boughs are bent with thickset fruit;
My heart is like a rainbow shell
 That paddles in a halcyon sea;
My heart is gladder than all these
 Because my love is come to me.

Raise me a dais of silk and down;
 Hang it with vair and purple dyes;
Carve it in doves and pomegranates,
 And peacocks with a hundred eyes;
Work it in gold and silver grapes,
 In leaves and silver fleurs-de-lys;
Because the birthday of my life
 Is come, my love is come to me.

Echo

Come to me in the silence of the night;
 Come in the speaking silence of a dream:
Come with soft rounded cheeks and eyes as bright
 As sunlight on a stream;
  Come back in tears,
O memory, hope, love of finished years.

Oh dream how sweet, too sweet, too bitter sweet,
 Whose wakening should have been in Paradise,
Where souls brimful of love abide and meet;
 Where thirsting longing eyes
  Watch the slow door
That opening, letting in, lets out no more.

Yet come to me in dreams, that I may live
 My very life again though cold in death:
Come back to me in dreams, that I may give
 Pulse for pulse, breath for breath:
  Speak low, lean low,
As long ago, my love, how long ago!

Song

When I am dead, my dearest,
    Sing no sad songs for me;
Plant thou no roses at my head,
    Nor shady cypress tree:
Be the green grass above me
    With showers and dewdrops wet,
And if thou wilt, remember,
    And if thou wilt, forget.

I shall not see the shadows,
    I shall not feel the rain;
I shall not hear the nightingale
    Sing on as if in pain:
And dreaming through the twilight
    That doth not rise nor set,
Haply, I may remember,
    And haply may forget.

Up-Hill

Does the road wind up-hill all the way?
    Yes, to the very end.
Will the day's journey take the whole long day?
    From morn to night, my friend.

But is there for the night a resting-place?
    A roof for when the slow dark hours begin.
May not the darkness hide it from my face?
    You cannot miss that inn.

Shall I meet other wayfarers at night?
    Those who have gone before.
Then must I knock, or call when just in sight?
    They will not keep you standing at that door.

Shall I find comfort, travel-sore and weak?
    Of labour you shall find the sum.
Will there be beds for me and all who seek?
    Yea, beds for all who come.

Thomas Edward Brown

My Garden

A garden is a lovesome thing, God wot!
  Rose plot,
  Fringed pool,
Ferned grot—
  The veriest school
  Of peace; and yet the fool
Contends that God is not—
Not God! in gardens! when the eve is cool?
  Nay, but I have a sign;
  'Tis very sure God walks in mine.

George A. Strong

From The Song of Milkanwatha

When he killed the Mudjokivis,
Of the skin he made him mittens,
Made them with the fur side inside,
Make them with the skin side outside,
He, to get the warm side inside,
Put the inside skin side outside;
He, to get the cold side outside,
Put the warm side fur side inside.
That's why he put the fur side inside,
Why he put the skin side outside,
Why he turned them inside outside.

Lewis Carroll

Jabberwocky

'Twas brillig, and the slithy toves
  Did gyre and gimble in the wabe:
All mimsy were the borogoves,
  And the mome raths outgrabe.

'Beware the Jabberwock, my son!
    The jaws that bite, the claws that catch!
Beware the Jubjub bird, and shun
    The frumious Bandersnatch!'

He took his vorpal sword in hand:
    Long time the manxome foe he sought—
So rested he by the Tumtum tree,
    And stood awhile in thought.

And, as in uffish thought he stood,
    The Jabberwock, with eyes of flame,
Came whiffling through the tulgey wood,
    And burbled as it came!

One, two! One two! And through and through
    The vorpal blade went snicker-snack!
He left it dead, and with its head
    He went galumphing back.

'And hast thou slain the Jabberwock?
    Come to my arms, my beamish boy!
O frabjous day! Callooh! Callay!'
    He chortled in his joy.

'Twas brillig, and the slithy toves
    Did gyre and gimble in the wabe:
All mimsy were the borogoves,
    And the mome raths outgrabe.

The Walrus and the Carpenter

The sun was shining on the sea,
    Shining with all his might:
He did his very best to make
    The billows smooth and bright—
And this was odd, because it was
    The middle of the night.

The moon was shining sulkily,
    Because she thought the sun
Had got no business to be there
    After the day was done—
'It's very rude of him,' she said,
    'To come and spoil the fun!'

The sea was wet as wet could be,
  The sands were dry as dry.
You could not see a cloud, because
  No cloud was in the sky:
No birds were flying overhead—
  There were no birds to fly.

The Walrus and the Carpenter
  Were walking close at hand:
They wept like anything to see
  Such quantities of sand:
'If this were only cleared away,'
  They said, 'it *would* be grand!'

'If seven maids with seven mops
  Swept it for half a year,
Do you suppose', the Walrus said,
  'That they could get it clear?'
'I doubt it,' said the Carpenter,
  And shed a bitter tear.

'O Oysters, come and walk with us!'
  The Walrus did beseech.
'A pleasant walk, a pleasant talk,
  Along the briny beach:
We cannot do with more than four,
  To give a hand to each.'

The eldest Oyster looked at him,
  But never a word he said:
The eldest Oyster winked his eye,
  And shook his heavy head—
Meaning to say he did not choose
  To leave the oyster-bed.

But four young Oysters hurried up,
  All eager for the treat:
Their coats were brushed, their faces washed,
  Their shoes were clean and neat—
And this was odd, because, you know,
  They hadn't any feet.

Four other Oysters followed them,
  And yet another four;
And thick and fast they came at last,
  And more, and more, and more—

All hopping through the frothy waves,
  And scrambling to the shore.

The Walrus and the Carpenter
  Walked on a mile or so,
And then they rested on a rock
  Conveniently low:
And all the little Oysters stood
  And waited in a row.

'The time has come', the Walrus said,
  'To talk of many things:
Of shoes – and ships – and sealing wax—
  Of cabbages – and kings—
And why the sea is boiling hot—
  And whether pigs have wings.'

'But wait a bit,' the Oysters cried,
  'Before we have our chat;
For some of us are out of breath,
  And some of us are fat!'
'No hurry!' said the Carpenter.
  They thanked him much for that.

'A loaf of bread', the Walrus said,
  'Is what we chiefly need:
Pepper and vinegar besides
  Are very good indeed—
Now, if you're ready, Oysters dear,
  We can begin to feed.'

'But not on us!' the Oysters cried,
  Turning a little blue.
'After such kindness, that would be
  A dismal thing to do!'
    'The night is fine,' the Walrus said.
    'Do you admire the view?

'It was so kind of you to come!
  And you are very nice!'
The Carpenter said nothing but
    'Cut us another slice.
I wish you were not quite so deaf—
  I've had to ask you twice!'

'It seems a shame', the Walrus said,
  'To play them such a trick.
After we've brought them out so far,
  And made them trot so quick!'
The Carpenter said nothing but
  'The butter's spread too thick!'

'I weep for you,' the Walrus said:
  'I deeply sympathize.'
With sobs and tears he sorted out
  Those of the largest size,
Holding his pocket-handkerchief
  Before his streaming eyes.

'O Oysters,' said the Carpenter,
  'You've had a pleasant run!
Shall we be trotting home again?'
  But answer came there none—
And this was scarcely odd, because
  They'd eaten every one.

From The Hunting of the Snark

Fit the First: The Landing

'Just the place for a Snark!' the Bellman cried,
  As he landed his crew with care;
Supporting each man on the top of the tide
  By a finger entwined in his hair.

'Just the place for a Snark! I have said it twice:
  That alone should encourage the crew.
Just the place for a Snark! I have said it thrice:
  What I tell you three times is true.'

The crew was complete: it included a Boots—
  A maker of Bonnets and Hoods—
A Barrister, brought to arrange their disputes—
  And a Broker, to value their goods.

A Billiard-marker, whose skill was immense,
  Might perhaps have won more than his share—
But a Banker, engaged at enormous expense,
  Had the whole of their cash in his care.

There was also a Beaver, that paced on the deck,
  Or would sit making lace in the bow:
And had often (the Bellman said) saved them from wreck
  Though none of the sailors knew how.

There was one who was famed for the number of things
  He forgot when he entered the ship:
His umbrella, his watch, all his jewels and rings,
  And the clothes he had brought for the trip.

He had forty-two boxes, all carefully packed,
  With his name painted clearly on each:
But, since he omitted to mention the fact,
  They were all left behind on the beach.

The loss of his clothes hardly mattered, because
  He had seven coats on when he came,
With three pairs of boots — but the worst of it was,
  He had wholly forgotten his name.

He would answer to 'Hi!' or to any loud cry,
  Such as 'Fry me!' or 'Fritter my wig!'
To 'What-you-may-call-um!' or 'What-was-his-name!'
  But especially 'Thing-um-a-jig!'

While, for those who preferred a more forcible word,
  He had different names from these:
His intimate friends called him 'Candle-ends',
  And his enemies 'Toasted-cheese'.

'His form is ungainly — his intellect small—'
  (So the Bellman would often remark)
'But his courage is perfect! And that, after all,
  Is the thing that one needs with a Snark.'

He would joke with hyænas, returning their stare
  With an impudent wag of the head:
And he once went a walk, paw-in-paw, with a bear,
  'Just to keep up its spirits,' he said.

He came as a Baker: but owned, when too late—
  And it drove the poor Bellman half-mad—
He could only bake Bridecake — for which, I may state,
  No materials were to be had.

The last of the crew needs especial remark,
  Though he looked an incredible dunce:
He had just one idea — but, that one being 'Snark',
  The good Bellman engaged him at once.

He came as a Butcher: but gravely declared,
   When the ship had been sailing a week,
He could only kill Beavers. The Bellman looked scared,
   And was almost too frightened to speak:

But at length he explained, in a tremulous tone,
   There was only one Beaver on board;
And that was a tame one he had of his own,
   Whose death would be deeply deplored.

The Beaver, who happened to hear the remark,
   Protested, with tears in its eyes,
That not even the rapture of hunting the Snark
   Could atone for that dismal surprise!

It strongly advised that the Butcher should be
   Conveyed in a separate ship:
But the Bellman declared that would never agree
   With the plans he had made for the trip:

Navigation was always a difficult art,
   Though with only one ship and one bell;
And he feared he must really decline, for his part,
   Undertaking another as well.

The Beaver's best course was, no doubt, to procure
   A second-hand dagger-proof coat—
So the Baker advised it – and next, to insure
   Its life in some Office of note:

This the Baker suggested, and offered for hire
   (On moderate terms), or for sale,
Two excellent Policies, one Against Fire
   And one Against Damage From Hail.

Yet still, even after that sorrowful day,
   Whenever the Butcher was by,
The Beaver kept looking the opposite way,
And appeared unaccountably shy.

William Morris

A Garden by the Sea

I know a little garden-close
Set thick with lily and red rose,
Where I would wander if I might
From dewy dawn to dewy night,
And have one with me wandering.

And though within it no birds sing,
And though no pillared house is there,
And though the apple boughs are bare
Of fruit and blossom, would to God,
Her feet upon the green grass trod,
And I beheld them as before!

There comes a murmur from the shore,
And in the close two fair streams are,
Drawn from the purple hills afar,
Drawn down unto the restless sea;
Dark hills whose heath-bloom feeds no bee,
Dark shore no ship has ever seen,
Tormented by the billows green,
Whose murmur comes unceasingly
Unto the place for which I cry.
For which I cry both day and night,
For which I let slip all delight,
Whereby I grow both deaf and blind,
Careless to win, unskilled to find,
And quick to lose what all men seek.

Yet tottering as I am, and weak,
Still have I left a little breath
To seek within the jaws of death
An entrance to that happy place;
To seek the unforgotten face
Once seen, once kissed, once reft from me
Anigh the murmuring of the sea.

Anonymous

Frankie and Johnny

Frankie and Johnny were lovers, O lordy how they could love.
Swore to be true to each other, true as the stars above;
He was her man, but he done her wrong.

Frankie she was his woman, everybody knows.
She spent one hundred dollars for a suit of Johnny's clothes.
He was her man, but he done her wrong.

Frankie and Johnny went walking, Johnny in his bran' new suit,
'O good Lawd,' says Frankie, 'but don't my Johnny look cute?'
He was her man, but he done her wrong

Frankie went down to Memphis; she went on the evening train.
She paid one hundred dollars for Johnny a watch and chain.
He was her man, but he done her wrong.

Frankie went down to the corner, to buy a glass of beer;
She says to the fat bartender, 'Has my loving man been here?
He was my man but he done me wrong.'

'Ain't going to tell you no story, ain't going to tell you no lie,
I seen your man 'bout an hour ago with a girl named Alice Bly—
If he's your man, he's doing you wrong.'

Frankie went back to the hotel, she didn't go there for fun,
Under her long red kimono she toted a forty-four gun.
He was her man, but he done her wrong.

Frankie went down to the hotel, looked in the window so high,
There was her lovin' Johnny a-lovin' up Alice Bly;
He was her man, but he done her wrong.

Frankie went down to the hotel, she rang that hotel bell,
'Stand back all of you floozies or I'll blow you all to hell,
I want my man, he's doin' me wrong.'

Frankie threw back her kimono; took out the old forty-four;
Roota-toot-toot, three times she shot, right through that hotel
    door.
She shot her man, 'cause he done her wrong.

Johnny grabbed off his Stetson, 'O good Lawd, Frankie, don't
    shoot.'
But Frankie put her finger on the trigger, and the gun went roota-
    toot-toot.
He was her man, but she shot him down.

'Roll me over easy, roll me over slow,
Roll me over easy, boys, 'cause my wounds are hurting me so,
I was her man, but I done her wrong.'

With the first shot Johnny staggered; with the second shot he fell;
When the third bullet hit him, there was a new man's face in hell.
He was her man, but he done her wrong.

Frankie heard a rumbling away down under the ground.
Maybe it was Johnny where she had shot him down.
He was her man, and she done him wrong.

'Oh, bring on your rubber-tyred hearses, bring on your rubber-
    tyred hacks,
They're takin' my Johnny to the buryin' groun' but they'll never
    bring him back.
He was my man, but he done me wrong.'

The judge he said to the jury, 'It's plain as plain can be.
This woman shot her man, so it's murder in the second degree.
He was her man, though he done her wrong.'

Now it wasn't murder in the second degree, it wasn't murder in
    the third.
Frankie simply dropped her man, like a hunter drops a bird.
He was her man, but he done her wrong.

'Oh, put me in that dungeon. Oh, put me in that cell.
Put me where the northeast wind blows from the southeast corner
    of hell.
I shot my man 'cause he done me wrong.'

Frankie walked up to the scaffold, as calm as a girl could be,
She turned her eyes to heaven and said, 'Good Lord, I'm coming to
    thee.
He was my man, and I done him wrong.'

William Schwenck Gilbert

The Yarn of the Nancy Bell

'Twas on the shores that round our coast
  From Deal to Ramsgate span,
That I found alone, on a piece of stone,
  An elderly naval man.

His hair was weedy, his beard was long,
  And weedy and long was he;
And I heard this wight on the shore recite,
  In a singular minor key:

'O, I am a cook and a captain bold,
  And the mate of the Nancy brig,
And a bo'sun tight, and a midshipmite,
  And the crew of the Captain's gig.'

And he shook his fists and he tore his hair,
  Till I really felt afraid,
For I couldn't help thinking the man had been drinking,
  And so I simply said:

'O elderly man, it's little I know
  Of the duties of men of the sea,
And I'll eat my hand if I understand
  How you can possibly be

'At once a cook and a captain bold,
  And the mate of the Nancy brig,
And a bo'sun tight, and a midshipmite,
  And the crew of the captain's gig!'

Then he gave a hitch to his trousers, which
  Is a trick all seamen larn,
And having got rid of a thumping quid
  He spun this painful yarn:

''Twas in the good ship Nancy Bell
  That we sailed to the Indian sea,
And there on a reef we come to grief,
  Which has often occurred to me.

'And pretty nigh all o' the crew was drowned
  (There was seventy-seven o' soul);
And only ten of the Nancy's men
  Said 'Here' to the muster-roll.

'There was me, and the cook, and the captain bold,
　　And the mate of the Nancy brig,
And the bo'sun tight, and a midshipmite,
　　And the crew of the captain's gig.

'For a month we'd neither wittles nor drink,
　　Till a-hungry we did feel,
So we drawed a lot, and, accordin', shot
　　The captain for our meal.

'The next lot fell to the Nancy's mate;
　　And a delicate dish he made;
Then our appetite with the midshipmite
　　We seven survivors stayed.

'And then we murdered the bo'sun tight,
　　And he much resembled pig;
Then we wittled free, did the cook and me,
　　On the crew of the captain's gig.

'Then only the cook and me was left,
　　And the delicate question, "Which
Of us two goes to the kettle?" arose,
　　And we argued it out as sich.

'For I loved that cook as a brother, I did,
　　And the cook he worshipped me;
But we'd both be blowed if we'd either be stowed
　　In the other chap's hold, you see.

' "I'll be eat if you dines off me," says Tom.
　　"Yes, that," says I, "you'll be.
I'm boiled if I die, my friend," quoth I;
　　And "Exactly so," quoth he.

'Say he: "Dear James, to murder me
　　Were a foolish thing to do,
For don't you see that you can't cook me,
　　While I can – and will – cook you?"

'So he boils the water, and takes the salt
　　And the pepper in portions true
(Which he never forgot) and some chopped shalot,
　　And some sage and parsley too.

' "Come here," says he, with a proper pride,
　　Which his smiling features tell;
" 'Twill soothing be if I let you see
　　How extremely nice you'll smell."

'And he stirred it round, and round, and round,
    And he sniffed at the foaming froth;
When I ups with his heels, and smothers his squeals
    In the scum of the boiling broth.

'And I eat that cook in a week or less,
    And as I eating be
The last of his chops, why I almost drops,
    For a wessel in sight I see.

'And I never larf, and I never smile,
    And I never lark nor play;
But I sit and croak, and a single joke
    I have – which is to say:

'O, I am a cook and a captain bold
    And the mate of the Nancy brig,
And a bo'sun tight, and a midshipmite,
    And the crew of the captain's gig!'

Algernon Charles Swinburne

From A Forsaken Garden

In a coign of the cliff between lowland and highland,
    At the sea-down's edge between windward and lee,
Walled round with rocks as an inland island,
    The ghost of a garden fronts the sea.
A girdle of brushwood and thorn encloses
    The steep square slope of the blossomless bed
Where the weeds that grew green from the graves of its roses
        Now lie dead.

The fields fall southward, abrupt and broken,
    To the low last edge of the long lone land.
If a step should sound or a word be spoken,
    Would a ghost not rise at the strange guest's hand?
So long have the grey bare walks lain guestless,
    Through branches and briars if a man make way,
He shall find no life but the sea-wind's, restless
        Night and day.

Thomas Hardy

Weathers

This is the weather the cuckoo likes,
    And so do I;
When showers betumble the chestnut spikes,
    And nestlings fly:
And the little brown nightingale bills his best,
And they sit outside at 'The Travellers' Rest',
And maids come forth sprig-muslin drest,
And citizens dream of the south and west,
    And so do I.

This is the weather the shepherd shuns,
    And so do I;
When beeches drip in browns and duns,
    And thresh, and ply;
And hill-hid tides throb, throe on throe,
And meadow rivulets overflow,
And drops on gate-bars hang in a row,
And rooks in families homeward go,
    And so do I.

In Time of 'The Breaking of Nations'

Only a man harrowing clods
    In a slow silent walk
With an old horse that stumbles and nods
    Half asleep as they stalk.

Only thin smoke without flame
    From the heaps of couch-grass;
Yet this will go onward the same
    Though dynasties pass.

Yonder a maid and her wight
    Come whispering by:
War's annals will cloud into night
    Ere their story die.

Snow in the Suburbs

Every branch big with it,
  Bent every twig with it;
Every fork like a white web-foot;
Every street and pavement mute:
Some flakes have lost their way, and grope back upward, when
Meeting those meandering down they turn and descend again.
  The palings are glued together like a wall,
  And there is no waft of wind with the fleecy fall.

A sparrow enters the tree,
  Whereon immediately
A snow-lump thrice his own slight size
Descends on him and showers his head and eyes,
    And overturns him
    And near inurns him,
  And lights on a nether twig, when its brush
Starts off a volley of other lodging lumps with a rush.

The steps are a blanched slope,
  Up which, with feeble hope,
A black cat comes, wide-eyed and thin;
    And we take him in.

Joachin Miller

Columbus

Behind him lay the gray Azores,
    Behind the Gates of Hercules;
Before him not the ghost of shores,
    Before him only shoreless seas.
The good mate said: 'Now must we pray,
    For lo! the very stars are gone.
Brave Admiral, speak, what shall I say?'
    'Why, say, "Sail on! sail on! and on!" '

'My men grow mutinous day by day;
    My men grow ghastly wan and weak.'
The stout mate thought of home; a spray
    Of salt wave washed his swarthy cheek.
'What shall I say, brave Admiral, say,

If we sight naught but seas at dawn?'
'Why, you shall say at break of day,
   "Sail on! sail on! and on!" '

They sailed and sailed, as winds might blow,
   Until at last the blanched mate said:
'Why, now not even God would know
   Should I and all my men fall dead.
These very winds forget their way,
   For God from these dead seas is gone.
Now speak, brave Admiral, speak and say'—
   He said: 'Sail on! sail on! and on!'

They sailed. They sailed. Then spake the mate:
   'This mad sea shows his teeth to-night.
He curls his lip, he lies in wait,
   With lifted teeth, as if to bite!
Brave Admiral, say but one good word:
   What shall we do when hope is gone?'
The words leapt like a leaping sword:
   'Sail on! sail on! and on!'

Then, pale and worn, he kept his deck,
   And peered through darkness. Ah, that night
Of all dark nights! And then a speck—
   A light! A light! A light! A light!
It grew, a starlit flag unfurled!
   It grew to be time's burst of dawn.
He gained a world; he gave that world
   Its grandest lesson: 'On! sail on!'

Gerard Manley Hopkins

Heaven-haven
A Nun Takes the Veil

I have desired to go
   Where springs not fail,
To fields where flies no sharp and sided hail
   And a few lilies blow.

And I have asked to be
   Where no storms come,
Where the green swell is in the havens dumb,
   And out of the swing of the sea.

The Windhover
To Christ Our Lord

I caught this morning morning's minion, king-
dom of daylight's dauphin, dapple-dawn-drawn Falcon, in his
    riding
  Of the rolling level underneath him steady air, and striding
High there, how he rung upon the rein of a wimpling wing
In his ecstasy! then off, off forth on swing,
    As a skate's heel sweeps smooth on a bow-bend: the hurl and
    gliding
  Rebuffed the big wind. My heart in hiding
Stirred for a bird – the achieve of, the mastery of the thing!

Brute beauty and valour and act, oh, air, pride, plume, here
  Buckle! AND the fire that breaks from thee then, a billion
Times told lovelier, more dangerous, O my chevalier!

  No wonder of it: shéer plód makes plough down sillion
Shine, and blue-bleak embers, ah my dear,
  Fall, gall themselves, and gash gold-vermilion.

Pied Beauty

  Glory be to God for dappled things—
    For skies of couple colour as a brinded cow;
      For rose-moles all in stipple upon trout that swim;
Fresh-firecoal chestnut-falls; finches' wings;
    Landscape plotted and pieced – fold, fallow, and plough;
      And áll trádes, their gear and tackle and trim.

All things, counter, original, spare, strange;
  Whatever is fickle, freckled (who knows how?)
    With swift, slow; sweet, sour; adazzle, dim;
He fathers-forth whose beauty is past change:
        Praise him.

Robert Bridges

A Passer-by

Whither, O splendid ship, thy white sails crowding,
  Leaning across the bosom of the urgent West,
That fearest nor sea rising, nor sky clouding,
  Whither away, fair rover, and what thy quest?
  Ah! soon, when Winter has all our vales opprest,
When skies are cold and misty, and hail is hurling,
  Wilt thou glide on the blue Pacific, or rest
In a summer haven asleep, thy white sails furling.

I there before thee, in the country that well thou knowest,
  Already arrived am inhaling the odorous air:
I watch thee enter unerringly where thou goest,
  And anchor queen of the strange shipping there,
  Thy sails for awnings spread, thy masts bare:
Nor is aught from the foaming reef to the snow-capped grandest
  Peak, that is over the feathery palms, more fair
Than thou, so upright, so stately and still thou standest.

And yet, O splendid ship, unhailed and nameless,
  I know not if, aiming a fancy, I rightly divine
That thou hast a purpose joyful, a courage blameless,
  Thy port assured in a happier land than mine.
  But for all I have given thee, beauty enough is thine,
As thou, aslant with trim tackle and shrouding,
  From the proud nostril curve of a prow's line
In the offing scatterest foam, thy white sails crowding.

London Snow

When men were all asleep the snow came flying,
In large and white flakes falling on the city brown,
Stealthily and perpetually settling and loosely lying,
  Hushing the latest traffic of the drowsy town;
Deadening, muffling, stifling its murmurs failing;
Lazily and incessantly floating down and down:
  Silently sifting and veiling road, roof and railing;
Hiding difference, making unevenness even,
Into angles and crevices softly drifting and sailing.

All night it fell, and when full inches seven
It lay in the depth of its uncompacted lightness,
The clouds blew off from a high and frosty heaven;
    And all woke earlier for the unaccustomed brightness
Of the winter dawning, the strange unheavenly glare:
The eye marvelled – marvelled at the dazzling whiteness;
    The ear hearkened to the stillness of the solemn air;
No sound of wheel rumbling nor of foot falling,
And the busy morning cries came thin and spare.
    Then boys I heard, as they went to school, calling,
They gathered up the crystal manna to freeze
Their tongues with tasting, their hands with snowballing;
    Or rioted in a drift, plunging up to the knees;
Or peering up from under the white-mossed wonder,
'O look at the trees!' they cried, 'O look at the trees!'
    With lessened load a few carts creak and blunder,
Following along the white deserted way,
A country company long dispersed asunder:
    When now already the sun, in pale display
Standing by Paul's high dome, spread forth below
His sparkling beams, and awoke the stir of the day.
    For now doors open, and war is waged with the snow;
And trains of sombre men, past tale of number,
Tread long brown paths, as toward their toil they go:
    But even for them awhile no cares encumber
Their minds diverted; the daily word is unspoken,
The daily thoughts of labour and sorrow slumber
At the sight of the beauty that greets them, for the charm they have
    broken.

James Whitcomb Riley

When the Frost is on the Punkin

When the frost is on the punkin and the fodder's in the shock,
And you hear the kyouck and gobble of the struttin' turkey-cock,
And the clackin' of the guineys, and the cluckin' of the hens,
And the rooster's hallylooyer as he tiptoes on the fence;
O, it's then's the times a feller is a-feelin' at his best,
With the risin' sun to greet him from a night of peaceful rest,
As he leaves the house, bareheaded, and goes out to feed the stock,
When the frost is on the punkin and the fodder's in the shock.

They's something kinda' harty-like about the atmusfere
When the heat of summer's over and the coolin' fall is here—
Of course we miss the flowers, and the blossums on the trees,
And the mumble of the hummin'-birds and buzzin' of the bees;
But the air's so appetizin'; and the landscape through the haze
Of a crisp and sunny morning of the airly autumn days
Is a pictur' that no painter has the colourin' to mock—
When the frost is on the punkin and the fodder's in the shock.

The husky, rusty russel of the tossels of the corn,
And the raspin' of the tangled leaves, as golden as the morn;
The stubble in the furries – kinda' lonesome-like, but still A-
    preachin' sermuns to us of the barns they growed to fill;
The strawstack in the medder, and the reaper in the shed;
The hosses in theyr stalls below – the clover overhead—
O, it sets my hart a-clickin' like the tickin' of a clock,
When the frost is on the punkin and the fodder's in the shock!

Then your apples all is getherd, and the ones a feller keeps
Is poured around the celler-floor in red and yeller heaps;
And your cider-makin''s over, and your wimmern-folks is through
With theyr mince and apple-butter, and theyr souse and saussage,
    too! . . .
I don't know how to tell it – but ef sich a thing could be
As the Angels wantin' boardin', and they'd call around on *me*—
I'd want to 'commodate 'em – all the whole indurin' flock—
When the frost is on the punkin and the fodder's in the shock!

William Ernest Henley

Invictus

Out of the night that covers me,
    Black as the pit from pole to pole,
I thank whatever gods may be
    For my unconquerable soul.

In the fell clutch of circumstance
    I have not winced nor cried aloud.
Under the bludgeonings of chance
    My head is bloody, but unbowed.

Beyond this place of wrath and tears
  Looms but the horror of the shade,
And yet the menace of the years
  Finds, and shall find, me unafraid.

It matters now how strait the gate,
  How charged with punishments the scroll,
I am the master of my fate:
  I am the captain of my soul.

Robert Louis Stevenson

Requiem

Under the wide and starry sky
Dig the grave and let me lie.
Glad did I live and gladly die,
  And I laid me down with a will.

This be the verse you grave for me:
Here he lies where he longed to be;
Home is the sailor, home from sea,
  And the hunter home from the hill.

Ella Wheeler Wilcox

Solitude

Laugh, and the world laughs with you,
Weep, and you weep alone;
For the sad old earth must borrow its mirth,
But has trouble enough of its own.
Sing and the hills will answer,
Sigh, it is lost on the air;
The echoes bound to a joyful sound
And shrink from voicing care.

Rejoice, and men will seek you.
Grieve, and they turn and go;
They want full measure of all your pleasure,
But they do not need your woe.

Be glad, and your friends are many,
Be sad, and you lose them all;
There are none to decline your nectared wine,
But alone you must drink life's gall.

Feast, and your halls are crowded,
Fast, and the world goes by.
Succeed and give – and it helps you live,
But no man can help you die;
For there is room in the halls of pleasure
For a long and lordly train,
But one by one we must all file on
Through the narrow aisles of pain.

Worthwhile

It is easy enough to be pleasant,
When life flows by like a song,
But the man worth while is one who will smile,
When everything goes dead wrong.
For the test of the heart is trouble,
And it always comes with the years,
And the smile that is worth the praises of earth
Is the one that shines through tears.

It is easy enough to be prudent,
When nothing tempts you to stray,
When without or within no voice of sin
Is luring your soul away;
But it's only a negative virtue
Until it is tried by fire,
And the life that is worth the honour of earth
Is the one that resists desire.

By the cynic, the sad, the fallen,
Who had no strength for the strife,
The world's highway is cumbered to-day;
They make up the sum of life.
But the virtue that conquers passion,
And the sorrow that hides in a smile,
It is these that are worth the homage of earth
For we find them but once in a while.

Oscar Wilde

From The Ballad of Reading Gaol

He did not wear his scarlet coat,
  For blood and wine are red,
And blood and wine were on his hands
  When they found him with the dead,
The poor dead woman whom he loved,
  And murdered in her bed.

He walked amongst the Trial Men
  In a suit of shabby gray;
A cricket cap was on his head,
  And his step seemed light and gay;
But I never saw a man who looked
  So wistfully at the day.

I never saw a man who looked
  With such a wistful eye
Upon that little tent of blue
  Which prisoners call the sky,
And at every drifting cloud that went
  With sails of silver by.

I walked, with other souls in pain,
  Within another ring,
And was wondering if the man had done
  A great or little thing,
When a voice behind me whispered low,
  That fellow's got to swing.

Dear Christ! the very prison walls
  Suddenly seemed to reel,
And the sky above my head became
  Like a casque of scorching steel;
And, though I was a soul in pain,
  My pain I could not feel.

I only knew what hunted thought
  Quickened his step, and why
He looked upon the garish day
  With such a wistful eye;
The man had killed the thing he loved,
  And so he had to die.

Yet each man kills the thing he loves,
   By each let this be heard,
Some do it with a bitter look,
   Some with a flattering word,
The coward does it with a kiss,
   The brave man with a sword!

Some kill their love when they are young,
   And some when they are old;
Some strangle with the hands of Lust,
   Some with the hands of Gold:
The kindest use a knife, because
   The dead so soon grow cold.

Some love too little, some too long,
   Some sell, and others buy;
Some do the deed with many tears,
   And some without a sigh:
For each man kills the thing he loves,
   Yet each man does not die.

John Davidson

A Runnable Stag

When the pods went pop on the broom, green broom,
   And apples began to be golden-skinned,
We harboured a stag in the Priory coomb,
   And we feathered his trail up-wind, up-wind,
   We feathered his trail up-wind—
     A stag of warrant, a stag, a stag
     A runnable stag, a kingly crop,
     Brow, bay and tray and three on top,
     A stag, a runnable stag.

Then the huntsman's horn rang yap, yap, yap,
   And 'Forwards' we heard the harbourer shout;
But 'twas only a brocket that broke a gap
   In the beechen underwood, driven out,
   From the underwood antlered out
     By warrant and might of the stag, the stag,
     The runnable stag, whose lordly mind
     Was bent on sleep, though beamed and tined
     He stood, a runnable stag.

So we tufted the covert till afternoon
  With Tinkerman's Pup and Bell-of-the-North;
And hunters were sulky and hounds out of tune
  Before we tufted the right stag forth,
  Before we tufted him forth,
    The stag of warrant, the wily stag,
    The runnable stag with his kingly crop,
    Brow, bay and tray and three on top,
    The royal and runnable stag.

It was Bell-of-the-North and Tinkerman's Pup
  That stuck to the scent till the copse was drawn.
'Tally ho! tally ho!' and the hunt was up,
  The tufters whipped and the pack laid on,
  The resolute pack laid on,
    And the stag of warrant away at last,
    The runnable stag, the same, the same,
    His hoofs on fire, his horns like flame,
    A stag, a runnable stag.

'Let your gelding be: if you check or chide
  He stumbles at once and you're out of the hunt;
For three hundred gentlemen, able to ride,
  On hunters accustomed to bear the brunt,
  Accustomed to bear the brunt,
    Are after the runnable stag, the stag,
    The runnable stag with his kingly crop,
    Brow, bay and tray and three on top,
    The right, the runnable stag.'

By perilous paths in coomb and dell,
  The heather, the rocks, and the river-bed,
The pace grew hot, for the scent lay well,
  And a runnable stag goes right ahead,
  The quarry went right ahead—
    Ahead, ahead, and fast and far;
    His antlered crest, his cloven hoof,
    Brow, bay and tray and three aloof,
    The stag, the runnable stag.

For a matter of twenty miles and more,
  By the densest hedge and the highest wall,
Through herds of bullocks he baffled the lore
  Of harbourer, huntsman, hounds and all,
  Of harbourer, hounds and all—

The stag of warrant, the wily stag,
  For twenty miles, and five and five,
  He ran, and he never was caught alive,
This stag, this runnable stag.

When he turned at bay in the leafy gloom,
  In the emerald gloom where the brook ran deep,
He heard in the distance the rollers boom,
  And he saw in a vision of peaceful sleep,
  In a wonderful vision of sleep,
    A stag of warrant, a stag, a stag,
    A runnable stag in a jewelled bed,
    Under the sheltering ocean dead,
    A stag, a runnable stag.

So a fateful hope lit up his eye,
  And he opened his nostrils wide again,
And he tossed his branching antlers high
  As he headed the hunt down the Charlock glen,
  As he raced down the echoing glen
    For five miles more, the stag, the stag,
    For twenty miles, and five and five,
    Not to be caught now, dead or alive,
    The stag, the runnable stag.

Three hundred gentlemen, able to ride,
  Three hundred horses as gallant and free,
Beheld him escape on the evening tide,
  Far out till he sank in the Severn Sea,
  Till he sank in the depths of the sea—
    The stag, the buoyant stag, the stag
    That slept at last in a jewelled bed
    Under the sheltering ocean spread,
    The stag, the runnable stag.

Dorothy Frances Gurney

'The Lord God planted a garden'

The Lord God planted a garden
  In the first white days of the world,
And he set there an angel warden
  In a garment of light enfurled.

So near to the peace of Heaven,
  That the hawk might nest with the wren,
For there in the cool of the even
  God walked with the first of men.

The kiss of the sun for pardon,
  The song of the birds for mirth—
One is nearer God's heart in a garden
  Than anywhere else on earth.

Katharine Lee Bates

America the Beautiful

O beautiful for spacious skies,
  For amber waves of grain,
For purple mountain majestics
  Above the fruited plain.
America! America!
  God shed His grace on thee,
And crown thy good with brotherhood
  From sea to shining sea.

O beautiful for pilgrim feet,
  Whose stern impassioned stress
A thoroughfare for freedom beat
  Across the wilderness.
America! America!
  God mend thine every flaw,
Confirm thy soul in self-control,
  Thy liberty in law.

O beautiful for heroes proved
  In liberating strife,
Who more than self their country loved,
  And mercy more than life!
America! America!
  May God thy gold refine
Till all success be nobleness
  And every gain divine!

O beautiful for patriot dream
    That sees beyond the years,
Thine alabaster cities gleam,
    Undimmed by human tears.
America! America!
    God shed His grace on thee,
And crown thy good with brotherhood
    From sea to shining sea.

Francis Thompson

From The Hound of Heaven

I fled Him down the nights and down the days;
    I fled Him down the arches of the years;
I fled Him down the labyrinthine ways
    Of my own mind; and in the mist of tears
I hid from Him, and under running laughter.
        Up vistaed hopes I sped;
        And shot, precipitated
    Adown Titanic glooms of chasmed fears,
From those strong Feet that followed, followed after.
        But with unhurrying chase,
        And unperturbed pace,
    Deliberate speed, majestic instancy,
        They beat – and a Voice beat
        More instant than the Feet—
'All things betray thee, who betrayest Me.'

Alfred Edward Housman

'Loveliest of trees, the cherry now'

Loveliest of trees, the cherry now
Is hung with bloom along the bough,
And stands about the woodland ride
Wearing white for Eastertide.

Now, of my threescore years and ten,
Twenty will not come again,
And take from seventy springs a score,
It only leaves me fifty more.

And since to look at things in bloom
Fifty springs are little room,
About the woodlands I will go
To see the cherry hung with snow.

'Is my team ploughing'

'Is my team ploughing,
    That I was used to drive
And hear the harness jingle
    When I was man alive?'

Ay, the horses trample,
    The harness jingles now;
No change though you lie under
    The land you used to plough.

'Is football playing
    Along the river shore,
With lads to chase the leather,
    Now I stand up no more?'

Ay, the ball is flying,
    The lads play heart and soul,
The goal stands up, the keeper
    Stands up to keep the goal.

'Is my girl happy,
    That I thought hard to leave,
And has she tired of weeping
    As she lies down at eve?'

Ay, she lies down lightly,
    She lies not down to weep:
Your girl is well contented.
    Be still, my lad, and sleep.

'Is my friend hearty,
    Now I am thin and pine,
And has he found to sleep in
    A better bed than mine?'

Yes, lad, I lie easy,
   I lie as lads would choose;
I cheer a dead man's sweetheart,
   Never ask me whose.

'When I was one-and-twenty'

When I was one-and-twenty
   I heard a wise man say,
'Give crowns and pounds and guineas
   But not your heart away;
Give pearls away and rubies
   But keep your fancy free.'
But I was one-and-twenty,
   No use to talk to me.

When I was one-and-twenty
   I heard him say again,
'The heart out of the bosom
   Was never given in vain;
'Tis paid with sighs a plenty
   And sold for endless rue.'
And I am two-and-twenty,
   And oh, 'tis true, 'tis true.

Epitaph on an Army of Mercenaries

These, in the day when heaven was falling,
   The hour when earth's foundations fled,
Followed their mercenary calling
   And took their wages and are dead.

Their shoulders held the sky suspended;
   They stood, and earth's foundations stay;
What God abandoned, these defended,
   And saved the sum of things for pay.

Henry Newbolt

Drake's Drum

Drake he's in his hammock an' a thousand mile away,
  (Capten, art tha sleepin' there below?),
Slung atween the round shot in Nombre Dios Bay,
  An' dreamin' arl the time o' Plymouth Hoe.
Yarnder lumes the Island, yarnder lie the ships.
  Wi' sailor-lads a-dancin' heel-an'-toe,
An' the shore-lights flashin', and the night-tide dashin',
  He sees et arl so plainly as he saw et long ago.

Drake he was a Devon man, an' ruled the Devon seas,
  (Capten, art tha sleepin' there below?),
Rovin' tho' his death fell, he went wi' heart at ease,
  An' dreamin' arl the time o' Plymouth Hoe.
'Take my drum to England, hang et by the shore,
  Strike et when your powder's runnin' low;
If the Dons sight Devon, I'll quit the port o' Heaven,
  An' drum them up the Channel as we drummed them long ago.'

Drake he's in his hammock till the great Armadas come,
  (Capten, art tha sleepin' there below?),
Slung atween the round shot, listenin' for the drum,
  An' dreamin' arl the time o' Plymouth Hoe.
Call him on the deep sea, call him up the Sound,
  Call him when ye sail to meet the foe;
Where the old trade's plyin' an' the old flag flyin'
  They shall find him ware an' wakin', as they found him long
  ago!

Vitaï Lampada

There's a breathless hush in the Close to-night—
  Ten to make and the match to win—
A bumping pitch and a blinding light,
  An hour to play and the last man in.
And it's not for the sake of a ribboned coat,
  Or the selfish hope of a season's fame,
But his Captain's hand on his shoulder smote
  'Play up! play up! and play the game!'

The sand of the desert is sodden red,—
    Red with the wreck of a square that broke;—
The Gatling's jammed and the colonel dead,
    And the regiment blind with dust and smoke.
The river of death has brimmed his banks,
    And England's far, and Honour a name,
But the voice of a schoolboy rallies the ranks,
    'Play up! play up! and play the game!'

This is the word that year by year
    While in her place the School is set
Every one of her sons must hear,
    And none that hears it dare forget.
This they all with a joyful mind
    Bear through life like a torch in flame,
And falling fling to the host behind—
    'Play up! play up! and play the game!'

Rudyard Kipling

Danny Deever

'What are the bugles blowin' for?' said Files-on-Parade.
'To turn you out, to turn you out,' the Colour-Sergeant said.
'What makes you look so white, so white?' said Files-on-Parade.
'I'm dredin' what I've got to watch,' the Colour-Sergeant said.
    For they're hangin' Danny Deever, you can hear the Dead
        March play,
    The Regiment's in 'ollow square – they're hangin' him today;
    They've taken of his buttons off an' cut his stripes away,
    An' they're hangin' Danny Deever in the mornin'.

'What makes the rear-rank breathe so 'ard?' said Files-on-Parade.
'It's bitter cold, it's bitter cold,' the Colour-Sergeant said.
'What makes that front-rank man fall down?' said Files-on-Parade.
'A touch o' sun, a touch o' sun,' the Colour-Sergeant said.
    They are hangin' Danny Deever, they are marchin' of 'im round,
    They 'ave 'alted Danny Deever by 'is coffin on the ground;
    An' 'e'll swing in 'arf a minute for a sneakin' shootin' hound—
    O they're hangin' Danny Deever in the mornin'!

' 'Is cot was right-'and cot to mine,' said Files-on-Parade.
' 'E's sleepin' out an' far tonight,' the Colour-Sergeant said.
'I've drunk 'is beer a score o' time,' said Files-on-Parade.
' 'E's drinkin' better beer alone,' the Colour-Sergeant said.
  They are hangin' Danny Deever, you must mark 'im to his place,
  For 'e shot a comrade sleepin' – you must look 'im in the face;
  Nine 'undred of 'is county an' the Regiment's disgrace,
  While they're hangin' Danny Deever in the mornin'.

'What's that so black agin the sun?' said Files-on-Parade.
'It's Danny fightin' 'ard for life,' the Colour-Sergeant said.
'What's that that whispers over'ead?' said Files-on-Parade.
'It's Danny's soul that's passin' now,' the Colour-Sergeant said.
  For they're done with Danny Deever, you can 'ear the quick-step
    play,
  The Regiment's in column, an' they're marchin' us away;
  Ho! the young recruits are shakin', an' they'll want their beer
    today,
  After hangin' Danny Deever in the mornin'!

Gunga Din

    You may talk o' gin and beer
    When you're quartered safe out 'ere,
    An' you're sent to penny-fights an' Aldershot it;
    But when it comes to slaughter
    You will do your work on water,
    An' you'll lick the bloomin' boots of 'im that's got it.
    Now in Injia's sunny clime,
    Where I used to spend my time
    A-servin' of 'Er Majesty the Queen,
    Of all them blackfaced crew
    The finest man I knew
    Was our regimental *bhisti*, Gunga Din.
        He was 'Din! Din! Din!
      You limpin' lump o' brick-dust, Gunga Din!'
        Hi! Slippy *hitherao!*
        Water, get it! *Panee lao,*
      You squidgy-nosed old idol, Gunga Din.'

The uniform 'e wore
Was nothin' much before,
An' rather less than 'arf o' that be'ind,
For a peace o' twisty rag
An' a goatskin water-bag
Was all the field-equipment 'e could find.
When the sweatin' troop-train lay
In a sidin' through the day,
Where the 'eat would make your bloomin' eyebrows crawl,
We shouted 'Harry By!'
Till our throats were bricky-dry,
Then we wopped 'im 'cause 'e couldn't serve us all.
      It was 'Din! Din! Din!
  You eathen, where the mischief 'ave you been?
        You put some *juldee* in it
        Or I'll *marrow* you this minute
    If you don't fill up my helmet, Gunga Din!'

'E would dot an' carry one
Till the longest day was done;
An' 'e didn't seem to know the use o' fear.
If we charged or broke or cut,
You could bet your bloomin' nut,
'E'd be waitin' fifty paces right flank rear.
With 'is *mussick* on 'is back,
'E would skip with our attack,
An' watch us till the bugles made 'Retire',
An' for all 'is dirty 'ide
'E was white, clear white, inside
When 'e went to tend the wounded under fire!
      It was 'Din! Din! Din!'
  With the bullets kickin' dust-spots on the green.
      When the cartridges ran out,
      You could hear the front-ranks shout,
  'Hi! ammunition-mules an' Gunga Din!'
I shan't forgit the night
When I dropped be'ind the fight
With a bullet where my belt-plate should 'a' been.
I was chokin' mad with thirst,
An' the man that spied me first
Was our good old grinnin', gruntin' Gunga Din.
'E lifted up my 'ead,
   An' he plugged me where I bled,
   An' 'e guv me 'arf-a-pint o' water green,

It was crawlin' and it stunk,
But of all the drinks I've drunk,
I'm gratefullest to one from Gunga Din.
    It was 'Din! Din! Din!
'Ere's a begger with a bullet through 'is spleen;
    'E's chawin' up the ground,
    An' 'e's kickin' all around:
For Gawd's sake git the water, Gunga Din!'

'E carried me away
To where a *dooli* lay,
An' a bullet come an' drilled the beggar clean.
'E put me safe inside,
An' just before 'e died,
'I 'ope, you liked your drink,' sez Gunga Din.
So I'll meet 'im later on
At the place where 'e is gone—
Where it's always double drill and no canteen.
'E'll be squattin' on the coals
Givin' drink to poor damned souls
An' I'll get a swig in hell from Gunga Din!
        Yes, Din! Din! Din!
    You Lazarushian-leather Gunga Din!
        Though I've belted you and flayed you,
        By the livin' Gawd that made you,
    You're a better man than I am, Gunga Din!

Recessional

God of our fathers, known of old,
    Lord of our far-flung battle-line,
Beneath whose awful Hand we hold
    Dominion over palm and pine—
Lord God of Hosts, be with us yet,
Lest we forget – lest we forget!

The tumult and the shouting dies;
    The captains and the kings depart;
Still stands Thine ancient sacrifice,
    An humble and a contrite heart.
Lord God of Hosts, be with us yet,
Lest we forget – lest we forget!

Far-called, our navies melt away;
   On dune and headland sinks the fire:
Lo, all our pomp of yesterday
   Is one with Nineveh and Tyre!
Judge of the Nations, spare us yet,
Lest we forget – lest we forget!

If, drunk with sight of power, we loose
   Wild tongues that have not Thee in awe,
Such boastings as the gentiles use,
   Or lesser breeds within the law—
Lord God of Hosts, be with us yet,
Lest we forget – lest we forget!

For heathen heart that puts her trust
   In reeking tube and iron shard,
All valiant dust that builds on dust,
   And guarding, calls not Thee to guard,
For frantic boast and foolish word—
Thy mercy on Thy people, Lord!

The Way through the Woods

They shut the road through the woods
Seventy years ago.
Weather and rain have undone it again,
And now you would never know
There was once a road through the woods
Before they planted the trees.
It is underneath the coppice and heath
And the thin anemones.
Only the keeper sees
That, where the ring-dove broods,
And the badgers roll at ease,
There was once a road through the woods.

Yet, if you enter the woods
Of a summer evening late,
When the night-air cools on the trout-ringed pools
Where the otter whistles his mate,
(They fear not men in the woods,
Because they see so few.)
You will hear the beat of a horse's feet,

And the swish of a skirt in the dew,
Steadily cantering through
The misty solitudes,
As though they perfectly knew
The old lost road through the woods. . . .
But there is no road through the woods.

If—

If you can keep your head when all about you
    Are losing theirs and blaming it on you,
If you can trust yourself when all men doubt you,
    But make allowance for their doubting too;
If you can wait and not be tired of waiting,
    Or being lied about, don't deal in lies,
Or being hated, don't give way to hating,
    And yet don't look too good, nor talk too wise:

If you can dream – and not make dreams your master;
    If you can think – and not make thoughts your aim;
If you can meet with Triumph and Disaster
    And treat those two impostors just the same;
If you can bear to hear the truth you've spoken
    Twisted by knaves to make a trap for fools,
Or watch the things you gave your life to, broken,
    And stoop and build 'em up with worn-out tools:

If you can make one heap of all your winnings
    And risk it on one turn of pitch-and-toss,
And lose, and start again at your beginnings
    And never breathe a word about your loss;
If you can force your heart and nerve and sinew
    To serve your turn long after they are gone,
And so hold on when there is nothing in you
    Except the Will which says to them: 'Hold on!'

If you can talk with crowds and keep your virtue,
    Or walk with Kings – nor lose the common touch,
If neither foes nor loving friends can hurt you,
    If all men count with you, but none too much;
If you can fill the unforgiving minute
    With sixty seconds' worth of distance run,
Yours is the Earth and everything that's in it,
    And – which is more – you'll be a Man, my son!

Mandalay

By the old Moulmein Pagoda, lookin' eastward to the sea,
There's a Burma girl a-settin', and I know she thinks o' me;
For the wind is in the palm-trees, and the temple-bells they say:
'Come you back, you British soldier; come you back to
        Mandalay!'
        Come you back to Mandalay,
        Where the old Flotilla lay:
        Can't you 'ear their paddles chunkin' from Rangoon to
        Mandalay?
        On the road to Mandalay,
        Where the flyin'-fishes play,
        An' the dawn comes up like thunder outer China 'crost the
        Bay!

'Er petticoat was yaller an' 'er little cap was green,
An' 'er name was Supi-yaw-lat – jes' the same as Theebaw's Queen
An' I seed her first a-smokin' of a wackin' white cheroot,
An' a-wastin' Christian kisses on an 'eathen idol's foot:
        Bloomin' idol made o' mud—
        Wot they called the Great Gawd Budd—
        Plucky lot she cared for idols when I kissed 'er where she stud!
        On the road to Mandalay . . .

When the mist was on the rice-fields an' the sun was droppin'
        slow,
She'd git 'er little banjo an' she'd sing 'Kulla-lo-lo!'
With 'er arm upon my shoulder an' 'er cheek agin my cheek
We useter watch the steamers an' the hathis pilin' teak.
        Elephints a-pilin' teak
        In the slidgy, squidgy creek,
        Where the silence 'ung that 'eavy you was 'arf afraid to speak!
        On the road to Mandalay . . .

But that's all shove be'ind me – long ago an' fur away,
An' there ain't no 'busses runnin' from the Bank to Mandalay;
An' I'm learnin' 'ere in London what the ten-year soldier tells:
'If you've 'eard the East a-callin', you won't never 'eed naught
        else.'
        No! you won't 'eed nothin' else
        But them spicy garlic smells,
        An' the sunshine an' the palm-trees an' the tinkly temple-bells;
        On the road to Mandalay . . .

I am sick o' wastin' leather on these gritty pavin'-stones,
An' the blasted Henglish drizzle wakes the fever in my bones;
Tho' I walks with fifty 'ousemaids outer Chelsea to the Strand,
An' they talks a lot o' lovin', but wot do they understand?
    Beefy face an' grubby 'and—
    Law! wot do they understand?
    I've a neater, sweeter maiden in a cleaner, greener land!
    On the road to Mandalay . . .

Ship me somewheres east of Suez, where the best is like the worst,
Where there aren't no Ten Commandments an' a man can raise a
    thirst;
For the temple-bells are callin', an' it's there that I would be—
By the old Moulmein Pagoda, looking lazy at the sea;
    On the road to Mandalay,
    Where the old Flotilla lay,
    With our sick beneath the awnings when we went to
    Mandalay!
    O the road to Mandalay,
    Where the flyin'-fishes play,
    An' the dawn comes up like thunder outer China 'crost the
    Bay!

J. Milton Hayes

The Green Eye of the Yellow God

There's a one-eyed yellow idol to the north of Khatmandu,
There's a little marble cross below the town;
There's a broken-hearted woman tends the grave of Mad Carew,
And the Yellow God forever gazes down.

He was known as Mad Carew by the subs at Khatmandu,
He was hotter than they felt inclined to tell;
But for all his foolish pranks, he was worshipped in the ranks,
And the Colonel's daughter smiled on him as well.

He had loved her all along, with a passion of the strong,
The fact that she loved him was plain to all.
She was nearly twenty-one and arrangements had begun
To celebrate her birthday with a ball.

He wrote to ask what present she would like from Mad Carew;
They met next day as he dismissed a squad;
And jestingly she told him then that nothing else would do
But the green eye of the little Yellow God.

On the night before the dance, Mad Carew seemed in a trance,
And they chaffed him as they puffed at their cigars;
But for once he failed to smile, and he sat alone awhile,
Then went out into the night beneath the stars.

He returned before the dawn, with his shirt and tunic torn,
And a gash across his temple dripping red;
He was patched up right away, and he slept through all the day,
And the Colonel's daughter watched beside his bed.

He woke at last and asked if they could send his tunic through;
She brought it, and he thanked her with a nod;
He bade her search the pocket saying, 'That's from Mad Carew',
And she found the little green eye of the god.

She upbraided poor Carew in the way that women do,
Though both her eyes were strangely hot and wet;
But she wouldn't take the stone and Mad Carew was left alone
With the jewel that he'd chanced his life to get.

When the ball was at its height, on that still and tropic night,
She thought of him and hastened to his room;
As she crossed the barrack square, she could hear the dreamy air
Of a waltz tune softly stealing through the gloom.

His door was open wide, with silver moonlight shining through;
The place was wet and slippery where she trod;
An ugly knife lay buried in the heart of Mad Carew,
'Twas the 'Vengeance of the Little Yellow God'.

There's one-eyed yellow idol to the north of Khatmandu,
There's a little marble cross below the town;
There's a broken-hearted woman tends the grave of Mad Carew,
And the Yellow God forever gazes down.

William Butler Yeats

Down by the Salley Gardens

Down by the salley gardens my love and I did meet;
She passed the salley gardens with little snow-white feet.
She bid me take love easy, as the leaves grow on the tree;
But I, being young and foolish, with her would not agree.

In a field by the river my love and I did stand,
And on my leaning shoulder she laid her snow-white hand.
She bid me take life easy, as the grass grows on the weirs;
But I was young and foolish, and now am full of tears.

The Lake Isle of Innisfree

I will arise and go now, and go to Innisfree,
And a small cabin build there, of clay and wattles made:
Nine bean-rows will I have there, a hive for the honey-bee,
And live alone in the bee-loud glade.

And I shall have some peace there, for peace comes dropping slow,
Dropping from the veils of the morning to where the cricket sings;
There midnight's all a-glimmer, and noon a purple glow,
And evening full of the linnet's wings.

I will arise and go now, for always night and day
I hear lake water lapping with low sounds by the shore;
While I stand on the roadway, or on the pavements grey,
I hear it in the deep heart's core.

When You Are Old

When you are old and grey and full of sleep,
    And nodding by the fire, take down this book,
    And slowly read, and dream of the soft look
Your eyes had once, and of their shadows deep;

How many loved your moments of glad grace,
  And loved your beauty with love false or true,
  But one man loved the pilgrim soul in you,
And loved the sorrows of your changing face.

And bending down beside the glowing bars,
  Murmur, a little sadly, how Love fled
  And paced upon the mountains overhead,
And hid his face amid a crowd of stars.

An Irish Airman Foresees His Death

I know that I shall meet my fate
Somewhere among the clouds above;
Those that I fight I do not hate,
Those that I guard I do not love;
My country is Kiltartan Cross,
My countrymen Kiltartan's poor,
No likely end could bring them loss
Or leave them happier than before.
Nor law, nor duty bade me fight,
Nor public men, nor cheering crowds,
A lonely impulse of delight
Drove to this tumult in the clouds;
I balanced all, brought all to mind,
The years to come seemed waste of breath,
A waste of breath the years behind
In balance with this life, this death.

The Second Coming

Turning and turning in the widening gyre
The falcon cannot hear the falconer;
Things fall apart; the centre cannot hold;
Mere anarchy is loosed upon the world,
The blood-dimmed tide is loosed, and everywhere
The ceremony of innocence is drowned;
The best lack all conviction, while the worst
Are full of passionate intensity.

Surely some revelation is at hand;
Surely the Second Coming is at hand.
The Second Coming! Hardly are those words out
When a vast image out of *Spiritus Mundi*
Troubles my sight: somewhere in sands of the desert
A shape with lion body and the head of a man,
A gaze blank and pitiless as the sun,
Is moving its slow thighs, while all about it
Reel shadows of the indignant desert birds.
The darkness drops again; but now I know
That twenty centuries of stony sleep
Were vexed to nightmare by a rocking cradle,
And what rough beast, its hour come round at last,
Slouches towards Bethlehem to be born?

Sailing to Byzantium

That is no country for old men. The young
In one another's arms, birds in the trees
—Those dying generations – at their song,
The salmon-falls, the mackerel-crowded seas,
Fish, flesh, or fowl, commend all summer long
Whatever is begotten, born, and dies.
Caught in that sensual music all neglect
Monuments of unageing intellect.

An aged man is but a paltry thing,
A tattered coat upon a stick, unless
Soul clap its hands and sing, and louder sing
For every tatter in its mortal dress,
Nor is there singing school but studying
Monuments of its own magnificence;
And therefore I have sailed the seas and come
To the holy city of Byzantium.

O sages standing in God's holy fire
As in the gold mosaic of a wall,
Come from the holy fire, perne in a gyre,
And be the singing-masters of my soul.
Consume my heart away; sick with desire
And fastened to a dying animal
It knows not what it is; and gather me
Into the artifice of eternity.

Once out of nature I shall never take
My bodily form from any natural thing,
But such a form as Grecian goldsmiths make
Of hammered gold and gold enamelling
To keep a drowsy Emperor awake;
Or set upon a golden bough to sing
To lords and ladies of Byzantium
Of what is past, or passing, or to come.

Edwin Arlington Robinson

Richard Cory

Whenever Richard Cory went down town,
We people on the pavement looked at him:
He was a gentleman from sole to crown,
Clean favoured, and imperially slim.

And he was always quietly arrayed,
And he was always human when he talked;
But still he fluttered pulses when he said,
'Good-morning,' and he glittered when he walked.

And he was rich – yes, richer than a king—
And admirably schooled in every grace:
In fine, we thought that he was everything
To make us wish that we were in his place.

So on we worked, and waited for the light,
And went without the meat, and cursed the bread;
And Richard Cory, one calm summer night,
Went home and put a bullet through his head.

Miniver Cheevy

Miniver Cheevy, child of scorn,
　　Grew lean while he assailed the seasons;
He wept that he was ever born,
　　And he had reasons.

Miniver loved the days of old
  When swords were bright and steeds were prancing;
The vision of a warrior bold
  Would set him dancing.

Miniver sighed for what was not,
  And dreamed, and rested from his labours;
He dreamed of Thebes and Camelot,
  And Priam's neighbours.

Miniver mourned the ripe renown
  That made so many a name so fragrant;
He mourned Romance, now on the town,
  And Art, a vagrant.

Miniver loved the Medici,
  Albeit he had never seen one;
He would have sinned incessantly
  Could he have been one.

Miniver cursed the commonplace
  And eyed a khaki suit with loathing;
He missed the mediaeval grace
  Of iron clothing.

Miniver scorned the gold he sought,
  But sore annoyed was he without it;
Miniver thought, and thought, and thought,
  And thought about it.

Miniver Cheevy, born too late,
  Scratched his head and kept on thinking;
Miniver coughed, and called it fate,
  And kept on drinking.

Laurence Binyon

For the Fallen
(*September 1914*)

With proud thanksgiving, a mother for her children,
England mourns for her dead across the sea.
Flesh of her flesh they were, spirit of her spirit,
Fallen in the cause of the free.

Solemn the drums thrill: Death august and royal
Sings sorrow up into immortal spheres.
There is music in the midst of desolation
And a glory that shines upon our tears.

They went with songs to the battle, they were young,
Straight of limb, true of eye, steady and aglow.
They were staunch to the end against odds uncounted,
They fell with their faces to the foe.

They shall grow not old, as we that are left grow old:
Age shall not weary them, nor the years condemn.
At the going down of the sun and in the morning
We will remember them.

They mingle not with their laughing comrades again;
They sit no more at familiar tables of home;
They have no lot in our labour of the day-time;
They sleep beyond England's foam.

But where our desires are and our hopes profound,
Felt as a well-spring that is hidden from sight,
To the innermost heart of their own land they are known
As the stars are known to the night;

As the stars that shall be bright when we are dust,
Moving in marches upon the heavenly plain,
As the stars that are starry in the time of our darkness,
To the end, to the end, they remain.

From The Burning of the Leaves

Now is the time for the burning of the leaves.
They go to the fire; the nostril pricks with smoke
Wandering slowly into a weeping mist.
Brittle and blotched, ragged and rotten sheaves!
A flame seizes the smouldering ruin and bites
On stubborn stalks that crackle as they resist.

The last hollyhock's fallen tower is dust;
All the spices of June are a bitter reek,
All the extravagant riches spent and mean.
All burns! The reddest rose is a ghost;
Sparks whirl up, to expire in the mist: the wild
Fingers of fire are making corruption clean.

Now is the time for stripping the spirit bare,
Time for the burning of days ended and done,
Idle solace of things that have gone before:
Rootless hopes and fruitless desire are there;
Let them go to the fire, with never a look behind.
The world that was ours is a world that is ours no more.

They will come again, the leaf and the flower, to arise
From squalor of rottenness into the old spendour,
And magical scents to a wondering memory bring;
The same glory, to shine upon different eyes.
Earth cares for her own ruins, naught for ours.
Nothing is certain, only the certain spring.

Hilaire Belloc

Tarantella

Do you remember an Inn,
Miranda?
Do you remember an Inn?
And the tedding and the spreading
Of the straw for a bedding,
And the fleas that tease in the High Pyrenees,
And the wine that tasted of the tar?
And the cheers and the jeers of the young muleteers
(Under the dark of the vine verandah)?
Do you remember an Inn, Miranda,
Do you remember an Inn?
And the cheers and the jeers of the young muleteers
Who hadn't got a penny,
And who weren't paying any,
And the hammer at the doors and the Din?
And the Hip! Hop! Hap!
Of the clap
Of the hands to the twirl and the swirl
Of the girl gone chancing,
Glancing,
Dancing,
Backing and advancing,
Snapping of the clapper to the spin
Out and in—

And the Ting, Tong, Tang of the guitar!
Do you remember an Inn,
Miranda?
Do you remember an Inn?

Never more;
Miranda,
Never more.
Only the high peaks hoar:
And Aragon a torrent at the door.
No sound
In the walls of the Halls where falls
The tread
Of the feet of the dead to the ground.
No sound:
Only the boom
Of the far Waterfall like Doom.

Ballade of Genuine Concern

A child at Brighton has been left to drown:
A railway train has jumped the line at Crewe:
I haven't got the change for half a crown:
I can't imagine what on earth to do . . .
Three bisons have stampeded from the Zoo,
A German fleet has anchored in the Clyde.
By God the wretched country's up the flue!
The ice is breaking up on every side.

What! Further news? Rhodesian stocks are down?
England, my England, can the news be true!
Cannot the Duke be got to come to town?
Or will not Mr Hooper pull us through?
And now the Bank is stopping payment too,
The chief cashier has cut his throat and died,
And Scotland Yard has failed to find a clue:
The ice is breaking up on every side.

A raging mob inflamed by Charley Brown
Is tearing up the rails of Waterloo;
They've hanged the Chancellor in wig and gown,
The Speaker, and the Chief Inspector too!
Police! Police! Is this the road to Kew?
I can't keep up: my garter's come untied;
I shall be murdered by the savage crew.
The ice is breaking up on every side.

Envoi

Prince of the Empire, Prince of Timbuctoo,
Prince eight feet round and nearly four feet wide,
Do try to run a little faster, do.
The ice is breaking up on every side.

Matilda
Who Told Lies, and Was Burned to Death

Matilda told such Dreadful Lies,
It made one Gasp and Stretch one's Eyes;
Her Aunt, who, from her Earliest Youth,
Had kept a Strict Regard for Truth,
Attempted to Believe Matilda:
The effort very nearly killed her,
And would have done so, had not She
Discovered this Infirmity.
For once, towards the Close of Day,
Matilda, growing tired of play,
And finding she was left alone,
Went tiptoe to the Telephone
And summoned the Immediate Aid
Of London's Noble Fire-Brigade.
Within an hour the Gallant Band
Were pouring in on every hand,
From Putney, Hackney Downs, and Bow,
With Courage high and Hearts a-glow
They galloped, roaring through the Town:
'Matilda's House is Burning Down!'
Inspired by British Cheers and Loud
Proceeding from the Frenzied Crowd,
They ran their ladders through a score
Of windows on the Ball Room Floor;

And took Peculiar Pains to Souse
The Pictures up and down the House,
Until Matilda's Aunt succeeded
In showing them they were not needed
And even then she had to pay
To get the Men to go away!

It happened that a few Weeks later
Her Aunt was off to the Theatre
To see that Interesting Play
The Second Mrs Tanqueray.
She had refused to take her Niece
To hear this Entertaining Piece:
A Deprivation Just and Wise
To Punish her for Telling Lies.
That Night a Fire *did* break out—
You should have heard Matilda Shout!
You should have heard her Scream and Bawl,
And throw the window up and call
To People passing in the Street—
(The rapidly increasing Heat
Encouraging her to obtain
Their confidence; – but all in vain!
For every time she shouted: 'Fire!'
They only answered 'Little Liar!'
And therefore when her Aunt returned,
Matilda, and the House, were Burned.

William Henry Davies

Leisure

What is this life if, full of care,
We have no time to stand and stare?

No time to stand beneath the boughs
And stare as long as sheep or cows:

No time to see, when woods we pass,
Where squirrels hide their nuts in grass:

No time to see, in broad daylight,
Streams full of stars, like skies at night:

No time to turn at Beauty's glance,
And watch her feet, how they can dance:

No time to wait till her mouth can
Enrich that smile her eyes began?

A poor life this if, full of care,
We have no time to stand and stare.

Walter de la Mare

The Listeners

'Is there anybody there?' said the Traveller,
    Knocking on the moonlit door;
And his horse in the silence champed the grasses
    Of the forest's ferny floor:
And a bird flew up out of the turret,
    Above the Traveller's head:
And he smote upon the door again a second time;
    'Is there anybody there?' he said.
But no one descended to the Traveller;
    No head from the leaf-fringed sill
Leaned over and looked into his grey eyes,
    Where he stood perplexed and still.
But only a host of phantom listeners
    That dwelt in the lone house then
Stood listening in the quiet of the moonlight
    To that voice from the world of men:
Stood thronging the faint moonbeams on the dark stair
    That goes down to the empty hall,
Hearkening in an air stirred and shaken
    By the lonely Traveller's call.
And he felt in his heart their strangeness,
    Their stillness answering his cry,
While his horse moved, cropping the dark turf,
    'Neath the starred and leafy sky;
For he suddenly smote on the door, even
    Louder, and lifted his head—
'Tell them I came, and no one answered,
    That I kept my word,' he said.
Never the least stir made the listeners,

Though every word he spake
Fell echoing through the shadowiness of the still house
    From the one man left awake:
Ay, they heard his foot upon the stirrup,
    And the sound of iron on stone,
And how the silence surged softly backward,
    When the plunging hoofs were gone.

Fare Well

When I lie where shades of darkness
Shall no more assail mine eyes,
Nor the rain make lamentation
        When the wind sighs;
How will fare the world whose wonder
Was the very proof of me?
Memory fades, must the remembered
        Perishing be?

Oh, when this my dust surrenders
Hand, foot, lip, to dust again,
May these loved and loving faces
        Please other men!
May the rusting harvest hedgerow
Still the Traveller's Joy entwine,
And as happy children gather
        Posies once mine.

Look thy last on all things lovely,
Every hour. Let no night
Seal thy sense in deathly slumber
        Till to delight
Thou have paid thy utmost blessing;
Since that all things thou wouldst praise
Beauty took from those who loved them
        In other days.

The Scribe

What lovely things
  Thy hand hath made:
The smooth-plumed bird
  In its emerald shade,
The seed of the grass,
  The speck of stone
Which the wayfaring ant
  Stirs – and hastes on!

Though I should sit
  By some tarn in thy hills,
Using its ink
  As the spirit wills
To write of Earth's wonders,
  Its live, willed things,
Flit would the ages
  On soundless wings
Ere unto Z
  My pen drew nigh;
Leviathan told,
  And the honey-fly:
And still would remain
  My wit to try—
My worn reeds broken,
  The dark tarn dry,
All words forgotten—
  Thou, Lord, and I.

Gilbert Keith Chesterton

The Donkey

When fishes flew and forests walked
  And figs grew upon thorn,
Some moment when the moon was blood
  Then surely I was born;

With monstrous head and sickening cry
  And ears like errant wings,
The devil's walking parody
  On all four-footed things.

The tattared outlaw of the earth,
    Of ancient crooked will;
Starve, scourge, deride me: I am dumb,
    I kept my secret still.

Fools! For I also had my hour;
    One far fierce hour and sweet:
There was a shout about my ears,
    And palms before my feet.

From Lepanto

White founts falling in the courts of the sun,
And the Soldan of Byzantium is smiling as they run;
There is laughter like the fountains in that face of all men feared,
It stirs the forest darkness, the darkness of his beard,
It curls the blood-red crescent, the crescent of his lips,
For the inmost sea of all the earth is shaken with his ships.
They have dared the white republics up the capes of Italy,
They have dashed the Adriatic round the Lion of the Sea,
And the Pope has cast his arms abroad for agony and loss,
And called the kings of Christendon for swords about the Cross,
The cold Queen of England is looking in the glass;
The shadow of the Valois is yawning at the Mass;
From evening isles fantastical rings faint the Spanish gun,
And the Lord upon the Golden Horn is laughing in the sun.

Dim drums throbbing, in the hills half heard,
Where only on a nameless throne a crownless prince has stirred,
Where, risen from a doubtful seat and half attained stall,
The last knight of Europe takes weapons from the wall,
The last and lingering troubadour to whom the bird has sung,
That once went singing southward when all the world was young.
In that enormous silence, tiny and unafraid,
Comes up along a winding road the noise of the Crusade.
Strong gongs groaning as the guns boom far,
Don John of Austria is going to the war;
Stiff flags straining in the night-blasts cold,
In the gloom black-purple, in the glint old-gold,
Torchlight crimson on the copper kettle-drums,
Then the tuckets, then the trumpets, then the cannon, and he
    comes.

Don John laughing in the brave beard curled,
Spurning of his stirrups like the thrones of all the world,
Holding his head up for a flag of all the free.
Love-light of Spain – hurrah!
Death-light of Africa!
Don John of Austria
Is riding to the sea.

Robert Frost

Fire and Ice

Some say the world will end in fire,
Some say in ice.
From what I've tasted of desire
I hold with those who favour fire.
But if it had to perish twice,
I think I know enough of hate
To say that for destruction ice
Is also great
And would suffice.

The Road Not Taken

Two roads diverged in a yellow wood,
And sorry I could not travel both
And be one traveller, long I stood
And looked down one as far as I could
To where it bent in the undergrowth;

Then took the other, as just as fair,
And having perhaps the better claim,
Because it was grassy and wanted wear;
Though as for that the passing there
Had worn them really about the same,

And both that morning equally lay
In leaves no step had trodden black.
Oh, I kept the first for another day!
Yet knowing how way leads on to way,
I doubted if I should ever come back.

I shall be telling this with a sigh
Somewhere ages and ages hence:
Two roads diverged in a wood, and I—
I took the one less travelled by,
And that has made all the difference.

Mending Wall

Something there is that doesn't love a wall,
That sends the frozen-ground-swell under it,
And spills the upper boulders in the sun;
And makes gaps even two can pass abreast.
The work of hunters is another thing:
I have come after them and made repair
Where they have left not one stone on a stone,
But they would have the rabbit out of hiding,
To please the yelping dogs. The gaps I mean,
No one has seen them made or heard them made,
But at spring mending-time we find them there.
I let my neighbour know beyond the hill;
And on a day we meet to walk the line
And set the wall between us once again.
We keep the wall between us as we go.
To each the boulders that have fallen to each.
And some are loaves and some so nearly balls
We have to use a spell to make them balance:
'Stay where you are until our backs are turned!'
We wear our fingers rough with handling them.
Oh, just another kind of out-door game,
One on a side. It comes to little more:
There where it is we do not need the wall:
He is all pine and I am apple orchard.
My apple trees will never get across
And eat the cones under his pines, I tell him.
He only says, 'Good fences make good neighbours.'
Spring is the mischief in me, and I wonder
If I could put a notion in his head:
'Why do they make good neighbours? Isn't it
Where there are cows? But here there are no cows.
Before I built a wall I'd ask to know
What I was walling in or walling out,

And to whom I was like to give offence.
Something there is that doesn't love a wall,
That wants it down.' I could say 'Elves' to him,
But it's not elves exactly, and I'd rather
He said it for himself. I see him there
Bringing a stone grasped firmly by the top
In each hand, like an old-stone savage armed.
He moves in darkness as it seems to me,
Not of woods only and the shade of trees.
He will not go behind his father's saying,
And he likes having thought of it so well
He says again, 'Good fences make good neighbours.'

Robert Service

The Shooting of Dan McGrew

A bunch of the boys were whooping it up in the Malamute saloon;
The kid that handles the music-box was hitting a jag-time tune;
Back of the bar, in a solo game, sat Dangerous Dan McGrew,
And watching his luck was his light-o'-love, the lady that's known
    as Lou.
When out of the night, which was fifty below, and into the din and
    the glare,
There stumbled a miner fresh from the creeks, dog-dirty and
    loaded for bear.
He looked like a man with a foot in the grave, and scarcely the
    strength of a louse,
Yet he tilted a poke of dust on the bar, and he called for drinks for
    the house.
There was none could place the stranger's face, though we
    searched ourselves for a clue;
But we drank his health, and the last to drink was Dangerous Dan
    McGrew.

There's men that somehow just grip your eyes, and hold them hard
    like a spell;
And such was he, and he looked to me like a man who had lived in
    hell;
With a face most hair, and the dreary stare of a dog whose day is
    done.
As he watered the green stuff in his glass, and the drops fell one by
    one.

Then I got to figgering who he was, and wondering what he'd do.
And I turned my head — and there watching him was the lady
    that's known as Lou.

His eyes went rubbering round the room, and he seemed in a kind
    of daze,
Till at last that old piano fell in the way of his wandering gaze.
The rag-time kid was having a drink; there was no one else on the
    stool,
So the stranger stumbles across the room, and flops down there
    like a fool.
In a buckskin shirt that was glazed with dirt he sat, and I saw him
    sway;
Then he clutched the keys with his talon hands — my God! but that
    man could play!

Were you ever out in the Great Alone, when the moon was awful
    clear,
And the icy mountains hemmed you in with a silence you most
    could *hear*;
With only the howl of a timber wolf, and you camped there in the
    cold.
A half-dead thing in stark, dead world, clean made for the muck
    called gold;
While high overhead, green, yellow, and red, the North Lights
    swept in bars—
Then you've a hunch what the music meant . . . hunger and night
    and the stars.

And hunger not of the belly kind, that's banished with bacon and
    beans;
But the gnawing hunger of lonely men for a home and all that it
    means;
For a fireside far from the cares that are, four walls and a roof
    above;
But oh! so cramful of cosy joy, and crowned with a woman's love;
A woman dearer than all the world, and true as Heaven is true—
(God! how ghastly she looks through her rouge — the lady that's
    known as Lou.)

Then on a sudden the music changed, so soft that you scarce could
    hear;
But you felt that your life had been looted clean of all that it once
    held dear;
That some-one had stolen the woman you loved; that her love was
    a devil's lie;

That your guts were gone, and the best for you was to crawl away
    and die.
'Twas the crowning cry of a heart's despair, and it thrilled you
    through and through—
'I guess I'll make it a spread misere,' said Dangerous Dan
    McGrew.

The music almost died away . . . then it burst like a pent-up flood;
And it seemed to say, 'Repay, repay,' and my eyes were blind with
    blood.
The thought came back of an ancient wrong, and its stung like a
    frozen lash,
And the lust awoke to kill, to kill . . . then the music stopped with
    a crash,
And the stranger turned, and and his eyes they burned in a most
    peculiar way;
In a buckskin shirt that was glazed with dirt he sat, and I saw him
    sway;
Then his lips went in in a kind of grin, and he spoke, and his voice
    was calm;
And, 'Boys,' says he, 'you don't know me, and none of you care a
    damn;
But I want to state, and my words are straight and I'll bet my poke
    they're true,
That one of you is a hound of hell . . . and that one is Dan
    McGrew.'

Then I ducked my head, and the lights went out, and two guns
    blazed in the dark;
And a woman screamed, and the lights went up, and two men lay
    stiff and stark;
Pitched on his head, and pumped full of lead, was Dangerous Dan
    McGrew,
While the man from the creeks lay clutched to the breast of the
    lady that's known as Lou.

These are the simple facts of the case, and I guess I ought to know;
They say that the stranger was crazed with 'hooch', and I'm not
    denying it's so.
I'm not so wise as the lawyer guys, but strictly between us two—
The woman that kissed him and – pinched his poke – was the lady
    that's known as Lou.

Edward Thomas

Adlestrop

Yes. I remember Adlestrop—
The name, because one afternoon
Of heat the express-train drew up there
Unwontedly. It was late June.

The steam hissed. Someone cleared his throat.
No one left and no one came
On the bare platform. What I saw
Was Adlestrop – only the name

And willows, willow-herb, and grass,
And meadowsweet, and haycocks dry,
No whit less still and lonely fair
Than the high cloudlets in the sky.

And for that minute a blackbird sang
Close by, and round him, mistier,
Farther and farther, all the birds
Of Oxfordshire and Gloucestershire.

John Masefield

Cargoes

Quinquireme of Nineveh from distant Ophir
Rowing home to haven in sunny Palestine,
With a cargo of ivory,
And apes and peacocks,
Sandalwood, cedarwood, and sweet white wine.

Stately Spanish galleon coming from the Isthmus,
Dipping through the Tropics by the palm-green shores,
With a cargo of diamonds,
Emeralds, amethysts,
Topazes, and cinnamon, and gold moidores.

Dirty British coaster with a salt-caked smoke stack
Butting through the Channel in the mad March days,

With a cargo of Tyne coal,
Road-rail, pig-lead,
Firewood, iron-ware, and cheap tin trays.

Sea-Fever

I must go down to the seas again, to the lonely sea and the sky,
And all I ask is a tall ship and a star to steer her by,
And the wheel's kick and the wind's song and the white sail's
     shaking,
And a grey mist on the sea's face and a grey dawn breaking.

I must go down to the seas again, for the call of the running tide
Is a wild call and a clear call that may not be denied;
And all I ask is a windy day with the white clouds flying,
And the flung spray and the blown spume, and the sea-gulls crying.

I must go down to the seas again, to the vagrant gipsy life,
To the gull's way and the whale's way where the wind's like a
     whetted knife;
And all I ask is a merry yarn from a laughing fellow-rover,
And quiet sleep and a sweet dream when the long trick's over.

Alfred Noyes

The Highwayman
I

The wind was a torrent of darkness among the gusty trees,
The moon was a ghostly galleon tossed upon cloudy seas,
The road was a ribbon of moonlight over the purple moor,
And the highwayman came riding—
          Riding – riding—
The highwayman came riding, up to the old inn-door.

He'd a French cocked-hat on his forehead, a bunch of lace at his
     chin,
A coat of claret velvet, and breeches of brown doe-skin;
They fitted with never a wrinkle: his boots were up to the thigh!
And he rode with a jewelled twinkle,
          His pistol butts a-twinkle,
His rapier hilt a-twinkle, under the jewelled sky.

Over the cobbles he clattered and clashed in the dark inn-yard,
And he tapped with his whip on the shutters, but all was locked
    and barred;
He whistled a tune to the window, and who should be waiting
    there
But the landlord's black-eyed daughter,
        Bess, the landlord's daughter,
Plaiting a dark red love-knot into her long black hair.

And dark in the old inn-yard a stable-wicket creaked
Where Tim the ostler listened; his face was white and peaked;
His eyes were hollows of madness, his hair like mouldy hay,
But he loved the landlord's daughter,
        The landlord's red-lipped daughter;
Dumb as a dog he listened, and he heard the robber say—

'One kiss, my bonny sweetheart, I'm after a prize to-night,
But I shall be back with the yellow gold before the morning light;
Yet, if they press me sharply, and harry me through the day,
Then look for me by moonlight,
        Watch for me by moonlight,
I'll come to thee by moonlight, though hell should bar the way.'

He rose upright in the stirrups; he scarce could reach her hand,
But she loosened her hair i' the casement! His face burnt like a
    brand
As the black cascade of perfume came tumbling over his breast;
And he kissed its waves in the moonlight,
        (Oh, sweet black waves in the moonlight!)
Then he tugged at his rein in the moonlight, and galloped away to
    the west.

II

He did not come in the dawning; he did not come at noon;
And out o' the tawny sunset, before the rise o' the moon,
When the road was a gipsy's ribbon, looping the purple moor,
A red-coat troop came marching—
        Marching – marching—
King George's men came marching, up to the old inn-door.

They said no word to the landlord, they drank his ale instead,
But they gagged his daughter and bound her to the foot of her
    narrow bed;
Two of them knelt at her casement, with muskets at their side!

There was death at every window;
        And hell at one dark window;
For Bess could see, through her casement, the road that *he* would
    ride.

They had tied her up to attention, with many a sniggering jest;
They had bound a musket beside her, with the barrel beneath her
    breast!
'Now keep good watch!' and they kissed her.
        She heard the dead man say—
Look for me by moonlight;
        Watch for me by moonlight;
I'll come to thee by moonlight, though hell should bar the way!

She twisted her hands behind her; but all the knots held good!
She writhed her hands till her fingers were wet with sweat or
    blood!
They stretched and strained in the darkness, and the hours crawled
    by like years,
Till, now, on the stroke of midnight,
        Cold, on the stroke of midnight,
The tip of one finger touched it! The trigger at least was hers!

The tip of one finger touched it; she strove no more for the rest!
Up, she stood to attention, with the barrel beneath her breast,
She would not risk their hearing; she would not strive again;
For the road lay bare in the moonlight;
        Blank and bare in the moonlight;
And the blood of her veins in the moonlight throbbed to her love's
    refrain.

Tlot-tlot; tlot-tlot! Had they heard it? The horse-hoofs ringing
    clear;
Tlot-tlot, tlot-tlot, in the distance? Were they deaf that they did
    not hear?
Down the ribbon of moonlight, over the brow of the hill,
The highwayman came riding,
        Riding, riding!
The red-coats looked to their priming! She stood up, straight and
    still!

Tlot-tlot in the frosty silence! *tlot-tlot,* in the echoing night!
Nearer he came and nearer! Her face was like a light!
Her eyes grew wide for a moment; she drew one last deep breath,
Then her finger moved in the moonlight,
        Her musket shattered the moonlight,
Shattered her breast in the moonlight and warned him – with her
    death.

He turned; he spurred to the westward; he did not know who
    stood
Bowed, with her head o'er the musket, drenched with her own red
    blood!
Not till the dawn he heard it, and slowly blanched to hear
How Bess, the landlord's daughter,
        The landlord's black-eyed daughter,
Had watched for her love in the moonlight, and died in the
    darkness there.

Back, he spurred like a madman, shrieking a curse to the sky,
With the white road smoking behind him and his rapier
    brandished high!
Blood-red were his spurs i' the golden noon; wine-red was his
    velvet coat;
When they shot him down on the highway,
        Down like a dog on the highway,
And he lay his blood on the highway, with the bunch of lace at his
    throat.

And still of a winter's night, they say, when the wind is in the
    trees,
When the moon is a ghostly galleon tossed upon cloudy seas,
When the road is a ribbon of moonlight over the purple moor,
A highwayman comes riding—
        Riding – riding—
A highwayman comes riding, up to the old inn-door.

Over the cobbles he clatters and clangs in the dark inn-yard,
And he taps with his whip on the shutters, but all is locked and
    barred;
He whistles a tune to the window, and who should be waiting
    there
But the landlord's black-eyed daughter,
        Bess, the landlord's daughter,
Plaiting a dark red love-knot into her long black hair.

John Drinkwater

Moonlit Apples

At the top of the house the apples are laid in rows,
And the skylight lets the moonlight in, and those
Apples are deep-sea apples of green. There goes
   A cloud on the moon in the autumn night.

A mouse in the wainscot scratches, and scratches, and then
There is no sound at the top of the house of men
Or mice; and the cloud is blown, and the moon again
   Dapples the apples with deep-sea light.

They are lying in rows there, under the gloomy beams;
On the sagging floor; they gather the silver streams
Out of the moon, those moonlit apples of dreams,
   And quiet is the steep stair under.

In the corridors under there is nothing but sleep.
And stiller than ever on orchard boughs they keep
Tryst with the moon, and deep is the silence, deep
   On moon-washed apples of wonder.

William Carlos Williams

This is Just to Say

I have eaten
the plums
that were in
the icebox

and which
you were probably
saving
for breakfast

Forgive me
they were delicious
so sweet
and so cold

James Elroy Flecker

From Hassan

[Soldiers' Song]

We are they who come faster than fate: we are they who ride early
  or late:
We storm at your ivory gate: pale kings of the sunset beware!
Not on silk nor in samet we lie, not in curtained solemnity die
Among women who chatter and cry and children who mumble a
  prayer.
But we sleep by the ropes of the camp, and we rise with a shout
  and we tramp
With the sun or the moon for a lamp, and the spray of the wind in
  our hair.

From the lands where the elephants are to the forts of Merou and
  Balghar.
Our steel we have brought and our star to shine on the ruins of
  Rum.
We have marched from the Indus to Spain, and by God we will go
  there again;
We have stood on the shore of the plain where the Waters of
  Destiny boom.
A mart of destruction we made at Yalula where men were afraid,
For death was a difficult trade, and the sword was a broker of
  doom;
And the Spear was a Desert Physician, who cured not a few of
  ambition,
And drave not to few to perdition with medicine bitter and strong.

And the shield was a grief to the fool and as bright as a desolate
  pool,
And as straight as the rock of Stamboul when their cavalry
  thundered along:
For the coward was drowned with the brave when our battle
  sheered up like a wave,
And the dead to the desert we gave, and the glory to God in our
  song.

David Herbert Lawrence

Snake

A snake came to my water-trough
On a hot, hot day, and I in pyjamas for the heat,
To drink there.

In the deep, strange-scented shade of the great dark carob-tree
I came down the steps with my pitcher
And must wait, must stand and wait, for there he was at the
    trough before me.

He reached down from a fissure in the earth-wall in the gloom
And trailed his yellow-brown slackness soft-bellied down, over the
    edge of the stone trough
And rested his throat upon the stone bottom,
And where the water had dripped from the tap, in a small
    clearness,
He sipped with his straight mouth,
Softly drank through his straight gums, into his slack long body.
Silently.

Someone was before me at my water-trough,
And I, like a second comer, waiting.

He lifted his head from his drinking, as cattle do,
And looked at me vaguely, as drinking cattle do,
And flickered his two-forked tongue from his lips, and mused a
    moment,
And stooped and drank a little more,
Being earth-brown, earth-golden from the burning bowels of the
    earth
On the day of Sicilian July, with Etna smoking.

The voice of my education said to me
He must be killed,
For in Sicily the black, black snakes are innocent, the gold are
    venomous.

And voices in me said, If you were a man
You would take a stick and break him now, and finish him off.

But must I confess how I liked him,
How glad I was he had come like a guest in quiet, to drink at my
    water-trough

And depart peaceful, pacified, and thankless,
Into the burning bowels of this earth?

Was it cowardice, that I dared not kill him?
Was it perversity, that I longed to talk to him?
Was it humility, to feel so honoured?
I felt so honoured.

And yet those voices:
If you were not afraid, you would kill him!

And truly I was afraid, I was most afraid,
But even so, honoured still more
That he should seek my hospitality
From out the dark door of the secret earth.

He drank enough
And lifted his head, dreamily, as one who has drunken,
And flickered his tongue like a forked night on the air, so black,
Seeming to lick his lips,
And looked around like a god, unseeing, into the air,
And slowly turned his head,
And slowly, very slowly, as if thrice adream,
Proceeded to draw his slow length curving round
And climb again the broken bank of my wall-face.

And as he put his head into that dreadful hole,
And as he slowly drew up, snake-easing his shoulders, and entered
        farther,
A sort of horror, a sort of protest against his withdrawing into that
        horrid black hole,
Deliberately going into the blackness, and slowly drawing himself
        after,
Overcame me now his back was turned.

I looked round, I put down my pitcher,
I picked up a clumsy log
And threw it at the water-trough with a clatter.

I think it did not hit him,
But suddenly that part of him that was left behind convulsed in
        undignified haste,
Writhed like lightning, and was gone
Into the black hole, the earth-lipped fissure in the wall-front,
At which, in the intense still noon, I stared with fascination.

And immediately I regretted it,
I thought how paltry, how vulgar, what a mean act!
I despised myself and the voices of my accursed human education.

And I thought of the albatross,
And I wished he would come back, my snake.

For he seemed to me again like a king,
Like a king in exile, uncrowned in the underworld,
Now due to be crowned again.

And so, I missed my chance with one of the lords
Of life.
And I have something to expiate;
A pettiness.

Joyce Kilmer

Trees

I think that I shall never see
A poem lovely as a tree.

A tree whose hungry mouth is prest
Against the earth's sweet flowing breast;

A tree that looks at God all day,
And lifts her leafy arms to pray;

A tree that may in summer wear
A nest of robins in her hair;

Upon whose bosom snow has lain;
Who intimately lives with rain.

Poems are made by fools like me,
But only God can make a tree.

Frances Cornford

To a Fat Lady Seen from the Train

O why do you walk through the fields in gloves,
    Missing so much and so much?
O fat white woman, whom nobody loves,
Why do you walk through the fields in gloves,
When the grass is soft as the breast of doves

And shivering-sweet to the touch?
O why do you walk through the fields in gloves,
Missing so much and so much?

Siegfried Sassoon

Everyone Sang

Everyone suddenly burst out singing;
And I was filled with such delight
As prisoned birds must find in freedom
Winging wildly across·the white
Orchards and dark-green fields; on; on; and out of sight.

Everyone's voice was suddenly lifted,
And beauty came like the setting sun.
My heart was shaken with tears; and horror
Drifted away . . . O but everyone
Was a bird; and the song was wordless; the singing will never be
    done

Rupert Brooke

The Old Vicarage, Grantchester

(Café des Westens, Berlin, May 1912)

Just now the lilac is in bloom,
All before my little room;
And in my flower-beds, I think,
Smile the carnation and the pink;
And down the borders, well I know,
The poppy and the pansy blow . . .
Oh! there the chestnuts, summer through,
Beside the river make for you
A tunnel of green gloom, and sleep
Deeply above; and green and deep
The stream mysterious glides beneath,
Green as a dream and deep as death.
– Oh, damn! I know it! and I know

How the May fields all golden show,
And when the day is young and sweet,
Gild gloriously the bare feet
That run to bathe . . .
                    Du lieber Gott!

Here I am, sweating, sick, and hot,
And there the shadowed waters fresh
Lean up to embrace the naked flesh.
Temperamentvoll German Jews
Drink beer around — and *there* the dews
Are soft beneath a morn of gold.
Here tulips bloom as they are told;
Unkempt about those hedges blows
An English unofficial rose;
And there the unregulated sun
Slopes down to rest when day is done,
And wakes a vague unpunctual star,
A slippered Hesper; and there are
Meads towards Haslingfield and Coton
Where *das Betreten's* not *verboten.*

Ε᾿ίθε γευσίμην . . . would I were
In Grantchester, in Grantchester!
Some, it may be, can get in touch
With Nature there, or Earth, or such.
And clever modern men have seen
A Faun a-peeping through the green,
And felt the Classics were not dead,
To glimpse a Naiad's reedy head,
Or hear the Goat-foot piping low: . . .
But these are things I do not know.
I only know that you may lie
Day-long and watch the Cambridge sky,
And, flower-lulled in sleepy grass,
Hear the cool lapse of hours pass,
Until the centuries blend and blur
In Grantchester, in Grantchester . . .
Still in the dawnlit waters cool
His ghostly Lordship swims his pool,
And tries the strokes, essays the tricks,
Long learnt on Hellespont, or Styx.
Dan Chaucer hears his river still
Chatter beneath a phantom mill.

Tennyson notes, with studious eye,
How Cambridge waters hurry by . . .
And in that garden, black and white,
Creep whispers through the grass all night;
And spectral dance, before the dawn,
A hundred Vicars down the lawn;
Curates, long dust, will come and go
On lissom, clerical, printless toe;
And oft between the boughs is seen
The sly shade of a Rural Dean . . .
Till, at a shiver in the skies,
Vanishing with Satanic cries,
The prim ecclesiastic rout
Leaves but a startled sleeper-out,
Grey heavens, the first bird's drowsy calls,
The falling house that never falls.

God! I will pack, and take a train,
And get me to England once again!
For England's the one land, I know,
Where men with Splendid Hearts may go;
And Cambridgeshire, of all England,
The shire for Men who Understand;
And of *that* district I prefer
The lovely hamlet Grantchester.
For Cambridge people rarely smile,
Being urban, squat, and packed with guile;
And Royston men in the far South
Are black and fierce and strange of mouth;
At Over they fling oaths at one,
And worse than oaths at Trumpington,
And Ditton girls are mean and dirty,
And there's none in Harston under thirty,
And folks in Shelford and those parts
Have twisted lips and twisted hearts,
And Barton men make Cockney rhymes,
And Coton's full of nameless crimes,
And things are done you'd not believe
At Madingley, on Christmas Eve.
Strong men have run on for miles and miles,
When one from Cherry Hinton smiles;
Strong men have blanched, and shot their wives,
Rather than send them to St Ives;
Strong men have cried like babes, bydam,

To hear what happened at Babraham.
But Grantchester! ah, Grantchester!
There's peace and holy quiet there,
Great clouds along pacific skies,
And men and women with straight eyes,
Lithe children lovelier than a dream,
A bosky wood, a slumbrous stream,
And little kindly winds that creep
Round twilight corners, half asleep.
In Grantchester their skins are white;
They bathe by day, they bathe by night;
The women there do all they ought;
The men observe the Rules of Thought.
They love the Good; they worship Truth;
They laugh uproariously in youth;
(And when they get to feeling old,
They up and shoot themselves, I'm told) . . .

    Ah God! to see the branches stir
Across the moon at Grantchester!
To smell the thrilling-sweet and rotten
Unforgettable, unforgotten
River-smell, and hear the breeze
Sobbing in the little trees.
Say, do the elm-clumps greatly stand
Still guardians of that holy land?
The chestnuts shade, in reverend dream,
The yet unacademic stream?
Is dawn a secret shy and cold
Anadyomene, silver-gold?
And sunset still a golden sea
From Haslingfield to Madingley?
And after, ere the night is born,
Do hares come out about the corn?
Oh, is the water sweet and cool,
Gentle and brown, above the pool?
And laughs the immortal river still
Under the mill, under the mill?
Say, is there Beauty yet to find?
And Certainty? and Quiet kind?
Deep meadows yet, for to forget
The lies, and truths, and pain? . . . oh! yet
Stands the Church clock at ten to three?
And is there honey still for tea?

The Soldier

If I should die, think only this of me:
  That there's some corner of a foreign field
That is for ever England. There shall be
  In that rich earth a richer dust concealed;
A dust whom England bore, shaped, made aware,
  Gave, once, her flowers to love, her ways to roam,
A body of England's breathing English air,
  Washed by the rivers, blessed by suns of home.

And think, this heart, all evil shed away,
  A pulse in the eternal mind, no less
    Gives somewhere back the thoughts by England given;
Her sights and sounds; dreams happy as her day;
  And laughter, learnt of friends; and gentleness,
    In hearts at peace, under an English heaven.

Thomas Stearns Eliot

The Love Song of J. Alfred Prufrock

*S'io credessi che mia risposta fosse
a persona che mai tornasse al mondo,
questa fiamma staria senza più scosse.
Ma per ciò che giammai di questo fondo
non tornò vivo alcun, s'i'odo il vero,
senza tema d'infamia ti rispondo.*

Let us go then, you and I,
When the evening is spread out against the sky
Like a patient etherised upon a table;
Let us go, through certain half-deserted streets,
The muttering retreats
Of restless nights in one-night cheap hotels
And sawdust restaurants with oyster-shells:
Streets that follow like a tedious argument
Of insidious intent
To lead you to an overwhelming question . . .
Oh, do not ask, 'What is it?'
Let us go and make our visit.

In the room the women come and go
Talking of Michelangelo.

The yellow fog that rubs its back upon the window-panes,
The yellow smoke that rubs its muzzle on the window-panes,
Licked its tongue into the corners of the evening,
Lingered upon the pools that stand in drains,
Let fall upon its back the soot that falls from chimneys,
Slipped by the terrace, made a sudden leap,
And seeing that it was a soft October night,
Curled once about the house, and fell asleep.

And indeed there will be time
For the yellow smoke that slides along the street
Rubbing its back upon the window-panes;
There will be time, there will be time
To prepare a face to meet the faces that you meet;
There will be time to murder and create,
And time for all the works and days of hands
That lift and drop a question on your plate;
Time for you and time for me,
And time yet for a hundred indecisions,
And for a hundred visions and revisions,
Before the taking of a toast and tea.

In the room the women come and go
Talking of Michelangelo.

And indeed there will be time
To wonder, 'Do I care?' and, 'Do I dare?'
Time to turn back and descend the stair,
With a bald spot in the middle of my hair—
(They will say: 'How his hair is growing thin!')
My morning coat, my collar mounting firmly to the chin,
My necktie rich and modest, but asserted by a simple pin—
(They will say: 'But how his arms and legs are thin!')
Do I dare
Disturb the universe?
In a minute there is time
For decisions and revisions which a minute will reverse.

For I have known them all already, known them all—
Have known the evenings, mornings, afternoons,
I have measured out my life with coffee spoons;
I know the voices dying with a dying fall
Beneath the music from a farther room.
So how should I presume?

And I have known the eyes already, known them all—
The eyes that fix you in a formulated phrase,
And when I am formulated, sprawling on a pin,
When I am pinned and wriggling on the wall,
Then how should I begin
To spit out all the butt-ends of my days and ways?
    And how should I presume?

And I have known the arms already, known them all—
Arms that are braceleted and white and bare
(But in the lamplight, downed with light brown hair!)
Is it perfume from a dress
That makes me so digress?
Arms that lie along a table, or wrap about a shawl.
    And should I then presume?
    And how should I begin?

    ·   ·   ·   ·   ·

Shall I say, I have gone at dusk through narrow streets
And watched the smoke that rises from the pipes
Of lonely men in shirt-sleeves, leaning out of windows? . . .

I should have been a pair of ragged claws
Scuttling across the floors of silent seas.

    ·   ·   ·   ·   ·

And the afternoon, the evening, sleeps so peacefully!
Smoothed by long fingers,
Asleep . . . tired . . . or it malingers,
Stretched on the floor, here beside you and me.
Should I, after tea and cakes and ices,
Have the strength to force the moment to its crisis?
But though I have wept and fasted, wept and prayed,
Though I have seen my head (grown slightly bald) brought in
    upon a platter,
I am no prophet – and here's no great matter;
I have seen the moment of my greatness flicker,
And I have seen the eternal Footman hold my coat, and snicker,
And in short, I was afraid.

And would it have been worth it, after all,
After the cups, the marmalade, the tea,
Among the porcelain, among some talk of you and me,
Would it have been worth while,
To have bitten off the matter with a smile,
To have squeezed the universe into a ball

To roll it toward some overwhelming question,
To say: I am Lazarus, come from the dead,
Come back to tell you all, I shall tell you all'—
If one, settling a pillow by her head,
    Should say: 'That is not what I meant at all.
    That is not it, at all.'

    And would it have been worth it, after all,
Would it have been worth while,
After the sunsets and the dooryards and the sprinkled streets,
After the novels, after the teacups, after the skirts that trail along
    the floor—
And this, and so much more?—
It is impossible to say just what I mean!
But as if a magic lantern threw the nerves in patterns on a screen:
Would it have been worth while
If one, settling a pillow or throwing off a shawl,
And turning toward the window, should say:
    'That is not it at all,
    That is not what I meant, at all.'
        .   .   .   .   .

    No! I am not Prince Hamlet, nor was meant to be;
Am an attendant lord, one that will do
To swell a progress, start a scene or two,
Advise the prince; no doubt, an easy tool,
Deferential, glad to be of use,
Politic, cautious, and meticulous;
Full of high sentence, but a bit obtuse;
At times, indeed, almost ridiculous—
Almost, at times, the Fool

    I grow old . . . I grow old . . .
I shall wear the bottoms of my trousers rolled.

    Shall I part my hair behind? Do I dare eat a peach?
I shall wear white flannel trousers, and walk upon the beach.
I have heard the mermaids singing, each to each.

I do not think that they will sing to me.

I have seen them riding seaward on the waves
Combing the white hair of the waves blown back
When the wind blows the water white and black.

We have lingered in the chambers of the sea
By sea-girls wreathed with seaweed red and brown
Till human voices wake us, and we drown.

Journey of the Magi

'A cold coming we had of it,
Just the worst time of the year
For a journey, and such a long journey:
The ways deep and the weather sharp,
The very dead of winter.'
And the camels galled, sore-footed, refractory,
Lying down in the melting snow.
There were times we regretted
The summer palaces on slopes, the terraces,
And the silken girls bringing sherbet.
Then the camel men cursing and grumbling
And running away, and wanting their liquor and women,
And the night-fires going out, and the lack of shelters,
And the cities hostile and the towns unfriendly
And the villages dirty and charging high prices:
A hard time we had of it.
At the end we preferred to travel all night,
Sleeping in snatches,
With the voices singing in our ears, saying
That this was all folly.

Then at dawn we came down to a temperate valley,
Wet, below the snow line, smelling of vegetation,
With a running stream and water-mill beating the darkness,
And three trees on the low sky,
And an old white horse galloped away in the meadow.
Then we came to a tavern with vine-leaves over the lintel,
Six hands at an open door dicing for pieces of silver,
And feet kicking the empty wine-skins.
But there was no information, and so we continued
And arrived at evening, not a moment too soon
Finding the place; it was (you may say) satisfactory.

All this was a long time ago, I remember,
And I would do it again, but set down
This set down
This: were we led all that way for
Birth or Death? There was a Birth, certainly,
We had evidence and no doubt. I had seen birth and death,
But had thought they were different; this Birth was
Hard and bitter agony for us, like Death, our death.
We returned to our places, these Kingdoms,

But no longer at ease here, in the old dispensation,
With an alien people clutching their gods.
I should be glad of another death.

The Song of the Jellicles

Jellicle Cats come out to-night,
Jellicle Cats come one come all:
The Jellicle Moon is shining bright—
Jellicles come to the Jellicle Ball.

Jellicle Cats are black and white,
Jellicle Cats are rather small;
Jellicle Cats are merry and bright,
And pleasant to hear when they caterwaul.
Jellicle Cats have cheerful faces,
Jellicle Cats have bright black eyes;
They like to practise their airs and graces
And wait for the Jellicle Moon to rise.

Jellicle Cats develop slowly,
Jellicle Cats are not too big;
Jellicle Cats are roly-poly,
They know how to dance a gavotte and a jig.
Until the Jellicle Moon appears
They make their toilette and take their repose:
Jellicles wash behind their ears,
Jellicles dry between their toes.

Jellicle Cats are white and black,
Jellicle Cats are of moderate size;
Jellicles jump like a jumping-jack,
Jellicle Cats have moonlit eyes.
They're quiet enough in the morning hours,
They're quiet enough in the afternoon,
Reserving their terpsichorean powers
To dance by the light of the Jellicle Moon.

Jellicle Cats are black and white,
Jellicle Cats (as I said) are small;
If it happens to be a stormy night
They will practise a caper or two in the hall.
If it happens the sun is shining bright

You would say they had nothing to do at all:
They are resting and saving themselves to be right
For the Jellicle Moon and the Jellicle Ball.

Walter James Turner

Romance

When I was but thirteen or so
    I went into a golden land,
Chimborazo, Cotopaxi
    Took me by the hand.

My father died, my brother too,
    They passed like fleeting dreams.
I stood where Popocatapetl
    In the sunlight gleams.

I dimly heard the master's voice
    And boys far-off at play,
Chimborazo, Cotopaxi
    Had stolen me away.

I walked in a great golden dream
    To and fro from school—
Shining Popocatapetl
    The dusty streets did rule

I walked home with a gold dark boy,
    And never a word I'd say,
Chimborazo, Cotopaxi
    Had taken my speech away:

I gazed entranced upon his face
    Fairer than any flower—
O shining Popocatapetl
    It was thy magic hour:

The houses, people, traffic seemed
    Thin fading dreams by day,
Chimborazo, Cotopaxi
    They had stolen my soul away!

Edna St Vincent Millay

First Fig

My candle burns at both ends;
  It will not last the night;
But ah, my foes, and oh, my friends—
  It gives a lovely light!

Wilfred Owen

Strange Meeting

It seemed that out of battle I escaped
Down some profound dull tunnel, long since scooped
Through granites which titanic wars had groined.
Yet also there encumbered sleepers groaned,
Too fast in thought or death to be bestirred.
Then, as I probed them, one sprang up, and stared
With piteous recognition in fixed eyes,
Lifting distressful hands as if to bless.
And by his smile, I knew that sullen hall,
By his dead smile I knew we stood in Hell.
With a thousand pains that vision's face was grained;
Yet no blood reached there from the upper ground,
And no guns thumped, or down the flues made moan.
'Strange friend,' I said, 'here is no cause to mourn.'
'None,' said the other, 'save the undone years,
The hopelessness. Whatever hope is yours,
Was my life also; I went hunting wild
After the wildest beauty in the world,
Which lies not calm in eyes, or braided hair,
But mocks the steady running of the hour,
And if it grieves, grieves richlier than here.
For by my glee might many men have laughed,
And of my weeping something had been left,
Which must die now. I mean the truth untold,
The pity of war, the pity war distilled.
Now men will go content with what we spoiled.
Or, discontent, boil bloody, and be spilled.
They will be swift with swiftness of the tigress,

None will break ranks, though nations trek from progress.
Courage was mine, and I had mystery,
Wisdom was mine, and I had mastery;
To miss the march of the retreating world
Into vain citadels that are not walled.
Then, when much blood had clogged their chariot-wheels
I would go up and wash them from sweet wells,
Even with truths that lie too deep for taint.
I would have poured my spirit without stint
But not through wounds; not on the cess of war.
Foreheads of men have bled where no wounds were.
I am the enemy you killed, my friend.
I knew you in this dark; for so you frowned
Yesterday through me as you jabbed and killed.
I parried; but my hands were loath and cold.
Let us sleep now. . . .'

e. e. cummings

'anyone lived in a pretty how town'

anyone lived in a pretty how town
(with up so floating many bells down)
spring summer autumn winter
he sang his didn't he danced his did.

Women and men (both little and small)
cared for anyone not at all
they sowed their isn't they reaped their same
sun moon stars rain

children guessed (but only a few
and down they forgot as up they grew
autumn winter spring summer)
that noone loved him more by more

when by now and tree by leaf
she laughed his joy she cried his grief
bird by snow and stir by still
anyone's any was all to her

someones married their everyones
laughed their cryings and did their dance
(sleep wake hope and then) they
said their nevers they slept their dream

stars rain sun moon
(and only the snow can begin to explain
how children are apt to forget to remember
with up so floating many bells down)

one day anyone died i guess
(and noone stooped to kiss his face)
busy folk buried them side by side
little by little and was by was

all by all and deep by deep
and more by more they dream their sleep
noone and anyone earth by april
wish by spirit and if by yes.

Women and men (both dong and ding)
summer autumn winter spring
reaped their sowing and went their came
sun moon stars rain

'next to of course god america i'

'next to of course god america i
love you land of the pilgrims' and so forth oh
say can you see by the dawn's early my
country 'tis of centuries come and go
and are no more what of it we should worry
in every language even deafanddumb
thy sons acclaim your glorious name by gorry
by jingo by gee by gosh by gum
why talk of beauty what could be more beaut-
iful than these heroic happy dead
who rushed like lions to the roaring slaughter
they did not stop to think they died instead
then shall the voice of liberty be mute?'

He spoke. And drank rapidly a glass of water.

Robert Graves

Welsh Incident

'But that was nothing to what things came out
From the sea-caves of Criccieth yonder.'
'What were they? Mermaids? dragons? ghosts?'
'Nothing at all of any things like that.'
'What were they, then?'
       'All sorts of queer things,
Things never seen or heard or written about,
Very strange, un-Welsh, utterly peculiar
Things. Oh, solid enough they seemed to touch,
Had anyone dared it. Marvellous creation,
All various shapes and sizes, and no sizes,
All new, each perfectly unlike his neighbour,
Though all came moving slowly out together.'
'Describe just one of them.'
      'I am unable.'
'What were their colours?'
 'Mostly nameless colours,
Colours you'd like to see; but one was puce
Or perhaps more like crimson, but not purplish.
   Some had no colour.'
        'Tell me, had they legs?'
'Not a leg nor foot among them that I saw.'
'But did these things come out in any order?'
What o'clock was it? What was the day of the week?
Who else was present? How was the weather?
'I was coming to that. It was half-past three
On Easter Tuesday last. The sun was shining.
The Harlech Silver Band played *Marchog Jesu*
On thirty-seven shimmering instruments,
Collecting for Caernarvon's (Fever) Hospital Fund.
The populations of Pwllheli, Criccieth,
Portmadoc, Borth, Tremadoc, Penrhyndeudraeth,
Were all assembled. Criccieth's mayor addressed them
First in good Welsh and then in fluent English,
Twisting his fingers in his chain of office,
Welcoming the things. They came out on the sand,
Not keeping time to the band, moving seaward
Silently at a snail's pace. But at last

The most odd, indescribable thing of all,
Which hardly one man there could see for wonder,
Did something recognizably a something.'
'Well, what?'
               'It made a noise.'
                              'A frightening noise?'
'No, no.'
          'A musical noise? A noise of scuffling?'
'No, but a very loud, respectable noise—
Like groaning to oneself on Sunday morning
In Chapel, close before the second psalm.'
'What did the mayor do?'
        'I was coming to that.'

Ogden Nash

Peekaboo, I Almost See You

Middle-aged life is merry, and I love to lead it,
But there comes a day when your eyes are all right but your arm
    isn't long enough to hold the telephone book where you can
    read it,
And your friends get jocular, so you can go to the oculist,
And of all your friends he is the joculist,
So over his facetiousness let us skim,
Only noting that he has been waiting for you ever since you said
    Good evening to his grandfather clock under the impression
    that it was him,
And you look at his chart and it says SHRDLU QWERTYOP, and
    you say Well, why SHRDNTLU QWERTYOP? and he says
    one set of glasses won't do.
You need two,
One for reading Erle Stanley Gardner's *Perry Mason* and Keats's
    Endymion with,
And the other for walking around without saying Hallo to strange
    wymion with.
So you spend your time taking off your seeing glasses to put on
    your reading glasses, and then remembering that your reading
    glasses are upstairs or in the car,
And then you can't find your seeing glasses again because without
    them you can't see where they are.

Enough of such mishaps, they would try the patience of an ox,
I prefer to forget both pairs of glasses and pass my declining years
    saluting strange women and grandfather clocks.

Song of the Open Road

I think that I shall never see
A billboard lovely as a tree.
Indeed, unless the billboards fall
I'll never see a tree at all.

Stevie Smith

Not Waving but Drowning

Nobody heard him, the dead man,
But still he lay moaning:
I was much further out than you thought
And not waving but drowning.

Poor chap, he always loved larking
And now he's dead
It must have been too cold for him his heart gave way,
They said.

Oh, no no no, it was too cold always
(Still the dead one lay moaning)
I was much too far out all my life
And not waving but drowning.

Cecil Day Lewis

Birthday Poem for Thomas Hardy

Is it birthday weather for you, dear soul?
Is it fine your way,
With tall moon-daisies alight, and the mole
Busy, and elegant hares at play
By meadow paths where once you would stroll
In the flush of day?

I fancy the beasts and flowers there beguiled
By a visitation
That casts no shadow, a friend whose mild
Inquisitive glance lights with compassion,
Beyond the tomb, on all of this wild
And humbled creation.

It's hard to believe a spirit could die
Of such generous glow,
Or to doubt that somewhere a bird-sharp eye
Still broods on the capers of men below,
A stern voice asks the Immortals why
They should plague us so.

Dear poet, wherever you are, I greet you,
Much irony, wrong,
Innocence you'd find here to tease or entreat you,
And many the fate-fires have tempered strong,
But none that in ripeness of soul could meet you
Or magic of song.

Great brow, frail frame – gone. Yet you abide
In the shadow and sheen,
All the mellowing traits of a countryside
That nursed your tragi-comical scene;
And in us, warmer-hearted and brisker-eyed
Since you have been.

John Betjeman

A Subaltern's Love-song

Miss J. Hunter Dunn, Miss J. Hunter Dunn,
Furnish'd and burnish'd by Aldershot sun,
What strenuous singles we played after tea,
We in the tournament – you against me!

Love-thirty, love-forty, oh! weakness of joy,
The speed of a swallow, the grace of a boy,
With carefullest carelessness, gaily you won,
I am weak from your loveliness, Joan Hunter Dunn.

Miss Joan Hunter Dunn, Miss Joan Hunter Dunn,
How mad I am, sad I am, glad that you won.
The warm-handled racket is back in its press,
But my shock-headed victor, she loves me no less.

Her father's euonymus shines as we walk,
And swing past the summer-house, buried in talk,
And cool the verandah that welcomes us in
To the six-o'clock news and a lime-juice and gin.

The scent of the conifers, sound of the bath,
The view from my bedroom of moss-dappled path,
As I struggle with double-end evening tie,
For we dance at the Golf Club, my victor and I.

On the floor of her bedroom lie blazer and shorts
And the cream-coloured walls are be-trophied with sports,
And westering, questioning settles the sun
On your low-leaded window, Miss Joan Hunter Dunn.

The Hillman is waiting, the light's in the hall,
The pictures of Egypt are bright on the wall,
My sweet, I am standing beside the oak stair
And there on the landing's the light on your hair.

By roads 'not adopted,' by woodlanded ways,
She drove to the club in the late summer haze,
Into nine-o'clock Camberley, heavy with bells
And mushroomy, pine-woody, evergreen smells.

Miss Joan Hunter Dunn, Miss Joan Hunter Dunn,
I can hear from the car-park the dance has begun.
Oh! full Surrey twilight! importunate band!
Oh! strongly adorable tennis-girl's hand!

Around us are Rovers and Austins afar,
Above us, the intimate roof of the car,
And here on my right is the girl of my choice,
With the tilt of her nose and the chime of her voice,

And the scent of her wrap, and the words never said,
And the ominous, ominous dancing ahead.
We sat in the car park till twenty to one
And now I'm engaged to Miss Joan Hunter Dunn.

Hunter Trials

It's awf'lly bad luck on Diana,
　　Her ponies have swallowed their bits;
She fished down their throats with a spanner
　　And frightened them all into fits.

So now she's attempting to borrow.
　　Do lend her some bits, Mummy, *do*;
I'll lend her my own for to-morrow,
　　But to-day *I'll* be wanting them too.

Just look at Prunella on Guzzle,
　　The wizardest pony on earth;
Why doesn't she slacken his muzzle
　　And tighten the breech in his girth?

I say, Mummy, there's Mrs Geyser
　　And doesn't she look pretty sick?
I bet it's because Mona Lisa
　　Was hit on the hock with a brick.

Miss Blewitt says Monica threw it,
　　But Monica says it was Joan,
And Joan's very thick with Miss Blewitt,
　　So Monica's sulking alone.

And Margaret failed in her paces,
　　Her withers got tied in a noose,
So her coronets caught in the traces
　　And now all her fetlocks are loose.

Oh, it's me now. I'm terribly nervous.
　　I wonder if Smudges will shy.
She's practically certain to swerve as
　　Her Pelham is over one eye.

　　　　·　　·　　·　　·

Oh wasn't it naughty of Smudges?
　　Oh, Mummy, I'm sick with disgust.
She threw me in front of the Judges,
　　And my silly old collarbone's bust.

Louis MacNeice

Bagpipe Music

It's no go the merrygoround, it's no go the rickshaw,
All we want is a limousine and a ticket for the peepshow.
Their knickers are made of crêpe-de-chine, their shoes are made of
    python,
Their halls are lined with tiger rugs and their walls with heads of
    bison.

John MacDonald found a corpse, put it under the sofa,
Waited till it came to life and hit it with a poker,
Sold its eyes for souvenirs, sold its blood for whiskey,
Kept its bones for dumb-bells to use when he was fifty.

It's no go the Yogi-Man, it's no go Blavatsky,
All we want is a bank balance and a bit of skirt in a taxi.

Annie MacDougall went to milk, caught her foot in the heather,
Woke to hear a dance record playing of Old Vienna.
It's no go your maidenheads, it's no go your culture,
All we want is a Dunlop tyre and the devil mend the puncture.

The Laird o' Phelps spent Hogmanay declaring he was sober,
Counted his feet to prove the fact and found he had one foot over.
Mrs Carmichael had her fifth, looked at the job with repulsion,
Said to the midwife 'Take it away; I'm through with over-
    production.'

It's no go the gossip column, it's no go the ceilidh,
All we want is a mother's help and a sugar-stick for the baby.

Willie Murray cut his thumb, couldn't count the damage.
Took the hide of an Ayrshire cow and used it for a bandage.
His brother caught three hundred cran when the seas were lavish,
Threw the bleeders back in the sea and went upon the parish.

It's no go the Herring Board, it's no go the Bible,
All we want is a packet of fags when our hands are idle.

It's no go the picture palace, it's no go the stadium,
It's no go the country cot with a pot of pink geraniums,
It's no go the Government grants, it's no go the elections,
Sit on your arse for fifty years and hang your hat on a pension.

It's no go my honey love, it's no go my poppet;
Work your hands from day to day, the winds will blow the profit.
The glass is falling hour by hour, the glass will fall for ever,
But if you break the bloody glass you won't hold up the weather.

Prayer before Birth

I am not yet born; O hear me.
Let not the bloodsucking bat or the rat or the stoat or the
    clubfooted ghoul come near me.

I am not yet born; console me.
I fear that the human race may with tall walls wall me,
    with strong drugs dope me, and wise lies lure me,
        on black racks rack me, in blood-baths roll me.

I am not yet born; provide me
With water to dandle me, grass to grow for me, trees to talk
    to me, sky to sing to me, birds and a white light
        in the back of my mind to guide me.

I am not yet born; forgive me
For the sins that in me the world shall commit, my words
    when they speak me, my thoughts when they think me,
        my treason engendered by traitors beyond me,
            my life when they murder by means of my
                hands, my death when they live me.

I am not yet born; rehearse me
In the parts I must play and the cues I must take when
    old men lecture me, bureaucrats hector me, mountains
        frown at me, lovers laugh at me, the white
            waves call me to folly and the desert calls
                me to doom and the beggar refuses
                    my gift and my children curse me.

I am not yet born; O hear me.
Let not the man who is beast or who thinks he is God come near
    me.

I am not yet born; O fill me
With strength against those who would freeze my
    humanity, would dragoon me into a lethal automaton,
        would make me a cog in a machine, a thing with

one face, a thing, and against all those
who would dissipate my entirety, would
blow me like thistledown hither and
thither or hither and thither
like water held in the
hands would spill me

Let them not make me a stone and let them not spill me.
Otherwise kill me.

Wystan Hugh Auden

Lullaby

Lay your sleeping head, my love,
Human on my faithless arm;
Time and fevers burn away
Individual beauty from
Thoughtful children, and the grave
Proves the child ephemeral:
But in my arms till break of day
Let the living creature lie,
Mortal, guilty, but to me
The entirely beautiful.

Soul and body have no bounds:
To lovers as they lie upon
Her tolerant enchanted slope
In their ordinary swoon,
Grave the vision Venus sends
Of supernatural sympathy,
Universal love and hope;
While an abstract insight wakes
Among the glaciers and the rocks
The hermit's sensual ecstasy.

Certainty, fidelity
On the stroke of midnight pass
Like vibrations of a bell
And fashionable madmen raise
Their pedantic boring cry:
Every farthing of the cost,
All the dreaded cards foretell,

Shall be paid, but from this night
Not a whisper, not a thought,
Not a kiss nor look be lost.

Beauty, midnight, vision dies:
Let the winds of dawn that blow
Softly round your dreaming head
Such a day of sweetness show
Eye and knocking heart may bless,
Find the mortal world enough;
Noons of dryness see you fed
By the involuntary powers,
Nights of insult let you pass
Watched by every human love.

Stephen Spender

'I think continually of those
who were truly great'

I think continually of those who were truly great.
Who, from the womb, remembered the soul's history
Through corridors of light where the hours are suns,
Endless and singing. Whose lovely ambition
Was that their lips, still touched with fire,
Should tell of the Spirit, clothed from head to foot in song.
And who hoarded from the Spring branches
The desires falling across their bodies like blossoms.

What is precious is never to forget
The essential delight of the blood drawn from ageless springs
Breaking through rocks in worlds before our earth.
Never to deny its pleasure in the morning simple light
Nor its grave evening demand for love.
Never to allow gradually the traffic to smother
With noise and fog, the flowering of the Spirit.

Near the snow, near the sun, in the highest fields,
See how these names are fêted by the waving grass
And by the streamers of white cloud
And whispers of wind in the listening sky.
The names of those who in their lives fought for life,

Who wore at their hearts the fire's centre.
Born of the sun, they travelled a short while toward the sun
And left the vivid air signed with their honour.

Dylan Thomas

Do Not Go Gentle into That Good Night

Do not go gentle into that good night,
Old age should burn and rave at close of day;
Rage, rage against the dying of the light.

Though wise men at their end know dark is right,
Because their words had forked no lightning they
Do not go gentle into that good night.

Good men, the last wave by, crying how bright
Their frail deeds might have danced in a green bay,
Rage, rage against the dying of the light.

Wild men who caught and sang the sun in flight,
And learn, too late, they grieved it on its way,
Do not go gentle into that good night.

Grave men, near death, who see with blinding sight
Blind eyes could blaze like meteors and be gay,
Rage, rage against the dying of the light.

And you, my father, there on the sad height,
Curse, bless, me now with your fierce tears, I pray.
Do not go gentle into that good night.
Rage, rage against the dying of the light.

Poem in October

It was my thirtieth year to heaven
Woke to my hearing from harbour and neighbour wood
And the mussel pooled and the heron
Priested shore
The morning beckon
With water praying and call of seagull and rook

And the knock of sailing boats on the net webbed wall
  Myself to set foot
   That second
In the still sleeping town and set forth.

My birthday began with the water-
Birds and the birds of the winged trees flying my name
  Above the farms and the white horses
   And I rose
   In rainy autumn
And walked abroad in a shower of all my days.
High tide and the heron dived when I took the road
  Over the border
   And the gates
Of the town closed as the town awoke.

A springful of larks in a rolling
Cloud and the roadside bushes brimming with whistling
  Blackbirds and the sun of October
   Summery
  On the hill's shoulder,
Here were fond climates and sweet singers suddenly
Come in the morning where I wandered and listened
  To the rain wringing
   Wind blow cold
In the wood faraway under me.

Pale rain over the dwindling harbour
And over the sea wet church the size of a snail
  With its horns through mist and the castle.
   Brown as owls
   But all the gardens
Of spring and summer were blooming in the tall tales
Beyond the border and under the lark full cloud.
  There could I marvel
   My birthday
Away but the weather turned around.

It turned away from the blithe country
And down the other air and the blue altered sky
  Streamed again a wonder of summer
   With apples
   Pears and red currants
And I saw in the turning so clearly a child's
Forgotten mornings when he walked with his mother

Through the parables
    Of sunlight
And the legends of the green chapels

And the twice told fields of infancy
That his tears burned my cheeks and his heart moved in mine.
    These were the woods the river and sea
        Where a boy
    In the listening
Summertime of the dead whispered the truth of his joy
To the trees and the stones and the fish in the tide.
    And the mystery
        Sang alive
    Still in the water and singingbirds.

And there could I marvel my birthday
Away but the weather turned around. And the true
    Joy of the long dead child sang burning
        In the sun
    It was my thirtieth
Year to heaven stood there then in the summer noon
Though the town below lay leaved with October blood.
    O may my heart's truth
        Still be sung
    On this high hill in a year's turning.

And Death Shall Have No Dominion

And death shall have no dominion.
Dead men naked they shall be one
With the man in the wind and the west moon;
When their bones are picked clean and the clean bones gone,
They shall have stars at elbow and foot;
Though they go mad they shall be sane,
Though they sink through the sea they shall rise again;
Though lovers be lost love shall not;
And death shall have no dominion.

And death shall have no dominion.
Under the windings of the sea
They lying long shall not die windily;
Twisting on racks when sinews give way,
Strapped to a wheel, yet they shall not break;

Faith in their hands shall snap in two,
And the unicorn evils run them through;
Split all ends up they shan't crack;
And death shall have no dominion.

And death shall have no dominion.
No more may gulls cry at their ears
Or waves break loud on the seashores;
Where blew a flower may a flower no more
Lift its head to the blows of the rain;
Though they be mad and dead as nails,
Heads of the characters hammer through daisies;
Break in the sun till the sun breaks down,
And death shall have no dominion.

Henry Reed

From Lessons of the War

I. Naming of Parts

To-day we have naming of parts. Yesterday,
We had daily cleaning. And to-morrow morning,
We shall have what to do after firing. But to-day,
To-day we have naming of parts. Japonica
Glistens like coral in all of the neighbouring gardens,
   And to-day we have naming of parts.

This is the lower sling swivel. And this
Is the upper sling swivel, whose use you will see,
When you are given your slings. And this is the piling swivel,
Which in your case you have not got. The branches
Hold in the gardens their silent, eloquent gestures,
   Which in our case we have not got.

This is the safety-catch, which is always released
With an easy flick of the thumb. And please do not let me
See anyone using his finger. You can do it quite easy
If you have any strength in your thumb. The blossoms
Are fragile and motionless, never letting anyone see
   Any of them using their finger.

And this you can see is the bolt. The purpose of this
Is to open the breech, as you see. We can slide it
Rapidly backwards and forwards: we call this
Easing the spring. And rapidly backwards and forwards
The early bees are assaulting and fumbling the flowers:
    They call it easing the Spring.

They call it easing the Spring: it is perfectly easy
If you have any strength in your thumb: like the bolt,
And the breech, and the cocking-piece, and the point of balance
Which in our case we have not got; and the almond blossom
Silent in all of the gardens and the bees going backwards and
    forwards,
    For to-day we have naming of parts.

Charles Causley

Nursery Rhyme of
Innocence and Experience

I had a silver penny
    And an apricot tree
And I said to the sailor
    On the white quay

'Sailor O sailor
    Will you bring me
If I give you my penny
    And my apricot tree

'A fez from Algeria
    An Arab drum to beat
A little gilt sword
    And a parakeet?'

And he smiled and he kissed me
    As strong as death
And I saw his red tongue
    And I felt his sweet breath

*'You may keep your penny
    And your apricot tree
And I'll bring your presents
    Back from sea.'*

O the ship dipped down
   On the rim of the sky
And I waited while three
   Long summers went by

Then one steel morning
   On the white quay
I saw a grey ship
   Come in from sea.

Slowly she came
   Across the bay
For her flashing rigging
   Was shot away

All round her wake
   The seabirds cried
And flew in and out
   Of the hole in her side

Slowly she came
   In the path of the sun
And I heard the sound
   Of a distant gun

And a stranger came running
   Up to me
From the deck of the ship
   And he said, said he

'O are you the boy
   Who would wait on the quay
With the silver penny
   And the apricot tree?

'I've a plum-coloured fez
   And a drum for thee
And a sword and a parakeet
   From over the sea.'

'O where is the sailor
   With bold red hair?
And what is that volley
   On the bright air?

'O where are the other
   Girls and boys?
And why have you brought me
   Children's toys?'

Philip Larkin

The Whitsun Weddings

That Whitsun, I was late getting away:
   Not till about
One-twenty on the sunlit Saturday
Did my three-quarters-empty train pull out,
All windows down, all cushions hot, all sense
Of being in a hurry gone. We ran
Behind the backs of houses, crossed a street
Of blinding windscreens, smelt the fish-dock; thence
The river's level drifting breadth began,
Where sky and Lincolnshire and water meet.

All afternoon, through the tall heat that slept
   For miles inland,
A slow and stopping curve southwards we kept.
Wide farms went by, short-shadowed cattle, and
Canals with floatings of industrial froth;
A hothouse flashed uniquely: hedges dipped
And rose: and now and then a smell of grass
Displaced the reek of buttoned carriage-cloth
Until the next town, new and nondescript,
Approached with acres of dismantled cars.

At first, I didn't notice what a noise
   The weddings made
Each station that we stopped at: sun destroys
The interest of what's happening in the shade,
And down the long cool platforms whoops and skirls
I took for porters larking with the mails,
And went on reading. Once we started, though,
We passed them, grinning and pomaded, girls
In parodies of fashion, heels and veils,
All posed irresolutely, watching us go,

As if out on the end of an event
   Waving good-bye
To something that survived it. Struck, I leant
More promptly out next time, more curiously,
And saw it all again in different terms:
The fathers with broad belts under their suits
And seamy foreheads; mothers loud and fat;

An uncle shouting smut; and then the perms,
The nylon gloves and jewellery-substitutes,
The lemons, mauves, and olive-ochres that

Marked off the girls unreally from the rest.
    Yes, from cafés
And banquet-halls up yards, and bunting-dressed
Coach-party annexes, the wedding-days
Were coming to an end. All down the line
Fresh couples climbed aboard: the rest stood round;
The last confetti and advice were thrown,
And, as we moved, each face seemed to define
Just what it saw departing: children frowned
At something dull; fathers had never known

Success so huge and wholly farcical;
    The women shared
The secret like a happy funeral;
While girls, gripping their handbags tighter, stared
At a religious wounding. Free at last,
And loaded with the sum of all they saw,
We hurried towards London, shuffling gouts of steam.
Now fields were building-plots, and poplars cast
Long shadows over major roads, and for
Some fifty minutes, that in time would seem

Just long enough to settle hats and say
    I nearly died,
A dozen marriages got under way.
They watched the landscape, sitting side by side
An Odeon went past, a cooling tower,
And someone running up to bowl – and none
Thought of the others they would never meet
Or how their lives would all contain this hour.
I thought of London spread out in the sun,
Its postal districts packed like squares of wheat:

There we were aimed. And as we raced across
    Bright knots of rail
Past standing Pullmans, walls of blackened moss
Came close, and it was nearly done, this frail
Travelling coincidence; and what it held
Stood ready to be loosed with all the power
That being changed can give. We slowed again,
And as the tightened brakes took hold, there swelled
A sense of falling, like an arrow-shower
Sent out of sight, somewhere becoming rain.

This Be the Verse

They fuck you up, your mum and dad.
    They may not mean to, but they do.
They fill you with the faults they had
    And add some extra, just for you.

But they were fucked up in their turn
    By fools in old-style hats and coats,
Who half the time were soppy-stern
    And half at one another's throats.

Man hands on misery to man.
    It deepens like a coastal shelf.
Get out as early as you can,
    And don't have any kids yourself.

Elizabeth Jennings

One Flesh

Lying apart now, each in a separate bed,
He with a book, keeping the light on late,
She like a girl dreaming of childhood,
All men elsewhere – it is as if they wait
Some new event: the book he holds unread,
Her eyes fixed on the shadows overhead

Tossed up like flotsam from a former passion,
How cool they lie. They hardly ever touch,
Or if they do it is like a confession
Of having little feeling – or too much.
Chastity faces them, a destination
For which their whole lives were a preparation.

Strangely apart, yet strangely close together,
Silence between them like a thread to hold
And not wind in. And time itself's a feather
Touching them gently. Do they know they're old,
These two who are my father and my mother
Whose fire from which I came, has now grown cold?

George MacBeth

Owl

is my favourite. Who flies
like a nothing through the night,
who-whoing. Is a feather
duster in leafy corners ring-a-rosy-ing
boles of mice. Twice

you hear him call. Who
is he looking for? You hear
him hoovering over the floor
of the wood. O would you be gold
rings in the driving skull

if you could? Hooded and
vulnerable by the winter suns
owl looks. Is the grain of bark
in the dark. Round beaks are at
work in the pellety nest,

resting. Owl is an eye
in the barn. For a hole
in the trunk owl's blood
is to blame. Black talons in the
petrified fur! Cold walnut hands

on the case of the brain! In the reign
of the chicken owl comes like
a god. Is a goad in
the rain to the pink eyes,
dripping. For a meal in the day

flew, killed, on the moor. Six
mouths are the seed of his
arc in the season. Torn meat
from the sky. Owl lives
by the claws of his brain. On the branch

in the sever of the hand's
twigs owl is a backward look.
Flown wind in the skin. Fine
rain in the bones. Owl breaks
like the day. Am an owl, am an owl.

Sylvia Plath

Daddy

You do not do, you do not do
Any more, black shoe
In which I have lived like a foot
For thirty years, poor and white,
Barely daring to breathe or Achoo.

Daddy, I have had to kill you.
You died before I had time——
Marble-heavy, a bag full of God,
Ghastly statue with one grey toe
Big as a Frisco seal

And a head in the freakish Atlantic
Where it pours bean green over blue
In the waters off beautiful Nauset.
I used to pray to recover you.
Ach, du.

In the German tongue, in the Polish town
Scraped flat by the roller
Of wars, wars, wars.
But the name of the town is common.
My Polack friend.

Says there are a dozen or two.
So I never could tell where you
Put your foot, your root,
I never could talk to you.
The tongue stuck in my jaw.

It stuck in a barb wire snare.
Ich, ich, ich, ich,
I could hardly speak.
I thought every German was you.
And the language obscene

An engine, an engine
Chuffing me off like a Jew.
A Jew to Dachau, Auschwitz, Belsen.
I began to talk like a Jew.
I think I may well be a Jew.

The snows of the Tyrol, the clear beer of Vienna
Are not very pure or true.
With my gypsy ancestress and my weird luck
And my Taroc pack and my Taroc pack
I may be a bit of a Jew.

I have always been scared of *you*,
With your Luftwaffe, your gobbledygoo.
And your neat moustache
And your Aryan eye, bright blue.
Panzer-man, panzer-man, O You——

Not God but a swastika
So black no sky could squeak through.
Every woman adores a Fascist,
The boot in the face, the brute
Brute heart of a brute like you.

You stand at the blackboard, daddy,
In the picture I have of you,
A cleft in your chin instead of your foot
But no less a devil for that, no not
Any less the black man who

Bit my pretty red heart in two.
I was ten when they buried you.
At twenty I tried to die
And get back, back, back to you.
I thought even the bones would do.

But they pulled me out of the sack,
And they stuck me together with glue.
And then I knew what to do.
I made a model of you,
A man in black with a Meinkampf look

And a love of the rack and the screw.
And I said I do, I do.
So daddy, I'm finally through.
The black telephone's off at the root,
The voices just can't worm through.

If I've killed one man, I've killed two——
The vampire who said he was you
And drank my blood for a year,
Seven years, if you want to know.
Daddy, you can lie back now.

There's a stake in your fat black heart
And the villagers never liked you.
They are dancing and stamping on you.
They always *knew* it was you.
Daddy, daddy, you bastard, I'm through.

Tony Harrison

Long Distance II

Though my mother was already two years dead
Dad kept her slippers warming by the gas,
put hot water bottles her side of the bed
and still went to renew her transport pass.

You couldn't just drop in. You had to phone.
He'd put you off an hour to give him time
to clear away her things and look alone
as though his still raw love were such a crime.

He couldn't risk my blight or disbelief
though sure that very soon he'd hear her key
scrape in the rusted lock and end his grief.
He *knew* she'd just popped out to get the tea.

I believe life ends with death, and that is all.
You haven't both gone shopping; just the same,
in my new black leather phone book there's your name
and the disconnected number I still call.

Roger McGough

Let Me Die a Youngman's Death

Let me die a youngman's death
not a clean & inbetween
the sheets holywater death
not a famous-last-words
peaceful out of breath death.

When I'm 73
& in constant good tumour
may I be mown down at dawn
by a bright red sports car
on my way home
from an allnight party

Or when I'm 91
with silver hair
& sitting in a barber's chair
may rival gangsters
with hamfisted tommyguns burst in
& give me a short back & insides

Or when I'm 104
& banned from the Cavern
may my mistress
catching me in bed with her daughter
& fearing her son
cut me up into little pieces
& throw away every piece but one

Let me die a youngman's death
not a free from sin tiptoe in
candle wax & waning death
not a curtains drawn by angels borne
'what a nice way to go' death

Pete Seeger

Where Have All the Flowers Gone?

Where have all the flowers gone?
Long time passing.
Where have all the flowers gone?
Long time ago.
Where have all the flowers gone?
Young girls picked them, every one.
When will they ever learn,
O when will they ever learn.

Where have all the young girls gone?
Long time passing.
Where have all the young girls gone?
Long time ago.

Where have all the young girls gone?
Gone to young men, every one.
When will they ever learn,
O when will they ever learn.

Where have all the young men gone?
Long time passing.
Where have all the young men gone?
Long time ago.
Where have all the young men gone?
Gone for soldiers, every one.
When will they ever learn,
O when will they ever learn.

Where have all the soldiers gone?
Long time passing.
Where have all the soldiers gone?
Long time ago.
Where have all the soldiers gone?
Gone to graveyards, every one.
When will they ever learn,
O when will they ever learn.

Where have all the graveyards gone?
Long time passing.
Where have all the graveyards gone?
Long time ago.
Where have all the graveyards gone?
Gone to flower every one.
When will they ever learn,
O when will they ever learn.

Where have all the flowers gone?
Long time passing.
Where have all the flowers gone?
Long time ago.
Where have all the flowers gone?
Young girls picked them, every one.
When will they ever learn,
O when will they ever learn.

Seamus Heaney

Personal Helicon

As a child, they could not keep me from wells
And old pumps with buckets and windlasses.
I loved the dark drop, the trapped sky, the smells
Of waterweed, fungus and dank moss.

One, in a brickyard, with a rotted board top.
I savoured the rich crash when a bucket
Plummeted down at the end of a rope.
So deep you saw no reflection in it.

A shallow one under a dry stone ditch
Fructified like any aquarium.
When you dragged out long roots from the soft mulch
A white face hovered over the bottom.

Others had echoes, gave back your own call
With a clean new music in it. And once
Was scaresome for there, out of ferns and tall
Foxgloves, a rat slapped across my reflection.

Now, to pry into roots, to finger slime,
To stare big-eyed Narcissus, into some spring
Is beneath all adult dignity. I rhyme
To see myself, to set the darkness echoing.

Wendy Cope

From From June to December

Summer Villanelle

You know exactly what to do—
Your kiss, your fingers on my thigh—
I think of little else but you.

It's bliss to have a lover who,
Touching one shoulder, makes me sigh—
You know exactly what to do.

You make me happy through and through,
The way the sun lights up the sky—
I think of little else but you.

I hardly sleep – an hour or two;
I can't eat much and this is why—
You know exactly what to do.

The movie in my mind is blue—
As June runs into warm July
I think of little else but you.

But is it love? And is it true?
Who cares? This much I can't deny:
You know exactly what to do;
I think of little else but you.

ACKNOWLEDGEMENTS

W.H. AUDEN 'Lullaby' reprinted by permission of Faber & Faber Ltd.

HILAIRE BELLOC 'Tarantella', 'Ballade of Genuine Concern' and 'Matilda' from *Complete Verse*, reprinted by permission of the Peters Fraser & Dunlop Group Ltd.

JOHN BETJEMAN 'A Subaltern's Love-Song' and 'Hunter Trials' from *Collected Poems*, reprinted by permission of John Murray (Publishers) Ltd.

LAURENCE BINYON 'For the Fallen (September 1914)' and extract from 'The Burning of the Leaves' reprinted by permission of Mrs Nicolete Gray and the Society of Authors on behalf of the Laurence Binyon Estate.

SYDNEY CARTER 'Lord of the Dance' reprinted by permission of Stainer & Bell Ltd.

CHARLES CAUSLEY 'Nursery Rhyme of Innocence and Experience' from *Collected Poems* (Macmillan London Ltd), reprinted by permission of David Higham Associates.

WENDY COPE 'From June to December, III: Summer Villanelle' from *Making Cocoa for Kingsley Amis*, reprinted by permission of Faber & Faber Ltd.

FRANCES CORNFORD 'To a Fat Lady Seen from a Train' from *Collected Poems*, reprinted by permission of the Estate of the author and Hutchinson.

e.e. cummings 'anyone lived in a pretty how town' reprinted by permission of Granada Publishing Ltd; and of Harcourt Brace Jovanovich, Inc., from *Complete Poems 1913–1962*. 'next to of course god america i' reprinted by permission of Granada Publishing Ltd; and of the Liveright Publishing Corporation of IS5 poems.

C. DAY LEWIS 'Birthday Poem for Thomas Hardy' reprinted by permission of the Executors of the Estate of C. Day Lewis, Jonathan Cape Ltd and the Hogarth Press Ltd, from *Collected Poems 1954*; and of Harper and Row (Publishers) Inc., from *Selected Poems*.

WALTER DE LA MARE 'The Listeners', 'Fare Well' and 'The Scribe' reprinted by permission of the Literary Trustees of Walter de la Mare and the Society of Authors as their representative.

T.S. ELIOT 'The Love Song of J. Alfred Prufrock' and 'Journey of the Magi' from *Collected Poems 1909–1962*, reprinted by permission of Faber & Faber Ltd. 'The Song of the Jellicles' from *Old Possum's Book of Practical Cats* reprinted by permission of Faber & Faber Ltd.

ROBERT FROST 'Fire and Ice', 'The Road Not Taken' and 'Mending

Wall' from *The Poetry of Robert Frost* edited by Edward Connery Lathem, reprinted by permission of the Estate of the author and Jonathan Cape Ltd.

ROBERT GRAVES 'Welsh Incident' from *Collected Poems 1975*, reprinted by permission of A.P. Watt Ltd on behalf of the Trustees of the Robert Graves Copyright Trust.

TONY HARRISON 'Long Distance II' reprinted by permission of the Peters Fraser & Dunlop Group Ltd.

SEAMUS HEANEY 'Personal Helicon' from *Death of a Naturalist*, reprinted by permission of Faber & Faber Ltd.

ELIZABETH JENNINGS 'One Flesh' from *Collected Poems* (Carcanet), reprinted by permission of David Higham Associates.

PHILIP LARKIN 'The Whitsun Weddings' from *The Whitsun Weddings*, reprinted by permission of Faber & Faber Ltd.

GEORGE MACBETH 'Owl' reprinted by permission of Scorpion Press.

LOUIS MACNEICE 'Bagpipe Music' and 'Prayer before Birth' from *The Collected Poems of Louis MacNeice*, reprinted by permission of Faber & Faber Ltd.

JOHN MASEFIELD 'Cargoes' and 'Sea-Fever' reprinted by permission of the Society of Authors as the literary representative of the Estate of John Masefield; and of Macmillan Publishing Co., Inc., from *Poems*.

ROGER MCGOUGH 'Let me Die a Youngman's Death' reprinted by permission of Tessa Sayle.

EDNA ST VINCENT MILLAY 'First Fig' from *Collected Poems* (Harper and Row), reprinted by permission of Norma Millay Ellis.

EDWIN MUIR 'The Combat' from *Collected Poems*, reprinted by permission of Faber & Faber Ltd.

OGDEN NASH 'Peekaboo, I Almost See You', 'What's the Use?' and 'Song of the Open Road' reprinted by permission of the Estate of Ogden Nash; and of Little, Brown and Company from *Verses from 1929 On*.

ALFRED NOYES 'The Highwayman' from *Collected Poems*, reprinted by permission of John Murray (Publishers) Ltd.

SYLVIA PLATH 'Daddy' from *Collected Poems* edited by Ted Hughes, reprinted by permission of Faber & Faber Ltd.

PETER PORTER 'Your attention please' from *Collected Poems*, reprinted by permission of Oxford University Press.

EZRA POUND 'The Temperaments' from *Collected Shorter Poems*, reprinted by permission of Faber & Faber Ltd.

HENRY REED 'Lessons of the War: 1. Naming of Parts' from *A Map of Verona*, reprinted by permission of Curtis Brown Ltd, London.

SIEGFRIED SASSOON 'Everyone Sang' from *Collected Poems 1908–1956*, reprinted by permission of G.T. Sassoon.

PETE SEEGER 'Where Have All The Flowers Gone?' reprinted by permission of Essex Music Group/Bucks Music, London.

ROBERT SERVICE 'The Shooting of Dan McGrew' from *Songs of a Sourdough*, reprinted by permission of Ernest Benn; and of Dodd,

Mead and Co., Inc., and McGraw-Hill Ryerson Ltd from *The Collected Poems of Robert Service*.

STEVIE SMITH 'Not Waving but Drowning' from *The Collected Poems of Stevie Smith* (Penguin Books), reprinted by permission of James MacGibbon.

STEPHEN SPENDER 'The Truly Great' from *Collected Poems*, reprinted by permission of Faber & Faber Ltd.

DYLAN THOMAS 'Do Not Go Gentle', 'Poem in October' and 'And Death Shall Have No Dominion' from *The Poems* (J.M. Dent & Sons), reprinted by permission of David Higham Associates.

W.J. TURNER 'Romance' reprinted by permission of Sidgwick and Jackson Ltd.

WILLIAM CARLOS WILLIAMS 'This is just to say' from *Collected Poems*, reprinted by permission of Carcanet.

INDEX OF AUTHORS

Allingham, William (1824–1889) 207
Arnold, Matthew (1822–1888) 204
Auden, Wystan Hugh (1907–1973) 306

Babington, Thomas (*see* Macaulay)
Bates, Katharine Lee (1859–1929) 241
Belloc, Hilaire (1870–1953) 261
Betjeman, John (1906–1985) 301
Bickerstaffe, Isaac (*c*.1735–*c*.1812) 96
Binyon, Laurence (1869–1943) 259
Blake, William (1757–1827) 97
Breton, Nicholas (*c*.1542–*c*.1626) 13
Bridges, Robert (1844–1930) 232
Brontë, Emily (1818–1848) 197
Brooke, Rupert (1887–1915) 284
Brown, Thomas Edward (1830–1897) 215
Browning, Elizabeth Barrett (1806–1861) 151
Browning, Robert (1812–1889) 191
Bunyan, John (1628–1688) 75
Burns, Robert (1759–1796) 101
Byron, George Gordon, Lord (1788–1824) 126

Campbell, Thomas (1777–1844) 121
Campion, Thomas (1567–*c*.1619) 50
Carey, Henry (*c*.1687–1743) 82
Carroll, Lewis (1832–1898) 215
Causley, Charles (1917–) 312
Chaucer, Geoffrey (*c*.1340–1400) 1
Chesterton, Gilbert Keith (1874–1936) 267
Clough, Arthur Hugh (1819–1861) 200
Coleridge, Samuel Taylor (1772–1834) 116
Cope, Wendy (1945–) 323
Cornford, Frances (1886–1960) 283
Cory, William Johnson (1823–1892) 206
Cowper, William (1731–1800) 93
cummings, e. e. (1894–1962) 296

Davidson, John (1857–1909) 238
Davies, William Henry (1871–1940) 264
Day Lewis, Cecil (1904–1972) 300
de la Mare, Walter (1873–1956) 265
Dickinson, Emily (1830–1886) 210
Donne, John (*c*.1572–1631) 53
Drayton, Michael (1563–1631) 19

Drinkwater, John (1882–1937)   279
Dryden, John (1631–1700)   77
Dyer, Edward (c.1555–1607)   18

Eliot, Thomas Stearns (1888–1965)   288
Emerson, Ralph Waldo (1803–1882)   150

FitzGerald, Edward (1809–1883)   170
Flecker, James Elroy (1884–1915)   280
Frost, Robert (1875–1963)   269

Gay, John (1685–1732)   79
Gilbert, William Schwenck (1836–1911)   225
Goldsmith, Oliver (c.1728–1774)   91
Gordon, George (see Byron)
Graham, James, Marquis of Montrose (1612–1650)   71
Graves, Robert (1895–1985)   298
Gray, Thomas (1716–1771)   87
Gurney, Dorothy Frances (1858–1932)   240

Hardy, Thomas (1840–1928)   228
Harrison, Tony (1937–)   320
Hawker, Robert Stephen (1803–1875)   151
Hayes, J. Milton (1884–1940)   253
Heaney, Seamus (1939–)   323
Hemans, Felicia D. (1793–1835)   134
Henley, William Ernest (1849–1903)   234
Herbert, George (1593–1632)   58
Herrick, Robert (1591–1674)   56
Holmes, Oliver Wendell (1809–1894)   190
Hood, Thomas (1799–1845)   142
Hopkins, Gerard Manley (1844–1889)   230
Housman, Alfred Edward (1859–1936)   242
Howe, Julia Ward (1819–1910)   203
Hunt, Leigh (1784–1859)   124

Jennings, Elizabeth (1926–)   316
Jonson, Ben (c. 1572–1637)   51

Keats, John (1795–1821)   135
Key, Francis Scott (1779–1843)   123
Kilmer, Joyce (1886–1918)   283
Kingsley, Charles (1819–1875)   198
Kipling, Rudyard (1865–1936)   246

Landor, Walter Savage (1775–1864)   122
Larkin, Philip (1922–1985)   314
Lawrence, David Herbert (1885–1930)   281
Lear, Edward (1812–1888)   195
Longfellow, Henry Wadsworth (1807–1882)   154
Lovelace, Richard (c.1618–c.1657)   72

Macaulay, Thomas Babington, Lord (1800–1859)   146
MacBeth, George (1932–1992)   317

MacNeice, Louis (1907–1963)   304
Marlowe, Christopher (1564–1593)   23
Marvell, Andrew (1621–1678)   72
Masefield, John (1878–1967)   274
McGough, Roger (1937–)   320
Millay, Edna St Vincent (1892–1950)   295
Miller, Joachin (c.1837–1913)   229
Milton, John (1608–1674)   63
Montrose, Marquis of (see Graham)
Moore, Thomas (1779–1852)   122
Morris, William (1834–1896)   222
Munday, Anthony (1553–1633)   17

Nash, Ogden (1902–1971)   299
Newbolt, Henry (1862–1938)   245
Noyes, Alfred (1880–1958)   275

Owen, Wilfred (1893–1918)   295

Payne, John Howard (1791–1852)   131
Peacock, Thomas Love (1785–1866)   125
Plath, Sylvia (1932–1963)   318
Poe, Edgar Allan (1809–1849)   166
Pope, Alexander (1688–1744)   80
Procter, Adelaide Anne (1825–1864)   207

Raleigh, Walter (c.1552–1618)   14, 25
Reed, Henry (1914–1986)   311
Riley, James Whitcomb (1849–1916)   233
Robinson, Edwin Arlington (1869–1935)   258
Rossetti, Christina (1830–1894)   211
Rossetti, Dante Gabriel (1828–1882)   208

Sassoon, Siegfried (1886–1967)   284
Scott, Walter (1771–1832)   115
Seeger, Pete (1919–)   321
Service, Robert (1874–1958)   271
Shakespeare, William (1564–1616)   25
Shelley, Percy Bysshe (1792–1822)   132
Sheridan, Richard Brinsley (1751–1816)   96
Shirley, James (1596–1666)   62
Sidney, Philip (1554–1586)   18
Smith, Samuel Francis (1808–1895)   165
Smith, Stevie (1902–1971)   300
Southey, Robert (1774–1843)   118
Spender, Stephen (1909–)   307
Spenser, Edmund (c.1552–1599)   15
Stevenson, Robert Louis (1850–1894)   235
Strong, George A. (1832–1912)   215
Suckling, John (1609–1642)   70
Swinburne, Algernon Charles (1837–1909)   227

Tennyson, Alfred, Lord (1809–1892)   172
Thomas, Dylan (1914–1953)   308

Thomas, Edward (1878–1917)   274
Thompson, Francis (1859–1907)   242
Thomson, James (1700–1748)   85
Turner, Walter James (1889–1946)   294

Vaughan, Henry (c.1621–1695)   75

Waller, Edmund (1606–1687)   62
Watts, Isaac (1674–1748)   78
Whitman, Walt (1819–1892)   201
Wilcox, Ella Wheeler (c.1855–1919)   235
Wilde, Oscar (1856–1900)   237
Williams, William Carlos (1883–1963)   279
Wolfe, Charles (1791–1823)   130
Wordsworth, William (1770–1850)   106
Wotton, Henry (1568–1639)   51
Wyatt, Thomas (c.1503–1542)   13

Yeats, William Butler (1865–1939)   255

INDEX OF FIRST LINES
AND TITLES

(titles are printed in italics)

A bunch of the boys were whooping it up in the Malamute saloon   271
A child at Brighton has been left to drown   262
'A cold coming we had of it   292
A garden is a lovesome thing, God wot!   215
A good sword and a trusty hand!   151
A little black thing among the snow   99
A little learning is a dangerous thing   80
A slumber did my spirit seal   107
A snake came to my water-trough   281
A sweet disorder in the dress   56
A thing of beauty is a joy for ever   136
Abou Ben Adhem   124
Abou Ben Adhem (may his tribe increase!)   124
Absalom and Achitophel (extract)   77
Acis and Galatea (song)   79
Adlestrop   274
Ae fond kiss, and then we sever   105
Against Idleness and Mischief   78
Alas, my love! ye do me wrong   10
All the world's a stage   35
America   165
America the Beautiful   241
And Death Shall Have No Dominion   310
And death shall have no dominion   310
And did those feet in ancient time   101
And wilt thou leave me thus?   13
Annabel Lee   169
Antony and Cleopatra (extract)   47
anyone lived in a pretty how town   296
Armada, The (extract)   149
As a child, they could not keep me from wells   323
As I was walking all alane   4
As You Like It (extract and songs)   35
At Flores in the Azores Sir Richard Grenville lay   186
At the top of the house the apples are laid in rows   279
Auguries of Innocence (extract)   99
Auld Lang Syne   101
Awake! for Morning in the Bowl of Night   170
Ay, tear her tattered ensign down!   190

Bagpipe Music   304
Ballad of Reading Gaol, The (extract)   237

Ballade of Genuine Concern   262
Barbara Allan   6
Batter my heart, three-personed God; for you   55
Battle-Hymn of the Republic   203
Beauty sat bathing by a spring   17
Because I could not stop for death   210
Beggar's Opera, The (song)   79
Behind him lay the gray Azores   229
Behold her, single in the field   113
Beside yon straggling fence that skirts the way   91
Birthday, A   213
Birthday Poem for Thomas Hardy   300
Blessed Damozel, The (extract)   208
Blow, blow, thou winter wind   37
Book of the Tales of Caunterbury, The (extract)   1
Break, break, break   178
Breathes there the man, with soul so dead   115
Brook, The (extract)   185
Burial of Sir John Moore after Corunna, The   130
Burning of the Leaves, The (extract)   260
Busy old fool, unruly sun   54
'But that was nothing to what things came out   298
By the old Moulmein Pagoda, lookin' eastward to the sea   252
By the rude bridge that arched the flood   150
By the shores of Gitchee Gumee   161

Calm was the day, and through the trembling air   15
Cargoes   274
Casabianca   134
Character of a Happy Life, The   51
Charge of the Light Brigade, The   181
Cherry-Ripe   58
Cherry ripe, ripe, ripe, I cry   58
Childe Harold's Pilgrimage (extract: The Eve of Waterloo)   127
Chimney Sweeper, The   99
Close by those meads, for ever crowned with flowers   81
Collar, The   59
Columbus   229
Come into the garden, Maud   183
Come live with me and be my love   24
Come to me in the silence of the night   213
Come unto these yellow sands   49
Composed upon Westminster Bridge   114
'Courage!' he said, and pointed toward the land   176
Crabbed age and youth cannot live together   25
Cymbeline (songs)   48
Cynthia's Revels (extract)   51

Daddy   318
Danny Deever   246
Death, be not proud, though some have called thee   55

Delight in Disorder   56
Deserted Village, The (extract)   91
Destruction of Sennacherib, The   129
Do Not Go Gentle into That Good Night   308
Do not go gentle into that good night   308
Do you remember an Inn   261
Does the road wind up-hill all the way?   214
Donkey, The   267
Down by the Salley Gardens   255
Down by the salley gardens my love and I did meet   255
Dover Beach   205
Dr Faustus (extract)   23
Drake he's in his hammock an' a thousand mile away   245
Drake's Drum   245
Drink to me only with thine eyes   52

Earth has not anything to show more fair   114
Echo   213
Edward, Edward   5
Eftsoones they heard a most melodious sound   16
Elegy Written in a Country Churchyard   87
Endymion (extract)   136
England, with all thy faults, I love thee still   93
Epitaph on an Army of Mercenaries   244
Essay on Criticism, An (extract)   80
Essay on Man, An (extract)   81
Every branch big with it   229
Everyone Sang   284
Everyone suddenly burst out singing   284
Excelsior   163

Faerie Queene, The (extract)   16
Fair daffodils, we weep to see   57
Fair stood the wind for France   20
Fare Well   266
Farewell! thou art too dear for my possessing   27
Fear no more the heat o' the sun   48
Fire and Ice   269
First Fig   295
Five years have past; five summers, with the length   108
For the Fallen   259
Forsaken Garden, A (extract)   227
Four Ducks on a Pond   207
Four ducks on a pond   207
Frankie and Johnny   223
Frankie and Johnny were lovers, O lordy how they could love   223
Friends, Romans, countrymen, lend my your ears   38
From June to December (extract)   323
Full fathom five thy father lies   49
Full many a glorious morning have I seen   27

Gallop apace, you fiery-footed steeds   31
Garden by the Sea, A   222

Gather ye rosebuds, while ye may   56
Give me my scallop-shell of quiet   14
Glory be to God for dappled things—   231
Go, and catch a falling star   53
Go, lovely rose!   62
Goblin Market (extract)   211
God moves in a mysterious way   93
God of our fathers, known of old   249
God save great George our King   86
God Save the King   86
Green Eye of the Yellow God, The   253
Greensleeves   10
Grief   151
Gunga Din   247

Had we but world enough, and time   73
Hail to thee, blithe Spirit!   132
Half a league, half a league   181
Hamlet (extracts and songs)   40
Happy the man, whose wish and care   80
Hark, hark! the lark at heaven's gate sings   48
Hassan (extract: Soldiers' Song)   280
He did not wear his scarlet coat   237
He jests at scars that never felt a wound   29
He that is down needs fear no fall   75
Heaven-haven   230
Henry V (extracts)   34
Heraclitus   206
Her eyes the glow-worm lend thee   57
Here's to the maiden of bashful fifteen   96
Hero and Leander (extract)   23
High in front advanced   69
Highwayman, The   275
Home, Sweet Home   131
Home-Thoughts, from Abroad   193
Home-Thoughts, from the Sea   194
Hope dumbly then: with trembling pinions soar   81
Horatius (extract)   146
Hound of Heaven, The (extract)   242
Houses and rooms are full of perfumes, the shelves are crowded with
    perfumes   201
How do I love thee? Let me count the ways   153
How doth the little busy bee   78
How happy is he born and taught   51
How should I your true love know   42
How They Brought the Good News from Ghent to Aix   191
Hunter Trials   303
Hunting of the Snark, The (extract)   219
Hymn (Sung at the Completion of the Concord Monument 19 April
    1836)   150

I am monarch of all I survey   95
I am not yet born; O hear me   305

I caught this morning morning's minion king—   231
I come from haunts of coot and hern   185
I envy not in any moods   180
I fled Him down the nights and down the days   242
I had a silver penny   312
I have been here before   209
I have desired to go   230
I have eaten   279
I know a little garden-close   222
I know that I shall meet my fate   256
I met a traveller from an antique land   132
I must go down to the seas again, to the lonely sea and the sky   275
I remember, I remember   145
I sprang to the stirrup, and Joris, and he   191
I strove with none, for none was worth my strife   122
I struck the board, and cried, No more   59
I tell you, hopeless grief is passionless   151
I think continually of those who were truly great   307
I think that I shall never see (Kilmer)   283
I think that I shall never see (Nash)   380
I wandered lonely as a cloud   108
I will arise and go now, and go to Innisfree   255
If—   251
If all the world and love were young   25
If all the world were paper   61
If I should die, think only this of me   288
If music be the food of love, play on   43
If 'twere done when 'tis done, then 'twere well   45
If you can keep you head when all about you   251
In a coign of the cliff between lowland and highland   227
In good King Charles's golden days   84
In Memoriam (extracts)   180
In pious times ere priest-craft did begin   77
In Scarlet Town, where I was born   6
In the merry month of May   13
In Time of 'The Breaking of Nations'   228
In Xanadu did Kubla Khan   116
Inchcape Rock, The   118
Infant Sorrow   99
Invictus   234
Irish Airman Forsees His Death, An   256
Is it birthday weather for you, dear soul?   300
is my favourite. Who flies   317
'Is my team ploughing   243
'I there anybody there?' said the Traveller   265
Is this a dagger which I see before me   46
It is easy enough to be pleasant   236
It lies not in our power to love, or hate   23
It seemed that out of battle I escaped   295
It was a lover and his lass   37

It was many and many a year ago   169
It was my thirtieth year to heaven   308
It was the schooner Hesperus   158
It's awf'lly bad luck on Diana   303
It's no go the merrygoround, it's no go the rickshaw   304

Jabberwocky   215
Jellicle Cats come out to-night   293
Journey of the Magi   292
Julius Caesar (extracts)   38
Jumblies, The   196
Just for a handful of silver he left us   193
Just now the lilac is in bloom   284
'Just the place for a Snark!' the Bellman cried   219

Kubla Khan   116

La Belle Dame Sans Merci   136
Lady of Shalott, The   172
Lake Isle of Innisfree, The   253
Lamb, The   97
Lars Porsena of Clusium   146
Last Buccaneer, The   199
Laugh, and the world laughs with you   235
Lay of the Last Minstrel, The (extract)   115
Lay your sleeping head, my love   306
Leisure   264
Lepanto (extract)   268
Lessons of War (extract)   311
Let Me Die a Youngman's Death   320
Let me not to the marriage of true minds   28
Let us go then, you and I   288
Lines Composed a Few Miles above Tintern Abbey   108
Listen, my children, and you shall hear   155
Listeners, The   265
Little Lamb, who made thee?   97
Lochinvar   115
London 1802   114
London Snow   232
Long Distance II   320
Lord Randal   8
Lord Chord, A   207
Lost Leader, The   193
Lotos-Eaters, The   177
Love in a Village (extract)   96
Love Song of J. Alfred Prufrock, The   288
Loveliest of trees, the cherry now   242
Lullaby (Auden)   306
Lycidas   63
Lying apart now, each in a separate bed   316
Lykewake Dirge, A   3

Macbeth (extracts)   45
Mandalay   252
Matilda   263
Matilda told such Dreadful Lies   263
Maud (extract)   183
May Queen, The (extract)   176
Meeting at Night   194
Mending Wall   270
Merchant of Venice, The (extract and song)   33
'Mid pleasures and palaces though we may roam   131
Middle-aged life is merry, and I love to lead it   299
Midsummer Night's Dream, A (extract)   31
Milton (extract)   101
Milton! thou shouldst be living at this hour   114
Mine eyes have seen the glory of the coming of the Lord   203
Miniver Cheevy   258
Miniver Cheevy, child of scorn   258
Miss J. Hunter Dunn, Miss J. Hunter Dunn   301
Moonlit Apples   279
Morning and evening   211
Much have I travelled in the realms of gold   135
Music, when soft voices die   133
Musical Instrument, A   152
My candle burns at both ends   295
My country, 'tis of thee   165
My dear and only love, I pray   71
My Garden   215
My heart aches, and a drowsy numbness pains   138
My heart is like a singing bird   213
My heart leaps up when I behold   106
My life closed twice before its close   211
My luve is like a red, red rose   102
My mind to me a kingdom is   18
My mother groaned, my father wept   99
My soul, there is a country   75
My true love hath my heart, and I have his   18

next to of course god america i   297
Night sank upon the dusky beach, and on the purple sea   149
Night-Piece, to Julia   57
No coward soul is mine   197
No stir in the air, no stir in the sea   116
Nobly, nobly Cape Saint Vincent to the North-west died away   194
Nobody heard him, the dead man   300
Not a drum was heard, not a funeral note   130
Not Waving but Drowning   300
Now is the time for the burning of the leaves   260
Now is the winter of our discontent   28
Nursery Rhyme of Innocence and Experience   312
Nymph's Reply to the Shepherd, The   25

O beautiful for spacious skies   241
O blithe new-comer! I have heard   106
O Captain! My Captain!   201
O Captain! my Captain! our fearful trip is done   201
O Mary, go and call the cattle home   198
O mistress mine, where are you roaming?   43
O, pardon me, thou bleeding piece of earth   38
O Rose, thou art sick!   98
O ruddier than the cherry   79
O say, can you see, by the dawn's early light   123
O soft embalmer of the still midnight   138
O to be in England   193
O what can ail thee knight-at-arms   136
'O where hae ye been, Lord Randal, my son?   8
O why do you walk through the fields in gloves   283
O, young Lochinvar is come out of the west   115
Ode on a Grecian Urn   140
Ode on Solitude   80
Ode to a Nightingale   138
Of all the girls that are so smart   82
Of man's first disobedience, and the fruit   68
Oft in the stilly night   122
Oh, England is a pleasant place for them that's rich and high   198
Old Ironsides   190
Old Man's Comforts, The   120
Old Vicarage, Grantchester, The   284
On a Favourite Cat, Drowned in a Tub of Gold Fishes   90
On either side the river lie   172
On First Looking into Chapman's Homer   135
Once more into the breach, dear friends, once more   34
Once upon a midnight dreary, while I pondered, weak and weary   166
One Flesh   316
One word is too often profaned   133
Only a man harrowing clods   228
Othello (song)   44
Out of the night that covers me   234
Out upon it, I have loved   70
Owl   317
Owl and the Pussy-Cat, The   195
Ozymandias   132

Paradise Lost: Book 1 (extract)   68
Paradise Lost: Book XII (extract)   69
Parting at Morning   195
Passer-by, A   232
Passionate Man's Pilgrimage, The (extract)   14
Passionate Pilgrim, The (extract)   25
Passionate Shepherd to His Love, The   24
Paul Revere's Ride   155
Peace   75
Peekaboo, I Almost See You   299

Personal Helicon   323
Pied Beauty   231
Pilgrim's Progress, The (songs)   75
Pippa Passes (song)   191
Poem in October   308
Prayer before Birth   305
Princess, The (extracts)   178
Prothalamion (extract)   15
Psalm of Life, A   164
Pulley, The   60

Queen, and Huntress, chaste, and fair   51
Quinquireme of Nineveh from distant Ophir   274

Rape of the Lock, The (extract)   81
Raven, The   166
Recessional   249
Remember   212
Remember me when I am gone away   212
Requiem   235
Requiescat   206
Revenge, The, A Ballad of the Fleet   186
Richard II (extract)   32
Richard III (extract)   28
Richard Cory   258
Ring out, wild bells, to the wild sky   180
Road Not Taken, The   269
Romance   294
Romeo and Juliet (extracts)   29
Round the cape of a sudden came the sea   195
Rubáiyát of Omar Khayyám of Naishapur, The (extract)   170
Rule Britannia   85
Runnable Stag, A   238

Sailing to Byzantium   257
Sands of Dee, The   198
Say not the struggle nought availeth   200
School for Scandal (song)   96
Scots, wha hae wi' Wallace bled   104
Scribe, The   267
Sea-Fever   275
Season of mists and mellow fruitfulness   141
Seated one day at the organ   207
Second Coming, The   256
Shall I compare thee to a summer's day?   26
She dwelt among the untrodden ways   107
She Walks in Beauty   129
She walks in beauty, like the night   129
Shooting of Dan McGrew, The   271
Should auld acquaintance be forgot   101
Sick Rose, The   98

Silent Woman, The (song)   53
Since there's no help, come, let us kiss and part   19
Sing cuccu nu! Sing cuccu!   1
Sir Patrick Spens   9
Sluggard, The   78
Snake   281
Snow in the Suburbs   229
So, on the bloody sand, Sohrab lay dead   204
So, we'll go no more a roving   130
Sohrab and Rustum (extract)   204
Soldier, The   288
Solitary Reaper, The   113
Solitude   235
Some say the world will end in fire   269
Something there is that doesn't love a wall   270
Song (Burns)   102
Song (Donne)   53
Song (C. Rossetti)   214
Song of Hiawatha, The (extract)   161
Song of Milkanwatha, The (extract)   215
Song of Myself (extract)   201
Song of the Jellicles, The   293
Song of the Open Road   300
Song of the Shirt, The   142
Song of the Western Men, The   151
Songs of Experience (selected)   98
Songs of Innocence (selected)   97
Sonnet (On Milton's Blindness)   68
Sonnets (selected: Shakespeare)   26
Star-Spangled Banner, The   123
Still to be neat, still to be dressed   53
Stange Meeting   295
Strew on her roses, roses   206
Subaltern's Love-Song, A   301
Success is counted sweetest   211
Sudden Light   209
Sumer is icumen in   1
Summer Villanelle   323
Sun Rising, The   54
Sweet day, so cool, so calm, so bright   58

Tarantella   261
Task, The (extract)   93
Tears, idle tears, I know not what they mean   179
Tell me not, in mournful numbers   164
Tell me not (Sweet) I am unkind   72
Tell me where is fancy bred   33
Tempest, The (extract and songs)   49
That is no country for old men. The young   257
That Whitsun, I was late getting away   314

The Assyrian came down like the wolf on the fold   129
The barge she sat in, like a burnished throne   47
The blessed damozel leaned out   208
The boy stood on the burning deck   134
The curfew tolls the knell of parting day   87
The glories of our blood and state   62
The grey sea and the long black land   194
The king sits in Dunfermline toun   9
The Lord God planted a garden   240
The lunatic, the lover, and the poet   31
The mountain sheep are sweeter   125
The Owl and the Pussy-cat went to sea   195
The poor soul sat sighing by a sycamore tree   44
The quality of mercy in not strained   33
The raven himself is hoarse   45
The sea is calm to-night   205
The shades of night were falling fast   163
The splendour falls on castle walls   178
The sun was shining on the sea   216
The wind was a torrent of darkness among the gusty trees   275
The world is too much with us; late and soon   112
The year's at the spring   191
There is a garden in her face   50
There is a lady sweet and kind   12
There was a jolly miller once   96
There was a sound of revelry by night   127
There's a breathless hush in the Close to-night   245
There's a one-eyed yellow idol to the north of Khatmandu   253
These, in the day when heaven was falling   244
They fuck you up, your mum and dad   316
They shut the road through the woods   250
They told me, Heraclitus, they told me you were dead   206
They went to sea in a Sieve, they did   196
This ae night, this ae night   3
This Be the Verse   316
This day is called the feast of Crispian   35
This is the weather the cuckoo likes   228
This Is Just to Say   279
This royal throne of kings, this sceptred isle   32
Thou still unravished bride of quietness   140
Though my mother was already two years dead   320
Tiger, The   98
Tiger! Tiger! burning bright   98
'Tis the voice of the sluggard; I heard him complain   78
To a Fat Lady Seen from the Train   283
To a Mouse   103
To a Skylark (extract)   132
To Althea, from Prison   72
To Autumn   141

To be, or not to be – that is the question 41
To Celia 52
To Daffodils 57
To His Coy Mistress (Marvell) 73
To His Mistress (James Graham) 71
To Lucasta, Going to the Wars 72
To see a world in a grain of sand 99
To Sleep 138
To the Cuckoo 106
To the Virgins, to Make Much of Time 56
To-day we have naming of parts. Yesterday 311
To-morrow, and to-morrow, and to-morrow 47
To-morrow is Saint Valentine's day 42
Trees 283
Turning and turning in the widening gyre 256
Twa Corbies, The 4
'Twas brillig, and the slithy toves 215
'Twas on a lofty vase's side 90
'Twas on the shores that round our coast 225
Twelfth Night (extract and songs) 43
Two Gentlemen of Verona, The (song) 29
Two roads diverged in a yellow wood 269

Under a spreading chestnut-tree 154
Under the greenwood tree 36
Under the wide and starry sky 235
Up-Hill 214
Upon Julia's Clothes 56

Vicar of Bray, The 84
Vicar of Wakefield, The (song) 92
Village Blacksmith, The 154
Virtue 58
Vitaï Lampada 245

Walrus and the Carpenter, The 216
War Song of Dinas Vawr, The 125
Was this the face that launched a thousand ships 23
Way through the Woods, The 250
We are they who come faster than fate: we are they who ride early or late 280
Weathers 228
Wee, sleeket, cowrin, tim'rous beastie 103
Welsh Incident 298
Were I laid on Greenland's coast 79
Whan that April with his shoures soote 1
'What are the bugles blowin' for?' said Files-on-Parade 246
What is this life if, full of care 264
What lovely things 267
What was he doing, the great god Pan 152
When as in silks my Julia goes 58
When Britain first, at heaven's command 85

When fishes flew and forests walked   267
When God at first made man   60
When he killed the Mudjokivis   215
When I am dead, my dearest   214
When I consider how my light is spent   68
When I lie where shades of darkness   266
When I was but thirteen or so   294
When I was one-and-twenty   244
When in the chronicle of wasted time   27
When love with unconfined wings   72
When lovely woman stoops to folly   92
When men were all asleep the snow came flying   232
When that I was and a little tiny boy   43
When the Frost Is on the Punkin   233
When the frost is on the punkin and the fodder's in the shock   233
When the pods went pop on the broom, green broom   238
When to the sessions of sweet silent thought   26
When we two parted   126
When You Are Old   255
When you are old and grey and full of sleep   255
Whenever Richard Cory went down town   258
Where Have All the Flowers Gone?   321
Where have all the flowers gone?   321
Where the bee sucks, there suck I   49
White founts falling in the courts of the sun   268
Whither, O splendid ship, thy white sails crowding   232
Whitsun Weddings, The   314
Who is Silvia? what is she   29
Who would true valour see   76
'Why dois your brand sae drap wi' bluid   5
Why so pale and wan, fond lover?   70
Windhover, The   231
With fingers weary and worn   142
With proud thanksgiving, a mother for her children   259
Worthwhile   236
Wreck of the 'Hesperus', The   158

Yarn of the Nancy Bell, The   225
Ye mariners of England   121
Yes. I remember Adlestrop –   274
Yet here, Laertes! aboard, aboard, for shame!   40
Yet once more, O ye laurels, and once more   63
You are old, Father William, the young man cried   120
You do look, my son, in a moved sort   50
You do not do, you do not do   318
You know exactly what to do –   323
You may talk o' gin and beer   247
You must wake and call me early, call me early, mother dear   176